ON THIS DAY IN AMERICA

ON THIS DAY IN AMERICA

An Illustrated Almanac of
History, Sports, Science, and Culture

BY JOHN WAGMAN

GALLERY BOOKS
An Imprint of W. H. Smith Publishers Inc.
112 Madison Avenue
New York City 10016

Acknowledgements

The author would like to thank all the people at
JL Design for their efforts in producing this book,
especially: Judith Wach (born Nov 10), Barbara
Conklin (born Jan 8), Susan Tessmer (born Feb 21),
Richard Taverna (born Mar 15), and Paula Dennis
(born May 29).

Joan Carroll at AP/Wide World Photos (born Jan
25), also deserves special mention as does Sandra
Still (born May 9), who went beyond the call of
duty in editing this book.

And last but not least, Rita Rosenkranz (born Aug
22), who boosted my morale when it needed
boosting.

Author's note

Many reference works, almanacs, and encyclope-
dias were used in researching this book, and all
efforts have been made to insure the accuracy of
the information. In some cases there are differences
as to the exact day an event took place, particularly
in the sixteenth and seventeenth centuries. For this
volume, I used the most widely accepted dates.

This edition first published in the United States in
1990 by Gallery Books, an imprint of W.H. Smith
Publishers, Inc., 112 Madison Avenue, New York,
New York 10016

Gallery Books are available for bulk purchase for
sales promotions and premium use. For details
write or telephone the Manager of Special Sales,
W.H. Smith Publishers, Inc., 112 Madison Avenue,
New York, New York 10016. (212) 532-6600

ISBN-0-8317-6624-7

Picture Credits

AP/Wide World Photos

Jan 2, 5, 7, 11, 12, 14, 19, 20, 21, 22, 23, 27, 28, 31, 31 (full page)
Feb 3, 4, 7, 9, 11, 14, 19, 20, 25, 29 (full page)
Mar 8, 13, 18, 20, 21, 27, 30, 31 (full page)
Apr 6, 11, 13, 15, 17, 18, 23, 25 27, 29
May 2, 4, 7, 16, 18, 22, 23, 28, 30, 31 (full page)
Jun 4, 6, 9, 18, 20, 22
Jul 6, 10, 15, 16, 17, 19, 20, 22, 27, 31 (full page)
Aug 4, 5, 6, 7, 10, 14, 15, 17, 25, 28, 31, 31 (full page)
Sep 2, 5, 6, 11, 12, 19, 20, 23, 28, 29, 30
Oct 1, 2, 3, 11, 18, 19, 20, 24, 30, 31 (full page)
Nov 3, 4, 10, 11, 12, 13, 14, 15, 22, 27, 29
Dec 1, 5, 6, 7, 9, 11, 18, 22, 27, 28, 30, 31 (full page)

New York Public Library

Jan 3, 8, 9, 10, 15, 17, 18, 24, 25, 26, 29, 30
Feb 6, 8, 10, 12, 13, 15, 18, 21, 22, 23, 24, 26, 27, 29
Mar 1, 5, 6, 7, 9, 10, 12, 16, 17, 22, 23, 24, 25, 28, 29, 31
Apr 2, 3, 5, 9, 10, 16, 19, 20, 21, 22, 24, 26
May 3, 6, 8, 9, 10, 11, 12, 13, 14, 17, 20, 21, 24, 29, 31
Jun 1, 2, 7, 8, 11, 12, 14, 17, 19, 23, 25, 26
Jul 3, 8, 9, 23, 24, 26, 29, 30, 31
Aug 1, 2, 3, 9, 11, 12, 13, 16, 18, 20, 21, 24, 27, 29, 30
Sep 3, 4, 7, 8, 9, 10, 13, 14, 15, 17, 18, 21, 22, 24, 25, 26
Oct 6, 8, 12, 13, 17, 21, 22, 23, 25, 26, 27, 29, 31
Nov 1, 2, 5, 7, 8, 9, 16, 17, 18, 19, 21, 24, 28, 30
Dec 2, 4, 10, 12, 13, 14, 15, 17, 19, 21, 23, 25, 26, 31

John Wagman Collection

Jan 4, 6, 16
Feb 5, 16, 17, 28
Mar 4, 11, 14, 26
May 19, 25, 27
Jun 3, 5, 10, 13, 16, 21, 24, 29
Jul 5, 7, 12, 13, 14, 18, 25
Aug 22, 23, 26
Sep 16
Oct 4, 5
Nov 23, 25, 26
Dec 3, 8, 16, 20, 24

Sandra Still Collection

Aug 19

U.S. Department of the Interior, National Park Service, Edison National Historic Site

Feb 1
Aug 8

New York Historical Society

Jan 13
Feb 2
Mar 19
Apr 28
Jul 11, 23
Oct 14, 28
Nov 6

Anyone who has had to memorize dates in American history knows that sinking feeling when called upon to tell the class when the Gadsden Purchase took place.

Could it be that knowing that date would somehow help in later life? If I remembered when the cotton gin was invented, would it give me some future business insight? Would anyone ever ask me when the Mississippi River was discovered?

The answer to these questions is yes.

That's why no citizen should be without this book. With it, you'll never be caught short or be at a loss for words when someone comes up to you and asks if you know what happened in American history on that day.

You simply produce your copy of ON THIS DAY IN AMERICA and reply that in 1776, the British burned Norfolk, Virginia, during the Revolutionary War; in 1863 President Lincoln's Emancipation Proclamation went into effect; in 1902 Michigan beat Stanford in the first Rose Bowl game; and in 1966 *The Sounds of Silence* by Simon & Garfunkle was the number one record in the United States.

I can assure you that the look on that person's face will more than make up for your having carried this book around for seven months.

Now, some twenty years after the end of my own formal education, I have written a book consisting of dates in American history.

After beginning my research (I had forgotten just about every date I had had to memorize for those spot quizzes and mid-terms, so I had to look them all up *again*), I discovered that reviewing the almost five hundred years of the American experience on a day-by-day basis provides a unique and fascinating perspective on the many events, both large and small, that make up our heritage.

We all know (or should) that on June 6, 1944, the Allies invaded Normandy to begin the liberation of Western Europe during World War II. But did you know that on that day in 1716, the first Black slaves arrived in Louisiana? Or that in 1884, the Coney Island roller coaster opened? On June 6, 1933, the first drive-in theater opened in Camden, New Jersey; in 1934, President Roosevelt created the Securities and Exchange Commission; in 1942, the Battle of Midway, the largest naval battle the world had ever seen, was fought in the Pacific; and in 1968, presidential candidate Robert F. Kennedy was shot after winning the California Primary.

Every year we celebrate the birthday of George Washington who was born on February 22, 1732. But did you realize that on that day in 1630, popcorn was invented in New England? Or that on that day in 1631, the first Thanksgiving was celebrated in the Massachusetts Bay Colony? On February 22, 1856, the Republican Party held its first national meeting; in 1879, Woolworth's Department Store opened; and in 1944, United States Marines completed their takeover of the Marshall Islands during World War II.

Who can forget (except possibly President Bush) that on December 7, 1941, the Japanese launched their surprise attack on the United States' fleet at Pearl Harbor, a day that President Roosevelt said would "live in infamy"? But were you aware that on that day in 1787, Delaware became the firt state to ratify the Constitution? Or that on that day in 1917, the United States declared war on Austria-Hungary during World War I? On December 7, 1931, bread lines began forming in the United States during the Depression, and in 1946, one hundred twenty-seven people were killed in a fire at the Winecoff Hotel in Atlanta, one of the worst fires in this country.

All this makes American history actually interesting, something you previously thought impossible. So pull up your favorite chair, make yourself a snack (how about an *American* cheese sandwich?), look up what happened on your birthday, and start reading. There might be a short quiz.

John Wagman

New York City
1990

January

1637
The first mounted mail service is inaugurated, between Boston and New York.

1776
The British burn Norfolk, Virginia, during the Revolutionary War.

1776
The American flag is raised for the first time on land, at Prospect Hill in Sommerville, Massachusetts.

1816
The public debt reaches over $100 million for the first time.

1831
William Lloyd Garrison of Boston begins publication of *The Liberator*, the leading abolitionist journal in the United States.

1863
President Lincoln's Emancipation Proclamation becomes effective.

1892
The receiving station for immigrants at Ellis Island opens in New York harbor.

1902
Michigan defeats Stanford 49-0 in the first Rose Bowl football game in Pasadena, California.

1914
The Tampa Airboat Line becomes the first airline to offer regularly scheduled passenger service.

1928
The Milam Building in San Antonio, Texas, becomes the first office building in the United States to have air-conditioning.

1933
Miami defeats Manhattan 7-0 in the first Orange Bowl game.

1935
Tulane defeats Temple 20-14 in the first Sugar Bowl game.

1937
Texas Christian defeats Marquette 16-6 in the first Cotton Bowl.

1945
The German Air Force loses over 200 aircraft in attacks over Belgium and Holland, during World War II.

1951
Chinese Communist troops take Inchon and Kimpo Airfield, during the Korean War.

1955
The United States begins foreign aid to South Vietnam, Cambodia, and Laos.

1966
Traffic comes to a standstill as the first New York transit strike begins.

1966
The Sounds of Silence by Simon and Garfunkel becomes the number one record in the United States.

1977
Jacqueline Means becomes the first woman Episcopal priest in the United States.

1979
The United States and the People's Republic of China establish full diplomatic relations.

January

1788
Georgia becomes the fourth state to ratify the Constitution.

1861
President Buchanan orders the reinforcing of the Federal garrison at Fort Sumter in Charleston Harbor.

1863
The Battle of Murfreesboro, Tennessee ends with the Federals, commanded by General William S. Rosecrans, and the Confederates, commanded by General Braxton Bragg, holding their ground after sustaining over 11,000 casualties, during the Civil War.

1888
Marvin Chester Stone of Washington, D.C., is awarded a patent for the drinking straw.

1915
Congress passes a bill requiring immigrants to pass a literacy test.

1942
General Douglas MacArthur is forced to evacuate his troops, as the Japanese take Manila in the Philippines, during World War II.

1943
Japanese forces occupy Manila, as the Americans establish defensive positions on Bataan, during World War II.

1959
Fidel Castro takes control of Cuba after the collapse of the Batista regime.

1971
President Nixon signs the Omnibus Crime Control Act, authorizing Federal aid for state and local law enforcement.

General Douglas MacArthur in the Philippines

January

1777
General George Washington defeats a British force at the Battle of Princeton, New Jersey, during the Revolutionary War.

1921
The Supreme Court rules that labor unions can be prosecuted for restraint of interstate commerce.

1922
Orphans of the Storm, a film by D.W. Griffith starring Lillian and Dorothy Gish, premieres at the Apollo Theater in New York.

1933
Minnie Davenport Craig of North Dakota becomes the first woman Speaker of the House in a state legislature.

1942
Chiang Kai-shek is named Commander in Chief of all Allied forces in China, during World War II.

1958
The United States Air Force establishes two missile squadrons equipped with intermediate range ballistic missiles.

1959
Alaska joins the Union as the forty-ninth state.

1961
The United States breaks diplomatic relations with Cuba.

1970
Raindrops Keep Fallin' on My Head by B.J. Thomas becomes the number one record in the United States.

1986
President Reagan orders economic sanctions against Libya in retaliation for its involvement in terrorist attacks in Rome and Vienna.

The Battle of Princeton

January

1896
The Hartford Convention ends with the five New England states secretly adopting strong states rights positions.

1846
General Mariano Paredes becomes the President of Mexico, announcing he will defend all territory he considers Mexico's.

1862
Confederates commanded by Stonewall Jackson enter and occupy Bath in western Virginia, during the Civil War.

1863
General Grant's controversial Order No. 11, expelling Jews from his department, is revoked by President Lincoln, during the Civil War.

1896
Utah joins the Union as the forty-fifth state.

1904
The Supreme Court rules that Puerto Rican citizens can not be refused admission to the United States.

1936
The first popular music chart based on record sales is published by *The Billboard*, in New York.

1955
The United States agrees to pay Japan two million dollars in damages resulting from atomic tests in the Marshall Islands.

1960
The United Steel Workers end the longest strike in the United States, begun on July 15, 1959.

1987
Fifteen people are killed in a train accident in Chase, Maryland, the worst in Amtrak's history.

Mariano Paredes

January

1776
The New Hampshire Colony adopts the first state constitution.

1782
The British withdraw from Wilmington, North Carolina.

1818
The *James Monroe*, the first ocean liner, sails from New York on its maiden voyage to Liverpool, England.

1838
President Martin Van Buren issues a neutrality proclamation forbidding Americans to take part in the Canadian insurrection.

1861
Alabama state troops take possession of Forts Morgan and Gaines at the entrance to Mobile Bay, during the Civil War.

1933
Calvin Coolidge, thirtieth President of the United States, dies.

1943
The Russians capture Prokhladny in the Soviet Union to further consolidate their gains, during World War II.

1957
The Eisenhower Doctrine is proposed, offering protection to any nation in the Middle East against Communist aggression.

1968
Pediatrician Dr. Benjamin Spock is convicted of conspiracy to aid and abet draft evasion.

1982
A Federal Judge in Arkansas reverses a state law requiring the teaching of both creationism and evolutionism in public schools.

The Russian Army capturing Prokhladny

January

1861
Florida troops seize the Federal arsenal at Apalachicola.

1895
Former Hawaiian Queen Liliuokalani is arrested after a failed coup against the republican government of Sanford Dole.

1912
New Mexico joins the Union as the forty-seventh state.

1919
Theodore Roosevelt, twenty-sixth President of the United States, dies in Oyster Bay, New York.

1941
President Roosevelt introduces the term *Four Freedoms*: freedom of speech and expression, freedom of worship, freedom from fear, and freedom from want in a speech before Congress.

1945
Over 75 Japanese aircraft are destroyed at Kamikaze airfields on Luzon by American land and carrier based forces, during World War II.

1958
At The Hop by Danny and the Juniors becomes the number one record in the United States.

1958
E. E. Cummings wins the Bollingen Prize for Poetry.

1973
You're So Vain by Carly Simon becomes the number one record in the United States.

1978
The United States returns the Crown of St. Stephen to Hungary, after taking custody of it, following World War II.

State militia preparing to seize a Federal arsenal

January

1699
Hostilities end in King William's War, with the signing of a treaty at Casco, Maine.

1784
The first seed supply business is opened by David Landreth, in Philadelphia.

1800
Millard Fillmore, thirteenth President of the United States, is born in Cayuga County, New York.

1817
The second Bank of the United States opens in Philadelphia.

1839
The Washington Mining Company of North Carolina becomes the first silver mining company in the United States.

The first ship through the Panama Canal

1863
Confederate forces commanded by General Sterling Price attack and capture Springfield, Missouri, during the Civil War.

1914
The *Alexander la Valley* becomes the first boat to go through the Panama Canal.

1916
Germany notifies the United States of its intention to abide by international rules of naval warfare.

1927
Commercial transatlantic telephone service is inaugurated between New York and London.

1935
The Petrified Forest by Robert E. Sherwood premieres at the Broadhurst Theater in New York.

1941
President Roosevelt creates the Office of Production Management to supervise defense production.

1959
The United States recognizes the new Government of Cuba led by Fidel Castro.

1960
President Eisenhower projects a $200,000,000 budget surplus.

1975
Shenandoah, by Gary Geld and Peter Udell, opens at the Alvin Theater in New York.

1986
President Reagan imposes economic sanctions on Libya for its role in international terrorism.

January

1815
The United States force commanded by General Andrew Jackson defeats the British at the Battle of New Orleans, two weeks after the Treaty of Ghent ends the War of 1812.

1856
John Veatch discovers Borax at a Spring in California, the first find of this mineral in the United States.

1867
Congress passes a bill giving suffrage to Blacks in Washington, D.C., over President Johnson's veto.

1889
Dr. Herman Hollerith of New York is awarded a patent for the first computer designed for data processing.

1918
President Wilson outlines his 14 points for a just and lasting peace after the end of World War I.

1925
The first State Supreme Court composed entirely of women, sits in Texas.

1934
Days Without End by Eugene O'Neil opens at Henry Miller's Theater in New York.

1963
Leonardo DaVinci's painting, *The Mona Lisa*, goes on exhibition for the first time in the United States, at the Metropolitan Museum of Art in New York.

1967
Operation Cedar Falls begins against the Iron Triangle north of Saigon, the largest military operation to date during the Vietnam War.

1982
Ending an eight-year suit by the Justice Department, American Telephone & Telegraph Company divests itself of its twenty-two Bell systems.

The Battle of New Orleans

January

1788
Connecticut becomes the fifth state to ratify the Constitution.

1793
The first balloon flight in America is made by Frenchman Jean-Pierre Francois Blanchard, in Philadelphia.

1802
Western University, which becomes Ohio University two years later, is founded in Athens, Ohio.

1861
Mississippi secedes from the Union.

1861
The Union ship, *Star of the West*, is fired on by the South Carolina state battery in Charleston Harbor, on its way to resupply the garrison at Fort Sumter.

1913
Richard M. Nixon, thirty-seventh President of the United States, is born in Yorba Linda, California.

1928
Marco Millions by Eugene O'Neill opens at the Guild Theater in New York.

1945
The United States Sixth Army lands on Luzon in the Philippines, during World War II.

1960
The Protestant Episcopal Church approves some forms of birth control.

1964
The United States breaks diplomatic relations with Panama after riots in the Canal Zone.

1968
Surveyor 7 makes a soft landing on the Moon and begins transmitting pictures.

Official broadside of Blanchard's baloon

January

1769
The Northern and Southern Colonies are linked, as regular monthly mail service begins by boat, between New York and Charleston.

1776
Common Sense is published by Thomas Paine, containing the first call for total independence from England.

1847
General Kearney takes Los Angeles, ending hostilities in California, during the Mexican War.

1861
Florida secedes from the Union.

1863
Union gunboats begin a bombardment of Galveston, Texas, during the Civil War.

1876
The Standard Oil Company of Ohio is formed by John D. Rockefeller.

1901
The Spindletop claim near Beaumont, Texas, becomes the first major oil strike in the Southwest.

1923
United States troops, stationed in Germany since the end of World War I, are recalled.

1946
The first United Nations General Assembly meeting is held, in London.

1984
The United States restores diplomatic relations with the Vatican, which were broken off in 1867.

Thomas Paine

1775
Francis Salvador is elected to South Carolina's Provincial Congress, becoming the first Jew to hold elective office in America.

1785
New York becomes the temporary Capital of the United States.

1861
Alabama secedes from the Union.

1862
President Lincoln appoints Edwin M. Stanton Secretary of War, during the Civil War.

1863
Union troops commanded by General John A. McClernand seize Fort Hindman, Arkansas, during the Civil War.

1925
Symphony for Organ and Orchestra by Aaron Copeland is premiered by the New York Symphony Orchestra.

1935
Amelia Earhart becomes the first woman to fly solo from California to Hawaii.

1949
Snow falls for the first recorded time in Los Angeles, California.

1955
Inherit the Wind by Jerome Lawrence opens at the Theater '55 in Dallas, Texas.

1970
The Kansas City Chiefs defeat the Minnesota Vikings to win Super Bowl IV.

Amelia Earhart arrives back in California

January

12

1773
The first museum in the Colonies opens, in Charleston, South Carolina.

1792
Thomas Pinckney is appointed the first United States Minister to England.

1812
The first steamboat to sail down the Mississippi River arrives in New Orleans.

1828
The United States and Mexico agree to a common boundary along the Sabine River.

1839
Anthracite coal is used to smelt iron for the first time, in Mauch Chunk, Pennsylvania.

1942
President Roosevelt creates the War Labor Board in order to maintain the flow of war materials by settling labor disputes.

1960
Dolph Schayes of the Syracuse Nationals, becomes the first basketball player to score 15,000 points.

1962
The Pennsylvania and New York Central railroads, two of the nation's largest, merge.

1969
The New York Jets defeat the Baltimore Colts 16-7 to become the first AFL team to win the Super Bowl.

1975
The Pittsburgh Steelers defeat the Minnesota Vikings to win Super Bowl IX.

Joe Namath passing during Super Bowl III

January

1794
Congress authorizes the addition of two more stars and stripes to the American flag, in recognition of Vermont and Kentucky.

1854
Pacific University is founded in Forest Grove, Oregon.

1863
The United States authorizes the raising of Negro troops for the South Carolina Volunteer Infantry, during the Civil War.

1910
Cavalleria Rusticana, broadcast by the De Forest Radio Telephone Company from the Metropolitan Opera House in New York, becomes the first opera presented on radio.

1942
Allied representatives announce that Axis war criminals will be punished, at a meeting in London, during World War II.

1974
The Miami Dolphins defeat the Minnesota Vikings to win Super Bowl VIII.

1976
Sarah Caldwell conducts Verdi's *La Traviata* at the Metropolitan Opera House in New York, becoming the first woman to conduct there.

1982
An Air Florida jet crashes into a bridge over the Potomac River in Washington, D.C., killing 78 people.

1987
Seven Mafia leaders are convicted of criminal activities and given 100-year sentences.

ASSAULT OF THE SECOND LOUISIANA (COLORED) REGIMENT ON THE REBEL WORKS AT PORT HUDSON, MAY 27 — FROM A SKETCH BY OUR SPECIAL ARTIST.

Black Union troops in action

January

1639
Roger Ludlow of Connecticut composes the first constitution in the Colonies.

1790
Treasury Secretary Alexander Hamilton submits his first report on public credit to Congress.

1861
Union troops garrison Fort Taylor in Key West, Florida.

1864
Union forces commanded by General William T. Sherman occupy Meridian, Mississippi, during the Civil War.

1878
The Supreme Court rules unconstitutional any state law requiring railroads to provide equal accommodations for passengers, regardless of race or color.

1943
President Roosevelt and other allied leaders attend the Casablanca Conference, to map out strategy for 1943, during World War II.

1943
The Soviets capture Pitomnik Airfield near Stalingrad, held by the Germans since the invasion, during World War II.

1968
The Green Bay Packers defeat the Oakland Raiders to win Super Bowl II.

1973
The Miami Dolphins defeat the Washington Redskins to win Super Bowl VII.

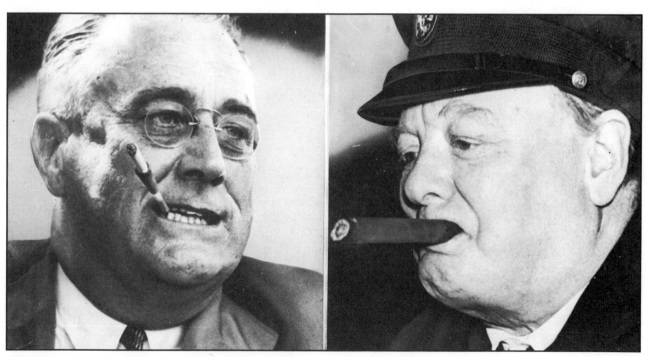

President Roosevelt and Prime Minister Churchill

January

1771
The North Carolina assembly passes the "Bloody Act," making rioters guilty of treason.

1780
The Continental Congress establishes the Court of Appeals.

1804
New Jersey becomes the last Northern State to abolish slavery.

1831
Best Friend becomes the first American-built locomotive to pull a passenger train, in South Carolina.

1844
The University of Notre Dame is founded in South Bend, Indiana.

1857
Abolitionist William Lloyd Garrison declares, "No union with slaveholders," at the State Disunion Convention in Worcester, Massachusetts.

1865
The last Confederate port is closed, as Union forces take Fort Fisher, North Carolina, during the Civil War.

1870
Harper's Weekly publishes the first political cartoon depicting a donkey as a symbol of the Democratic Party.

1927
The Academy of Motion Picture Arts and Sciences is founded in Hollywood, California.

1929
Congress passes the Kellogg-Briand Peace Pact, signed by 62 nations outlawing war.

1943
The Pentagon Building opens in Arlington, Virginia.

1962
In an effort to improve relations with the Soviet Union, the United States withdraws its tanks from the Berlin Wall.

1967
The Green Bay Packers defeat the Kansas City Chiefs 35-10 in the first Super Bowl.

1972
American Pie by Don McLean becomes the number one record in the United States.

Cartoon depicting the Democratic donkey

1855
The first Territorial Legislature of Nebraska meets in Omaha City.

1868
William Davis of Detroit, Michigan is granted a patent for his refrigerator car.

1883
Congress passes the Pendleton Act, specifying rules for filling government positions.

1893
Queen Liliuokalani of Hawaii is overthrown, as United States troops land in an effort to protect American lives and property on the island.

1945
The United States First and Third Armies link up at Houffalize in the Ardennes, during World War II.

1958
Two for the Seesaw by William Gibson opens at the Booth Theater in New York.

1964
Hello Dolly, by Michael Stewart and Jerry Herman, opens at the St. James Theater in New York.

1967
Lucius Amerson of Tuskegee, Alabama, becomes the first Black sheriff in the South since Reconstruction.

1969
Merck Laboratories and Rockefeller University announce the production of ribonuclease, the first synthesized enzyme.

1972
The Dallas Cowboys defeat the Miami Dolphins to win the Super Bowl VI.

Queen Liliuokalani

1781
American forces led by General Daniel Morgan defeat the British at the Battle of Cowpens, South Carolina, during the Revolutionary War.

1878
The United States and Samoa sign a commercial treaty.

1893
Rutherford B. Hayes, nineteenth President of the United States, dies in Fremont, Ohio.

1894
The United States Treasury floats a bond issue of $50 million in an effort to restore the gold reserve behind American currency.

1916
The Professional Golfers Association is formed.

1942
British forces take Halfaya in North Africa, capturing over 5500 German and Italian prisoners, during World War II.

1961
President Eisenhower warns of the power of the "military-industrial complex," in his farewell speech.

1966
Robert C. Weaver is named Secretary of Housing and Urban Development, becoming the first Black to hold a Cabinet position.

1971
The Baltimore Colts defeat the Dallas Cowboys to win Super Bowl V.

1977
Gary Gilmore is executed by a Utah firing squad, becoming the first convicted murderer to be executed in the United States in over 10 years.

The Battle of Cowpens

1778

English explorer Captain James Cook rediscovers the Hawaiian Islands, renaming them the Sandwich Islands.

1803

President Jefferson asks Congress for an appropriation of $2500 to fund the Lewis and Clark Expedition.

1861

Vassar Female College is founded in Poughkeepsie, New York.

1862

John Tyler, tenth President of the United States, dies in Richmond, Virginia.

1886

Congress passes the Presidential Succession Act, providing the order of succession for the heads of the executive departments to succeed to the presidency.

1911

Pilot Eugene Ely becomes the first man to land an airplane on the deck of a ship, the United States *Pennsylvania*.

1919

The Peace Conference opens in Paris.

1960

The United States and Japan sign a mutual security treaty.

1969

The United States, North Vietnam, South Vietnam, and the National Liberation Front begin peace talks in Paris.

1976

The Pittsburgh Steelers defeat the Dallas Cowboys to win Super Bowl X.

Captain Cook landing in the Sandwich Islands

January

1775
The first Continental Congress presents its petitions to the British Parliament.

1830
The Webster-Haynes debates take place in Congress, becoming a discussion on the nature of the Union.

1861
Georgia secedes from the Union.

1862
Federal troops commanded by General George H. Thomas defeat the confederates at the Battle of Mill Springs, Kentucky, during the Civil War.

1869
Susan B. Anthony is elected president of the American Equal Rights Association in Washington, D.C.

1941
The British, commanded by General Platt, begin an offensive against the Italians in the Sudan, during World War II.

1945
United States forces take Carmen on Luzon in the Philippines, after establishing a beachhead, during World War II.

1955
President Eisenhower conducts the first presidential press conference to be filmed.

1977
President Ford pardons Tokyo Rose, convicted during World War II for making propaganda broadcasts to American troops.

Tokyo Rose being escorted from jail

January

1801
John Marshall is appointed Chief Justice of the United States Supreme Court.

1847
The Governor of Taos, New Mexico, is killed by rebellious Mexicans, during the Mexican War.

1891
Liliuokalani becomes Queen of Hawaii after the death of her brother King Kalakaua.

1892
The first basketball game takes place, in Springfield, Massachusetts.

1954
The Caine Mutiny Court Martial by Herman Wouk opens at the Plymouth Theater in New York.

1969
Astronomers at the University of Arizona establish the first optical identification of a pulsar.

1980
President Carter announces the United States' boycott of the Summer Olympics in Moscow.

1980
The Pittsburgh Steelers defeat the Los Angeles Rams to win Super Bowl XIV.

1981
Iran releases the 52 American hostages seized at the United States Embassy in Teheran in November of 1979.

1985
The San Francisco 49ers defeat the Miami Dolphins to win Super Bowl XIX.

Four United States hostages in West Germany

January

1770
A group of Spanish explorers reaches southern California, near present-day San Diego.

1785
The Ottawa and Wyandot Indians cede their land in Ohio to the United States, in the Treaty of Fort McIntosh.

1789
The Power of Sympathy; or The Triumph of Nature is published, becoming the first American novel.

1832
Thomas Jefferson Randolph, the grandson of Thomas Jefferson, presents a plan of gradual emancipation to the Virginia Assembly.

1861
After making farewell speeches, Senators from Alabama, Mississippi, and Florida resign from the United States Senate.

1874
Morrison R. Waite becomes Chief Justice of the Supreme Court.

1888
The Amateur Athletic Union is formed.

1905
The United States and the Dominican Republic sign a protocol giving the United States control of the Dominican Republic's international debt.

1908
The Sullivan Ordinance is passed by the New York City legislature, making smoking by women in public places illegal.

1911
Senator Robert M. La Follette of Wisconsin establishes the National Progressive Republican League.

1924
Congress establishes the Mount Hood National Forest in Oregon.

1950
Alger Hiss is convicted of lying to a grand jury in connection with an espionage investigation.

1953
A Federal jury in New York convicts thirteen Communist leaders of plotting the overthrow of the United States Government.

1954
The U.S.S. *Nautilus* is launched in Groton, Connecticut, becoming the first atomic submarine in the United States.

1968
An American B-52 bomber crashes near Greenland, releasing radiation into the air from the four hydrogen bombs on board.

1970
Pan American Airways puts the first Boeing 747 wide-body jet into service.

1977
President Carter pardons Vietnam War draft resisters.

1979
The Pittsburgh Steelers defeat the Dallas Cowboys to win Super Bowl XIII.

1813

The British defeat an American militia force commanded by General James Winchester at the Battle of Raisin River, at the western end of Lake Erie, during the War of 1812.

1903

The United States and Columbia sign the Hay-Herran Treaty, giving the United States a 99-year lease and sovereignty over the Panama Canal Zone.

1912

United States troops begin the occupation of Tientsin, China, to protect American interests.

1917

President Wilson appears before Congress to outline a plan for a world league of peace.

1932

Congress establishes the Reconstruction Finance Corporation to lend money to failing banks and other hard-hit industries.

1944

Allied troops land in Anzio, Italy, in an attempt to outflank the retreating German Army, during World War II.

1957

Truth or Consequences becomes the first national television show to be videotaped.

1973

Lyndon B. Johnson, thirty-sixth President of the United States, dies in Johnson City, Texas.

1973

George Foreman stops Joe Frazier in the second round, to win the heavyweight boxing championship.

1973

In *Roe v. Wade*, the Supreme Court rules that state laws prohibiting abortions before the third month are unconstitutional.

Allied forces landing at Anzio

1845
Congress passes an act establishing a uniform election day for presidential elections.

1863
The Army of the Potomac withdraws to Fredericksburg after severe rains mire men and equipment in mud, making it impossible to advance, during the Civil War.

1911
Chantecler by Edmond Rostand opens at the Knickerbocker Theater in New York.

1926
The Great God Brown by Eugene O'Neill opens at the Greenwich Village Theater in New York.

1942
The Japanese land at Rabaul in New Britain and establish a major naval base there, during World War II.

1943
The British Eighth Army enters Tripoli in Libya, during World War II.

1945
Allied forces in France take St. Vith as the Germans retreat, during World War II.

1960
The *Trieste*, a bathyscaphe built by Auguste Piccard, sets a depth record of 10,916 meters off the Mariana Islands in the North Pacific.

1964
The Twenty-Fifth Amendment is ratified, abolishing the poll tax.

1968
The U.S.S. *Pueblo* is seized by North Korean patrol boats off the coast of North Korea.

Allied forces capturing St. Vith

1722
Edward Wigglesworth becomes the first divinity professor in the Colonies, at Harvard College.

1826
The United States signs the Treaty of Washington with the Creek Indians, granting the Indians the right to stay on their land for two years.

1848
Gold is discovered on land owned by John Sutter, setting off the California gold rush.

1861
Georgia troops seize the Federal arsenal in Augusta.

1897
The *Yellow Kid* becomes the first comic strip published in a newspaper, *The New York Journal*.

1902
The United States and Denmark sign a treaty for the purchase of the Virgin Islands in the Caribbean.

1903
The United States and England sign an agreement establishing a joint commission to decide the boundaries between Canada and Alaska.

1922
C.K. Nelson of Onawa, Iowa, is awarded a patent for the first ice cream bar, named the Eskimo Pie.

1942
American destroyers sink five Japanese transports off Balikpapan in the East Indies, during World War II.

1964
The first heart transplant attempt takes place at the University Hospital in Jackson, Mississippi, with the patient dying after 3 hours.

1975
A Puerto Rican terrorist group bombs Fraunces Tavern in New York, killing four people.

1982
The San Francisco 49ers defeat the Cincinnati Bengals to win Super Bowl XVI.

1986
Voyager 2 flies within 50,679 miles of the planet Uranus, discovering new rings and moons.

1987
Three American faculty members of Beirut University in Lebanon are taken captive by Moslem terrorists.

Sutter's Mill in California

January

1787
Massachusetts state militia puts down a rebellion led by Daniel Shays, a result of harsh financial conditions for local farmers.

1863
President Lincoln appoints General Joseph Hooker to replace General Ambrose E. Burnside as commander of the Union Army of the Potomac, during the Civil War.

1915
The Supreme Court rules that a Kansas law forbidding employers to require that employees be nonunion, is unconstitutional.

1915
The first transcontinental telephone call is made between New York and San Francisco.

1945
Grand Rapids, Michigan, becomes the first city in the United States to fluoridate its drinking water.

1961
President Kennedy conducts the first presidential press conference to be televised.

1964
Echo 2 is launched from Vandenberg Air Force Base in California, becoming the first joint United States-Soviet Union cooperative space effort.

1971
Charles Manson is convicted of the 1969 murders of actress Sharon Tate and six others.

1978
One thousand people are killed when a blizzard strikes the Midwest.

1981
The Oakland Raiders defeat the Philadelphia Eagles to win Super Bowl XV.

Shays's mob occupying the court house

1837
Michigan joins the Union as the twenty-sixth state.

1838
Tennessee passes the first prohibition law in the United States.

1861
Louisiana secedes from the Union.

1896
Major General Joseph Hooker takes comand of the Union Army of the Potomac, during the Civil War.

1870
Virginia is readmitted to the Union.

1875
George F. Green of Kalamazoo, Michigan, is awarded a patent for the first electric dental drill.

1907
Congress passes a law prohibiting corporate contributions to national candidates.

1915
Congress establishes Rocky Mountain National Park.

1942
Admiral Kimmel, the former Commander in Chief of the United States Fleet at Pearl Harbor, is found guilty of deriliction of duty by a Board of Inquiry investigating the Japanese attack, during World War II.

1954
A Stillness At Appomattox by Bruce Catton wins the National Book Award for history.

1986
The Chicago Bears defeat the New England Patriots to win Super Bowl XX.

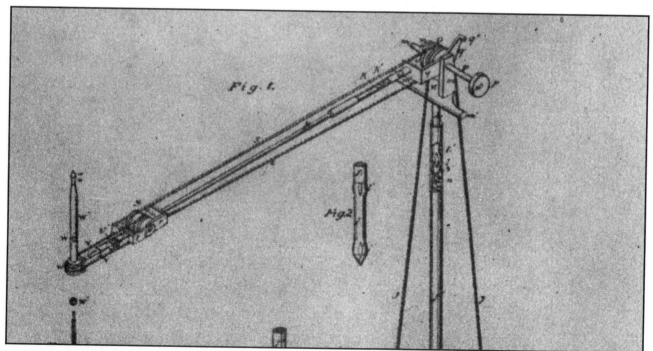

Drawing of the first electric dental drill

January

1785
The University of Georgia becomes the first state university in America.

1814
Congress authorizes the establishment of a United States Army of over 62,000 men.

1862
President Lincoln issues War order 51 calling for a general Union offensive, during the Civil War.

1863
A. D. Boileau, the owner of the Philadelphia *Journal*, is arrested by Federal authorities for printing anti-Northern articles, during the Civil War.

1943
The United States conducts its first bombing raid over a German target at Wilhelmshaven, losing three bombers, during World War II.

1951
An atomic bomb is exploded at the new test site of Yucca Flats, 65 miles northwest of Las Vegas, Nevada.

1967
The United States, the Soviet Union, and 60 other nations sign a treaty limiting the use of outer space for military purposes.

1967
Astronauts Virgil Grissom, Edward White, and Roger Chaffee are killed in a fire aboard their Apollo spacecraft, while still on the launchpad.

1973
The United States, North Vietnam, South Vietnam, and the Vietcong sign a pact calling for the withdrawal of all United States troops from Vietnam within 90 days.

Soldiers observing an A-bomb blast at Yucca Flats

January

1851
Northwestern University is established in Evanston, Illinois.

1909
The second military occupation of Cuba comes to an end.

1915
Congress establishes the United States Coast Guard.

1915
Louis D. Brandeis becomes the first Jew to serve on the Supreme Court.

1917
United States forces are withdrawn from Mexico after an unsuccessful search for revolutionary "Pancho" Villa.

1945
General "Vinegar Joe" Stilwell leads a truck convoy across the Burma-Chinese border, reopening the Burma Road, during World War II.

1950
Milton Berle wins the award as Best Kinescope performer at the Emmy Awards.

1979
Deng Xiaoping arrives in Washington, D.C., becoming the first Communist Chinese leader to visit the United States.

1986
The space shuttle, *Challenger*, explodes shortly after liftoff, killing all seven astronauts, including Christa McAuliff, a school teacher from Concord, New Hampshire.

The Space Shuttle *Challenger* exploding

1779

The British under Lieutenant Colonel Archibald Campbell capture Augusta, Georgia, during the Revolutionary War.

1802

John Beckley becomes the first Librarian of the Library of Congress.

1843

William McKinley, twenty-fifth President of the United States, is born in Niles, Ohio.

1850

Senator Henry Clay of Kentucky introduces eight resolutions in the Senate regarding free or slave status for new states, known as the Compromise of 1850.

1861

Kansas joins the Union as the thirty-fourth state.

1900

The American League is formed, to become the second professional baseball league in the United States.

1935

The United States Senate votes against American participation in the World Court.

1936

Ty Cobb, Babe Ruth, Honus Wagner, Walter Johnson, and Christy Matthewson become the first five members of the Baseball Hall of Fame in Cooperstown, New York.

1946

President Truman establishes the Central Intelligence Agency.

1964

A record 20,000 pound payload is boosted into orbit by a *Saturn* rocket launched from Cape Kennedy, Florida.

Henry Clay speaking before Congress

January

1799
Congress passes the Logan Act, making it illegal for a private citizen to conduct negotiations with a foreign government.

1835
The first assassination attempt on a president occurs when Richard Lawrence fires two shots at President Andrew Jackson, who is unhurt.

1862
The first Union ironclad warship, *Monitor*, is launched in New York, during the Civil War.

1875
The Hawaiian Reciprocity Act is signed, providing that Hawaiian territory not be turned over to a third power.

1882
Franklin D. Roosevelt, thirty-second President of the United States, is born in Hyde Park, New York.

1894
Brazilian revolutionaries fire on the United States flag in the harbor of Rio de Janiero.

1933
Adolph Hitler assumes office as Chancellor of Germany at the invitation of President Von Hindenburg.

1958
Sunrise at Campobello by Dore Schary opens at the Cort Theater in New York.

1963
Thirty American soldiers are killed when five United States helicopters are shot down over the Mekong Delta during the Vietnam War.

1968
The North Vietnamese begin the Tet Offensive, a massive assault in South Vietnam, during the Vietnam War.

1973
G. Gordon Liddy and James W. McCord are convicted of breaking into the Democratic National Committee's offices in the Watergate Building, in Washington, D.C.

1983
The Washington Redskins defeat the Miami Dolphins to win Super Bowl XVII.

1988
Brenda Webb sets a world indoor record of 15:25.04 for the 5000 meter run.

The attempted assassination of President Jackson

1862

President Lincoln issues Special War Order No. 1, calling for the Army of the Potomac to occupy Manassas Junction in Virginia, during the Civil War.

1863

Confederate gunboats, *Chicora* and *Palmetto State*, attack and destroy several Federal ships, temporarily breaking the naval blockade of Charleston, South Carolina, during the Civil War.

1915

Tear gas is used for the first time by the German army, in an attack against the Russians, during World War I.

1917

Germany announces the renewal of submarine warfare against neutral states.

1920

Joe Malone of the Quebec Bulldogs scores an NHL record 7 goals in a game against the Toronto St. Pats.

1934

Congress passes the Farm Mortgage Refinancing Act, providing easier credit terms to farmers.

1943

German General Paulus surrenders his army to the Soviets in Stalingrad, during World War II.

1950

President Truman authorizes the development of the hydrogen bomb.

1966

United States planes resume bombing of North Vietnam after a 37-day pause.

United States Marines during a gas attack

A B-52 dropping bombs over North Vietnam

February

1861
Texas secedes from the Union.

1863
Union troops attack and occupy Franklin, Tennessee, during the Civil War.

1865
Illinois becomes the first state to ratify the Thirteenth Amendment, abolishing slavery in the United States.

1865
Union forces commanded by General William T. Sherman march into South Carolina, during the Civil War.

1893
The first film production studio in the United States is opened by Thomas Alva Edison, in West Orange, New Jersey.

1898
The first automobile insurance is issued by the Travelers Insurance Company in Buffalo, New York.

1941
The United States Navy is reorganized into three fleets: the Atlantic, the Pacific, and the Asiatic, during World War II.

1950
The United Nations formally accuses Communist China of aggression in Korea.

1964
I Want to Hold Your Hand by the Beatles becomes the number one record in the United States.

Edison's first film studio

February

2

1811
A group of settlers from Russia land at Bodega Bay in northern California and establish Fort Ross.

1827
The Supreme Court rules that the President has the final authority to call out the militia.

1848
The United States and Mexico sign the Treaty of Guadalupe Hidalgo, ending the Mexican War.

1876
The National League is formed, becoming the first professional baseball league.

1901
Congress establishes the United States Army Dental Corps.

1913
Grand Central Terminal officially opens in New York.

1920
Beyond the Horizon by Eugene O'Neill opens at the Neighborhood Playhouse in New York.

1934
President Roosevelt establishes the Export-Import Bank to encourage commerce between the United States and foreign nations.

1944
The United States Fourth Marine Division takes Roi Island in the Marshall Islands, during World War II.

1962
John Uelses becomes the first man to pole vault over 16 feet, with a vault of 16′ ¼ ″ at Madison Square Garden in New York.

An early National League game

February

1690
Massachusetts issues the first paper money in America.

1783
Spain recognizes the independence of the United States.

1865
President Lincoln meets with Confederate peace commissioners aboard the *River Queen*, in Hampton Roads, Virginia, during the Civil War.

1887
Congress passes the Electoral Count Act, making each state responsible for its own electoral returns.

1908
The Supreme Court rules that antitrust laws apply to labor combinations as well as capital combinations.

1917
The United States breaks diplomatic relations with Germany.

1923
Many people are killed as five tidal waves sweep over Hawaii, inundating several villages.

1924
Woodrow Wilson, twenty-eighth President of the United States, dies in Washington, D.C.

1930
Charles Evans Hughes is appointed Chief Justice of the Supreme Court.

1951
The Rose Tattoo by Tennessee Williams opens at the Martin Beck Theater in New York.

1959
Buddy Holly and Richie Valens are killed in a plane crash in Ames, Iowa.

1962
President Kennedy orders a trade ban with Cuba.

1965
One hundred five United States Air Force Academy cadets resign as a result of cheating on examinations.

Buddy Holly

February

1789
Newly chosen electors cast their ballots in the first presidential election.

1861
The Confederate States of America is formed in Montgomery, Alabama.

1862
Union forces begin landing on the banks of the Tennessee River to prepare for an assault on Fort Henry, during the Civil War.

1887
The Interstate Commerce Commission is established, becoming the first regulatory commission in the United States.

1899
Philippine guerrillas fire on American Forces in Manila, beginning a rebellion against United States rule.

1915
Germany proclaims a war zone around the British Isles.

1932
The first Winter Olympics held in the United States opens in Lake Placid, New York.

1941
The United Service Organizations (USO) is formed, to serve the needs of American Soldiers around the world.

1978
Stayin' Alive by the Bee Gees becomes the number one record in the United States.

1987
United States yacht, *Stars & Stripes*, regains the America's Cup from Australia.

Hockey game at the first winter Olympics

1736
John Wesley arrives in Georgia to introduce Methodism to the colonies.

1862
Union forces commanded by General Ulysses S. Grant take Fort Henry on the Tennessee River, during the Civil War.

1862
The United States Senate votes to expel Senator Jesse D. Bright of Indiana for alleged complicity with the Confederacy, during the Civil War.

1932
Station W2XAB in New York becomes the first educational television station.

1941
British armored units capture 5000 Italians in North Africa, during World War II.

1943
Italian dictator Benito Mussolini dismisses Foreign Minister Count Ciano and assumes his duties, during World War II.

1972
In order to deter hijacking, the United States makes screening of all airline passengers and luggage mandatory.

1974
Publishing heiress, Patricia Hearst, is kidnapped by a group called the Symbionese Liberation Army.

1988
Panama's General Manuel Noriega is indicted by a grand jury in Miami on charges that he received more than $4.5 million in payoffs from large-scale drug dealers.

General Grant outside Fort Henry

February

1685
The Duke of York, proprietor of New York, becomes King James II of England.

1778
France recognizes the independence of the United States and signs a Treaty of Alliance.

1788
Massachusetts becomes the sixth state to ratify the Constitution.

1802
Congress empowers President Jefferson to arm United States ships in order to protect themselves against Tripolitan pirates.

1815
American inventor John Stevens is granted the first railroad charter.

1821
George Washington University is established in Washington, D.C.

1837
The House of Representatives rules that slaves do not have the right of petition that American citizens have under the Constitution.

1863
Union General S.F. Heintzelman is put in command of the Federal Department of Washington, during the Civil War.

1865
General Robert E. Lee becomes the commander of all Confederate armies, during the Civil War.

1869
Harper's Weekly runs the first caricature of Uncle Sam with whiskers.

1910
The Boys Scouts of America is established by William D. Boyce.

1911
Ronald Reagan, thirty-ninth President of the United States, is born in Tampico, Illinois.

1922
The Nine-Power Treaty is signed at the Washington Conference, endorsing the Open Door policy with China.

1941
Australian troops take Benghazi in North Africa after the withdrawal of the Italian army, during World War II.

1942
The first meeting of the combined Chiefs of Staff is held, in Washington, D.C., during World War II.

1956
Authorine Lucy becomes the first Black student to enroll at the University of Alabama.

1974
The House of Representatives approves an impeachment inquiry against President Nixon.

1977
American Buffalo by David Mamet opens at the Ethel Barrymore Theater in New York.

1982
Centerfold by the J. Geils Band becomes the number one record in the United States.

February

1827
The Deserter opens at the Bowery Theater in New York, becoming the first ballet in the United States.

1861
The Choctaw Indian Nation declares its allegiance to the Southern states.

1864
Union troops commanded by Major General Q.A. Gilmore occupy Jacksonville, Florida, during the Civil War.

1882
John L. Sullivan defeats Paddy Ryan to win the world heavyweight bare knuckle boxing championship.

1886
Federal troops are called in to restore order after more than 400 ethnic Chinese are driven from their homes in Seattle, Washington Territory.

1941
The Italian Army surrenders in Beda Fomm, North Africa during World War II.

1964
The English rock group, the Beatles, arrive at Kennedy Airport in New York to begin their first United States tour.

1976
Darryl Sittler of the Toronto Maple Leafs scores an NHL record 10 points in a game against the Boston Bruins.

1986
President-for-life Jean-Claude Duvalier of Haiti is flown to France on a United States jet after fleeing his country.

The Beatles at JFK International Airport

February

1690
French and Indian forces attack Schenectady, New York, during King William's War.

1693
The College of William & Mary is established in Virginia.

1735
The Hob In the Well becomes the first opera to be performed in the Colonies, in Charleston, South Carolina.

1862
The Confederate garrison at Roanoke Island, North Carolina, commanded by General Henry A. Wise, surrenders to Union forces, during the Civil War.

1887
President Cleveland signs the Dawes Severalty Act, dissolving Indian tribes as legal entities.

1915
D.W. Griffith's landmark motion picture, *The Birth of a Nation*, opens at Clune's Auditorium in Los Angeles.

1918
The first Army newspaper, *Stars and Stripes*, begins publication.

1924
Gee Jon becomes the first person to be executed in the gas chamber, at the Nevada State Prison.

1950
Man o' War is named the greatest race horse of the first half of the century by the Associated Press.

1962
The Defense Department sets up the Military Assistance Command in South Vietnam.

1969
The last issue of the *Saturday Evening Post* is published.

1971
The South Vietnamese Army, aided by United States air support, launches an attack into Laos, during the Vietnam War.

1980
Mary Slaney sets a world indoor record of 4:00.8 for the 1500 meter run.

Indians attacking Schenectady, New York

February

1773
William Henry Harrison, ninth President of the United States, is born in Berkely, Virginia.

1775
The British Parliament declares the Colony of Massachusetts to be in a state of rebellion.

1799
The American ship, *Constellation*, captures the French frigate, *L'Insurgente*, off the island of Nevis.

1825
After failing to receive an electoral majority in the presidential election of 1824, John Quincy Adams is chosen President by the House of Representatives.

1864
President Lincoln sits for the photograph which will be used for his image on the five dollar bill.

1871
Congress establishes the United States Weather Bureau.

1884
A tornado sweeps through the southern United States, killing over 700 people.

1922
Congress establishes a Foreign Debt Commission to settle the problem of debts incurred during World War I.

1926
The Board of Education in Atlanta, Georgia, prohibits the teaching of Darwin's theory of evolution in the public schools.

1945
United States Marines invade Iwo Jima, during World War II.

1964
The Beatles make their first appearance on the Ed Sullivan Show.

1971
Sixty-five people are killed as an earthquake strikes southern California.

1979
Thieves steal a Greek statue valued at $250,000 from the Metropolitan Museum of Art in New York, the first theft in the museum's history.

1980
Rick Barry of the Houston Rockets scores an NBA record of eight, 3-point field goals in a game against the Utah Jazz.

United States Marines landing on Iwo Jima

1676

Indians led by King Philip, a Wampanoag Indian Chief, attack the settlement at Lancaster, Massachusetts, during King Philip's War.

1763

The Treaty of Paris ends the French and Indian War.

1846

Brigham Young leads the Mormon migration west from Nauvoo, Illinois.

1855

United States citizenship laws are amended to provide citizenship to all children of American parents born outside the United States.

1907

The Colorado River is diverted to its old channel, causing it to empty into the Gulf of Mexico.

1915

President Wilson warns Germany that the United States will hold it accountable for lives lost or property damaged in submarine attacks.

1942

Glen Miller's *Chattanooga Choo Choo* becomes the first recording to receive a gold record in recognition of $1 million in sales.

1949

Death of a Salesman by Arthur Miller opens at the Morosco Theater in New York.

1962

The Soviet Union releases captured U-2 pilot, Francis Gary Powers, in exchange for Soviet spy, Rudolph Abel.

1962

Jim Beatty becomes the first American to run the mile in under 4 minutes indoors, at a meet in Los Angeles, California.

Brigham Young leading the Mormons

1766
The county court of Northampton, Virginia, declares the Stamp Act unconstitutional.

1790
The Society of Friends submits the first emancipation petition to Congress.

1811
President Madison orders trade with England ceased.

1812
Governor Elbridge Gerry of Massachusetts invents Gerrymandering, the restructuring of election districts for political purposes.

1839
The University of Missouri is founded in Columbia.

1890
President Harrison issues a proclamation throwing open 11 million acres of the Great Sioux Reservation for settlement.

1933
President Hoover establishes the Death Valley National Monument in California and Nevada.

1942
The Allied counterattack on Singapore is driven off by the Japanese after heavy losses, during World War II.

1945
The Yalta Conference ends in the Ukraine, with President Roosevelt, British Prime Minister Winston Churchill, and Soviet Premier Joseph Stalin agreeing on the postwar reorganization of Europe.

Churchill, Roosevelt and Stalin in Yalta

February

1793
Congress enacts a Fugitive Slave Act, allowing a slaveowner to recover a runaway.

1809
Abraham Lincoln, sixteenth President of the United States, is born in Hardin County, Kentucky.

1825
The Creek Indians cede all of their land in Georgia to the United States.

1846
Mexican President, Mariano Paredes, refuses to see Representative John Slidell of Louisiana, who has come to try to restore diplomatic relations between the United States and Mexico.

1863
The Confederate blockade runner, C.S.S. *Florida*, seizes and destroys the Union ship, *Jacob Bell*, in the West Indies, during the Civil War.

1908
The first around-the-world automobile race begins in New York.

1909
Over one million people attend ceremonies in New York, commemorating the 100th anniversary of Abraham Lincoln's birthday.

1924
Rhapsody in Blue by George Gershwin premieres at the Aeolian Hall in New York.

1964
The English rock group, the Beatles, perform their first concert in the United States at Carnegie Hall in New York.

Abraham Lincoln

February

1689
William and Mary of Orange are proclaimed King and Queen of England after the forced deposition of James II, concluding the Glorious Revolution.

1733
James Edward Oglethorpe of England founds Savannah, the first settlement in Georgia.

1741
The American Magazine becomes the first magazine published in North America.

1826
The American Society for the Promotion of Temperance, in Boston, becomes the first society in the United States to oppose the consumption of alcohol.

1851
The University of Minnesota is established in St. Paul.

1914
The American Society of Composers, Authors and Publishers (ASCAP) is founded in New York.

1929
Laund Loyalty, a collie, becomes the first puppy to win the Westminster Kennel Club dog show.

1929
Congress passes the Cruiser Act, authorizing construction of 19 cruisers and one aircraft carrier.

1948
Dick Button becomes the first American to win the men's singles title, at the World Figure Skating Championships in Davos, Switzerland.

1976
Dorothy Hamill wins the gold medal in figure skating at the Olympic Games in Innsbruck, Austria.

The founding of Georgia

February

1776
Spanish priest Father Garces reaches a Mohave settlement on the Colorado River.

1859
Oregon joins the Union as the thirty-third state.

1884
The Ohio River floods, cresting at 71 feet, the highest ever recorded.

1899
Congress approves the use of voting machines in Federal elections.

1903
The Department of Commerce and Labor is created by act of Congress.

1912
Arizona joins the Union as the forty-eighth state.

1919
President Wilson presents a draft of the League of Nations Covenant to the Peace Conference in Paris.

1929
Seven members of a Chicago gang are killed in a garage by rival gang members in the "St. Valentine's Day Massacre."

1951
Sugar Ray Robinson stops Jake LaMotta in the 13th round, to win the middleweight boxing championship.

1962
First Lady Jacqueline Kennedy conducts a televised tour of the White House.

1973
The first group of American prisoners of war, formally held by the North Vietnamese, arrive in the United States at Travis Air Force Base in California.

1975
The United States signs an agreement making the Marianas Islands in the Pacific Ocean a United States commonwealth.

1979
The United States Abassador to Afghanistan is killed when Afghan Government forces attempt to free him from kidnappers.

1986
Wayne Gretzky of the Edmonton Oilers gets an NHL record seven assists, for the third time, in a game against the Quebec Nordiques.

The St. Valentine's Day Massacre

February

15

1869
The University of Nebraska is founded in Lincoln.

1879
Women attorneys win the right to argue cases before the Supreme Court.

1898
The United States battleship, *Maine*, explodes in Havana, Cuba's harbor, killing 260 crewmembers.

1922
Samuel Dashiell Hammett resigns from the Pinkerton Detective Agency to begin his career as a writer of detective novels.

1933
President-elect Roosevelt is unhurt when Chicago mayor Anton Cermak is killed by a bullet fired by Giuseppe Zangara, while both are riding in a motorcade in Miami, Florida.

1945
Seventy thousand people are killed in Dresden, Germany, during a series of bombing raids by the United States and British air forces, during World War II.

1956
A Federal court bans all Louisiana laws opposing the Supreme Court ruling against segregation in public schools.

1957
Andrei A. Gromyko is appointed Foreign Minister of the Soviet Union.

1968
Henry Lewis is appointed director of the New Jersey Symphony, becoming the first Black to head a major orchestra.

1980
CBS anchorman, Walter Chronkite, announces his retirement.

The battleship *Maine* exploding

February

1804

Lt. Stephen Decatur, commanding the *Intrepid*, burns the United States frigate, *Philadelphia*, captured during the Tripolitan War, to keep it from falling into enemy hands.

1861

Texas state troops seize the Federal arsenal and barracks in San Antonio.

1862

Union forces commanded by General Ulysses S. Grant take Fort Donelson, near Nashville, Tennessee, during the Civil War.

1933

The Twenty-First Amendment is approved by the Senate, repealing the Eighteenth Amendment and ending prohibition.

1937

Dr. Wallace Carothers is awarded a patent for nylon fiber.

1938

Congress creates the Federal Crop Insurance Corporation to insure producers of wheat against losses due to bad weather.

1942

German U-boats attack Allied oil installations on the Island of Aruba in the Caribbean Sea, during World War II.

1943

The Soviets capture Kharkov in the Soviet Union, forcing German General Hausser's Panzer Corps to withdraw, during World War II.

1959

Fidel Castro becomes premier of Cuba.

1965

Four members of the Black Liberation Front are arrested for plotting to blow up the Statue of Liberty.

Union Navy attacking Fort Donelson

February

1834

The United States and Spain sign the Van Ness Convention, settling territorial claims.

1864

The Confederate vessel, *Hunley*, makes the first successful submarine attack, sinking the Federal sloop, *Housatonic*, during the Civil War.

1865

Union forces commanded by General William T. Sherman enter Columbia, South Carolina, after retreating Confederate troops set it on fire, during the Civil War.

1870

Esther Morris of South Pass, Wyoming, becomes the first woman judge in the United States.

1893

The University of Montana is established in Missoula.

1897

The National Congress of Mothers is established in Washington, D.C.

1944

American forces land on Eniwetok Atoll in the Marshall Islands, during World War II.

1956

Hayes Jenkins wins his fourth consecutive men's singles title at the World Figure Skating Championships in Germany.

1981

The Chrysler Corporation announces a record $1,700 million loss for the year 1980.

1988

Marine Colonel, William R. Higgins, is kidnapped by Moslem terrorists in southern Lebanon.

The burning of Charleston, South Carolina

1861
The Cheyenne and Arapaho Indians agree to give up their claims to most of Colorado.

1861
Jefferson Davis becomes President of the Confederate States of America.

1865
Union naval forces bombard Fort Anderson on the Cape Fear River in South Carolina, during the Civil War.

1878
The Lincoln County War begins as English rancher John Tunstall is killed by cattle rustlers in the New Mexico Territory.

1922
Congress passes the Capper-Volstead Act, allowing farmers to sell cooperatively without violating antitrust laws.

1927
The United States and Canada establish diplomatic relations.

1930
Astronomer Clyde W. Tombaugh discovers the planet Pluto at the Lowell Observatory in Flagstaff, Arizona.

1948
Mister Roberts, by Thomas Heggen and Joshua Logan, opens at the Alvin Theater in New York.

1960
The Winter Olympics open in Squaw Valley, California.

1978
Leon Spinks outpoints Muhammad Ali, to win the heavyweight boxing championship.

The inauguration of Jefferson Davis

February

1803
Ohio joins the Union as the seventeenth state.

1864
The Knights of Pythias is formed in Washington, D.C.

1866
Congress passes the New Freedmen's Bureau bill, providing for military trials for people accused of depriving Blacks of their civil rights.

1942
General Dwight D. Eisenhower is appointed Chief of War Plans Division of the United States Army General Staff, during World War II.

1949
Pisan Cantos by Ezra Pound wins the first Bollingen Prize for Poetry.

1953
Picnic by William Inge opens at the Music Box Theater in New York.

1968
More than half of Florida's public school teachers walk off the job in the first statewide teachers strike in the United States.

1986
Congress ratifies a United Nations treaty outlawing genocide that had been signed by the United States in 1948.

1987
President Reagan lifts trade sanctions against Poland after the Communist government releases political prisoners and restores its "most favored nation" status for commerce.

General Eisenhower with his staff

February

1755

British General, Edward Braddock, arrives in Virginia to become commander in chief of all British forces in America.

1839

Congress passes a law forbidding dueling in the District of Columbia.

1861

The Department of the Navy is established by the Confederate States of America.

1864

Confederate forces, commanded by General Joseph Finegan, defeat the Union troops, commanded by General Seymour, at the Battle of Olustee, Florida, during the Civil War.

1872

Silas Noble and James P. Cooley are awarded a patent for the toothpick.

1907

President Roosevelt signs the Immigration Act of 1907, restricting immigration by Japanese laborers.

1943

German forces commanded by General Irwin Rommel drive back American troops at the Kasserine Pass in Tunisia, during World War II.

1944

The United States Air Force launches a series of bombing raids on German aircraft industry centers, during World War II.

1962

John Glenn becomes the first American astronaut to make an orbital flight.

1971

An operator at the National Emergency Warning Center mistakenly runs an emergency alert tape, which is broadcast across the United States.

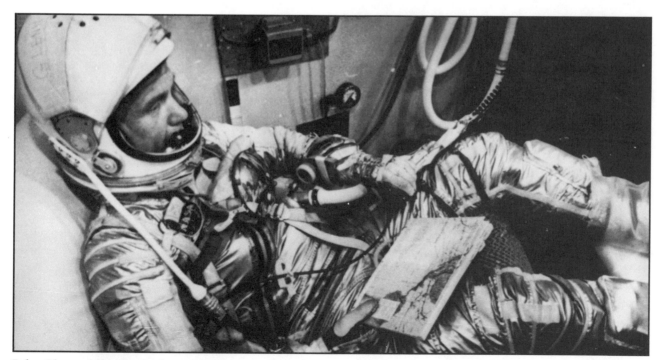

John Glenn riding to the launch pad

February

1787
Congress calls for a Constitutional Convention, to take place in Philadelphia.

1792
Congress passes the Presidential Succession Act.

1853
Congress passes the Coinage Act, authorizing the minting of three-dollar pieces.

1857
Congress passes an act declaring that foreign coins are no longer legal tender.

1862
Confederate forces, commanded by Colonel Henry H. Sibley, defeat Union troops, commanded by General R.S. Canby, in New Mexico, during the Civil War.

Placing the capstone on the Washington Monument

1865
Confederate troops commanded by General Braxton Bragg evacuate Wilmington, North Carolina, during the Civil War.

1885
The Washington Monument is dedicated in Washington, D.C.

1909
The 16-battleship naval fleet, known as the Great White Fleet, returns to Hampton Roads, Virginia, after a cruise around the world lasting over a year.

1925
The *New Yorker* Magazine edited by Harold Ross begins publication.

1965
Black Muslim leader, Malcolm X, is shot and killed during a speech in New York.

1972
President Nixon arrives in Peking, becoming the first American president to visit the Peoples Republic of China.

1972
West Coast longshoremen end a record 134-day dock strike.

1975
Former White House aides, H.R. Haldeman and John D. Ehrlichman, and former Attorney General, John Mitchell, are each sentenced to 30 months in prison for their roles in the Watergate cover-up.

February

1630
Popcorn is invented by Quadequina, in the Massachusetts Bay Colony.

1631
The first Thanksgiving is celebrated in the Massachusetts Bay Colony.

1732
George Washington, first President of the United States, is born in Virginia.

1819
Spain cedes its land in Florida to the United States, signing the Florida Purchase Treaty.

1856
The Republican Party holds its first national meeting in Pittsburgh, Pennsylvania.

1875
The American Manufactory of Woolens, Linens, and Cottons becomes the first joint stock company in America.

1879
Frank Winfield Woolworth establishes the first variety chain store in Utica, New York.

1923
The first successful chinchilla farm is established in Los Angeles.

1944
United States Marines take Parry Island, completing the Allied takeover of the Marshall Islands, during World War II.

1966
Operation White Wing, a search and destroy mission, ends with 1130 Communist troops killed, during the Vietnam War.

The first Thanksgiving

February

1836
President Santa Anna of Mexico raises an army of 6000 men to defend his concept of a central government for Mexican territories, including Texas.

1836
The Mexican Army commanded by General Santa Anna begins a siege of the Alamo.

1847
United States forces, commanded by General Zachary Taylor, defeat the Mexican Army, led by General Santa Anna, at the Battle of Buena Vista, during the Mexican War.

1848
John Quincy Adams, sixth President of the United States, dies in the House of Representatives in Washington, D.C.

The Battle of Buena Vista

1861
Texas secedes from the Union.

1862
Confederate forces evacuate Nashville, Tennessee, during the Civil War.

1870
Mississippi is readmitted to the Union.

1903
Cuba releases Guantanamo and Bahia Honda to the United States for use as naval stations.

1906
Tommy Burns outpoints Marvin Hart, to win the heavyweight boxing championship.

1915
Nevada passes a divorce bill, requiring only six months residence.

1927
President Coolidge signs the Radio Control Act, establishing a five-member Federal Radio Commission with wide regulatory authority.

1939
You Can't Take it With You wins the Academy Award for Best Picture of 1938.

1954
The inoculation of schoolchildren with a polio vaccine developed by Dr. Jonas Salk begins, in Pittsburgh.

1960
Demolition begins on Ebbets Field in Brooklyn, New York, the original home of the Brooklyn Dodgers.

February

1761

James Otis voices opposition to English colonial rule in a speech before the Supreme Court of Massachusetts.

1803

The Supreme Court rules an act of Congress null and void if it conflicts with the United States Constitution.

1813

The American sloop, *Hornet*, sinks the British sloop, *Peacock*, off the coast of Guiana, during the War of 1812.

1821

Mexico declares its independence from Spain.

1855

President Pierce signs an act creating the first United States Court of Claims.

1863

Congress establishes the Arizona Territory.

1868

The House of Representatives votes to impeach President Johnson.

1917

The British Secret Service intercepts the "Zimmerman telegram," revealing German plans to lure Mexico into World War I with promises of American territory.

1938

The first commercially produced nylon is made by the du Pont Company in Arlington, New Jersey.

1955

Silk Stockings by Cole Porter opens at the Imperial Theater in New York.

The impeachment of Andrew Johnson

February

1836
Samuel Colt is awarded a patent for his "six-shooter" revolver.

1837
Thomas Davenport of Rutland, Vermont, is awarded a patent for the first practical electric motor.

1863
Congress passes the National Banking Act, setting up a system of national banks.

1870
Senator Hiram R. Revels of Mississippi becomes the first Black to serve in Congress.

1885
Congress passes an act prohibiting the fencing of public lands.

Cassius Clay after beating Sonny Liston

1913
The Sixteenth Amendment, authorizing the levying of income taxes, is ratified.

1933
The U.S.S. *Ranger* becomes the United States' first aircraft carrier.

1949
The WAC-Corporal guided missile sets a flight altitude record of 250 miles, at White Sands, New Mexico.

1951
The first Pan-American Games begin, in Buenos Aires, Argentina.

1953
Wonderful Town, by Betty Comden, Adolph Green, and Leonard Bernstein, opens at the Winter Garden in New York.

1957
The Supreme Court voids a Michigan law banning the sale of books that might corrupt youth.

1960
Toys in the Attic by Lillian Hellman opens at the Hudson Theater in New York.

1964
Cassius Clay knocks out Sonny Liston in the sixth round, to win the heavyweight boxing championship.

1986
We Are The World, by USA for Africa, introduced to raise money for famine victims in Ethiopia, wins the Grammy Award as Best Record of 1985.

1775
British forces land in Salem, Massachusetts, and capture a Colonial arsenal.

1863
In support of the Union, the Cherokee Indian National Council repeals its ordinance of succession, during the Civil War.

1907
Congress passes the General Appropriation Act, increasing the salaries of members of Congress.

1926
President Coolidge signs the Revenue Act, reducing income taxes.

1942
How Green Was My Valley wins the Academy Award for Best Picture of 1941.

1951
The Twenty-Second Amendment is adopted, stipulating that a president may not serve more than two terms.

1960
A Thurber Carnival, based on the works of James Thurber, opens at the ANTA Theater in New York.

1984
Carl Lewis sets a world indoor record of 28' 10¼ " for the long jump at a track meet in New York.

1986
President Ferdinand Marcos of the Philippines is forced out of office after a fraudulent election, fleeing to Hawaii.

1986
Robert Penn Warren becomes the first Poet Laureate of the United States.

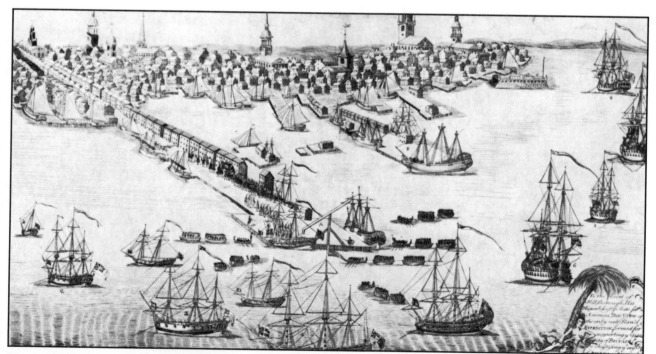

The British landing in Massachusetts

1782

The British Parliament votes against waging further war against the Colonies.

1860

Abraham Lincoln delivers a speech at Cooper Union in New York, projecting him into the lead for the Republican presidential nomination.

1920

Secretary of Commerce, Herbert Hoover, heads a conference establishing a system for allocating wavelengths for radio transmissions.

1923

Humoresque by Fannie Hurst opens at the Vanderbilt Theater in New York.

1931

The New York World-Telegram is created with the merger of *The New York World* and the *New York Telegram*.

1932

Congress passes the Glass-Steagall Banking Act, authorizing the Federal Reserve Bank to expand credit.

1939

The Supreme Court declares sitdown strikes illegal.

1941

Rebecca wins the Academy Award for Best Picture of 1940.

1979

Barbara Tuchman becomes the first woman President of the American Academy and Institute of Arts and Letters.

1987

Mike Conley sets a world indoor record of 58' 3¼ " for the triple jump at a track meet in New York.

Abraham Lincoln at Cooper Union

February

1847

The Missouri Mounted Volunteers commanded by Colonel Alexander Doniphan defeat the Mexicans at the Battle of Sacramento, Mexico, during the Mexican War.

1849

The first group of prospectors arrive in California, during the Gold Rush of '49.

1861

Congress establishes the Territory of Colorado.

1863

The Confederate ship, *Nashville*, is destroyed by the Union ironclad, *Montauk*, on the Ogeechee River in Georgia during the Civil War.

1920

Congress passes the Esch-Cummins Transportation Act, returning railroads to private ownership.

1943

Norwegian soldiers sabotage the Norsk Hydro Power Station, being used by the Germans to make "heavy water," vital to atomic research, during World War II.

1948

Mister Roberts, by Thomas Heggen and Joshua Logan, wins the Tony Award for Best Play of 1947-1948.

1973

Members of the American Indian Movement occupy Wounded Knee, South Dakota, to dramatize their cause.

1988

The XVth Olympic Winter Games end in Calgary, Canada with the United States winning only six medals, one of its worst performances in international competition.

American Dragoons in action during the Mexican War

1704
Abenaki Indians attack the frontier settlement of Deerfield, Massachusetts, killing over 50 colonists.

1904
President Roosevelt appoints a seven-member commission to oversee the construction of the Panama Canal.

1916
The German fleet is given orders to attack armed merchant shipping without warning, during World War I.

1940
Gone With The Wind wins the Academy Award for Best Picture of the year.

1940
Hattie McDaniel becomes the first Black actress to win an Academy Award, for her supporting role in *Gone With The Wind*.

1944
The Allies conduct heavy bombing raids over Berlin, Germany, during World War II.

1952
Dick Button wins his fifth straight singles title at the World Figure Skating Championships.

1964
Frank Rugani drives a badminton shuttlecock a record 79′ 8″.

1968
Sgt. Pepper's Lonely Hearts Club Band by the Beatles, wins the Grammy Award for Best Album of 1967.

1984
United States Marines complete their withdrawal from Beirut, Lebanon.

Abenaki Indians attacking Deerfield, Massachusetts

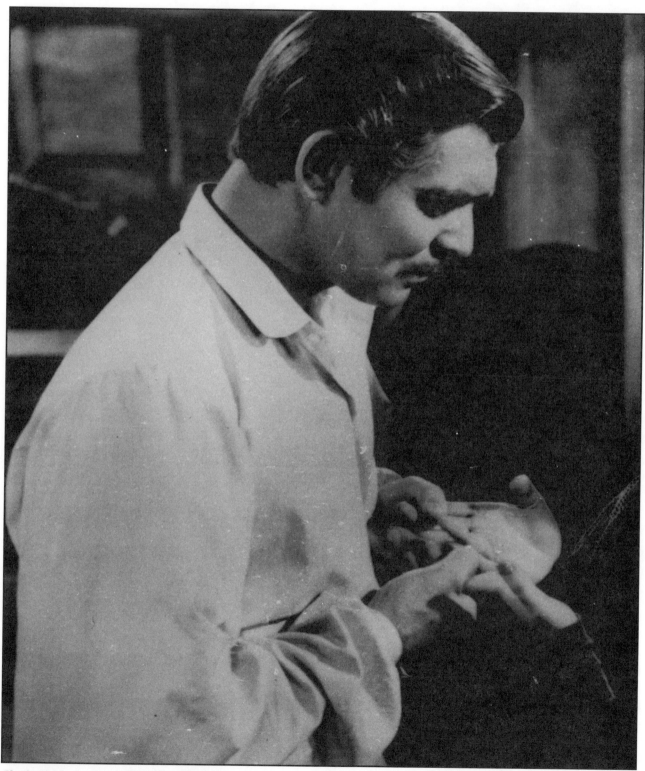

Clark Gable in *Gone With The Wind*

March

1543
Spanish explorer, Bartolome Ferrelo, sails north along the California coast, reaching Oregon.

1786
The Ohio Company is formed to purchase land and settle near the Upper Ohio River.

1790
Congress passes the Census Act, calling for regular censuses of the United States.

1867
Nebraska joins the Union as the thirty-seventh state.

1872
Congress establishes Yellowstone Park in Wyoming.

Yellowstone National Park

1893
Congress passes the Diplomatic Appropriation Act, creating the rank of ambassador.

1912
Albert Berry makes the first parachute jump from an airplane at Jefferson Barracks, Missouri.

1913
Congress passes the Webb-Kenyon Interstate Liquor Act, making it illegal to ship liquor into states where its sale is banned.

1932
Charles Lindbergh's 19-month old son is kidnapped from their home in Hopewell, New Jersey, one of the most highly publicized crimes in the United States.

1933
Six states declare Bank Holidays to prevent runs on bank assets.

1937
President Roosevelt signs the Reciprocal Trade Agreement Act, extending his ability to negotiate foreign trade agreements until June, 1940.

1942
The Battle of the Java Sea ends with the Japanese fleet defeating an American fleet commanded by Admiral Thomas C. Hart, during World War II.

1961
President Kennedy establishes the Peace Corps.

1971
The radical Weather Underground group sets off a bomb in the Capital building, causing over $300,000 in damage.

An early fort on the Oregon coast

Slaves on a Southern plantation

March

2

1807
Congress passes an act prohibiting the importation of slaves after January 1, 1808.

1824
Federal control of interstate commerce is established by the Supreme Court, in the *Gibbons v. Ogden* steamboat case.

1829
The New England Asylum for the Blind in Boston becomes the first school for the blind in the United States.

1836
Texas declares itself an independent republic.

1853
Congress forms the Washington Territory.

1861
Congress establishes the Nevada and Dakota Territories.

1867
Congress passes the first Reconstruction Act over President Johnson's veto, imposing martial law on the Southern States.

1877
An electoral commission awards all disputed votes in the presidential election of 1876 to Republican candidate Rutherford B. Hayes.

1889
Kansas passes the first antitrust law in the United States.

1901
Congress adopts the Platt Amendment, making Puerto Rico a protectorate.

1916
The *Eighth Symphony* by Gustav Mahler is premiered at the Bandbox in New York.

1917
Congress passes the Jones Act, making Puerto Rico a United States Territory.

1938
Floods and landslides in southern California kill 144 people.

1944
Casablanca wins the Academy Award for Best Picture of 1943.

1949
U.S. Air Force Captain, James Gallagher, completes the first nonstop flight around the world, refueling several times in mid-flight.

1952
The Supreme Court rules that people considered subversives can be barred from teaching in public schools.

1955
Bus Stop by William Inge opens at the Music Box Theater in New York.

1962
Wilt Chamberlain of the Philadelphia Warriors, scores an NBA record 100 points in a game against the New York Knickerbockers.

1971
William A. "Tony" Boyle, President of the United Mine Workers, is indicted for illegal campaign contributions and embezzlement.

March

1779
The Americans under General John Ashe lose more than 300 soldiers at the Battle of Briar Creek, Georgia, during the Revolutionary War.

1812
Congress approves the first foreign aid, for the relief of earthquake victims in Venezuela.

1815
Congress declares war against Algeria, a result of interference with American shipping by the Algerians.

1820
Congress passes the Missouri Compromise, with Maine to be admitted to the Union as a free state and Missouri as a slave state, along with restrictions on the spread of slavery into new territories.

1832
The Supreme Court rules that the Federal Government has jurisdiction over Indians within the states.

1837
Congress increases the membership in the Supreme Court from seven to nine justices.

1837
Congress recognizes the Republic of Texas.

1845
Florida joins the Union as the twenty-seventh state.

1947
Congress approves the use of adhesive postage stamps.

1849
Congress establishes the Minnesota Territory.

1849
The Department of Interior is created by act of Congress.

1853
Congress authorizes a survey to find the most practical route for a transcontinental railway.

1855
Congress appropriates $30,000 to introduce camels into the southwestern United States.

1863
Congress passes the first conscription act in the United States, during the Civil War.

1863
Congress establishes the Idaho Territory.

1865
Congress establishes the Freedmen's Bureau to help the freed Blacks in the South.

1871
Congress passes the Indian Appropriation Act, making all Indians national wards and nullifying all Indian treaties.

1885
The United States Post Office inaugurates special delivery mail service.

1917
Russia and Germany sign the Treaty of Brest-Litovsk, ending Russia's participation in World War I.

1931
President Hoover signs an act making the "Star Spangled Banner" the national anthem.

March

1634
The first tavern in America opens in Boston.

1681
William Penn receives a grant to establish the Colony of Pennsylvania.

1789
The first session of the United States Congress convenes.

1791
Vermont joins the Union as the fourteenth state.

1833
The First Regiment of Dragoons becomes the first cavalry unit under its own command in the United States.

1861
The Confederate flag is adopted in Montgomery, Alabama.

1861
Abraham Lincoln is inaugurated President of the United States.

1871
President Grant establishes the first Civil Service Commission in the United States.

1923
Congress passes the Intermediate Credit Act, to assist farmers in financing their crops.

1933
President Roosevelt appoints Frances Perkins, Secretary of Labor, the first woman to hold a Cabinet position.

1937
The Great Ziegfeld wins the Academy Award for Best Picture of 1936.

1943
The Battle of the Bismarck Sea ends with the sinking of an entire Japanese convoy of 22 ships, during World War II.

1943
Mrs. Miniver wins the Academy Award for Best Picture of 1942.

1964
International Brotherhood of Teamsters President, James R. Hoffa, is sentenced to eight years in prison for tampering with a Federal jury.

1973
The International Track Association launches its first season.

1976
John Pezzin rolls a record 33 consecutive strikes in an ABC league bowling tournament.

The Confederate flag

March

1770
The Boston Massacre occurs when British troops fire on a mob, killing five colonists.

1782
The English Parliament votes to negotiate peace with the United States.

1900
The Hall of Fame, commemorating great Americans, opens in New York.

1923
Montana and Nevada enact legislature establishing the first old age pension plans in the United States.

1948
A United States Navy rocket reaches a record speed of 3000 mph and an altitude of 78 miles, at White Sands, New Mexico.

1953
Soviet Premier Joseph Stalin dies in Moscow.

1966
The Ballad of the Green Berets by Staff Sergeant Barry Sadler becomes the number one record in the United States.

1979
Voyager I makes its closest approach to Jupiter —172,000 miles.

1979
The Supreme Court rules that alimony laws requiring payments by divorced husbands, but not divorced wives, are unconstitutional.

1983
Billie Jean by Michael Jackson becomes the number one record in the United States.

The Boston Massacre

1778

English explorer Captain James Cook arrives off the coast of present day Oregon, seeking the Northwest Passage.

1836

Mexican General Santa Anna takes the Alamo in San Antonio, Texas, killing all of the defenders, including frontiersman Davy Crockett.

1857

The Supreme Court rules that a slave taken into a free state cannot sue for freedom, in the Dred Scott decision.

1865

Confederate General Joseph E. Johnston assumes command of all troops in the Carolinas, during the Civil War.

1902

Congress establishes the Bureau of the Census.

1943

The Germans lose 50 tanks in the unsuccessful attack on the British at Medenine in Tunisia, during World War II.

1944

Eight hundred United States Flying Fortresses drop 2000 pounds of bombs on Berlin, during World War II.

1983

The United States Football League opens its first season.

1984

Dale Hawerchuk of the Winnipeg Jets gets an NHL record five assists in one period in a game against the Los Angeles Kings.

1987

Greg Foster sets a world indoor record of 7.46 for the 60 meter hurdles.

The fall of the Alamo

1825

Joel R. Poinsett becomes the first United States Minister to Mexico.

1859

The Supreme Court rules that a state cannot interfere in a Federal case, in *Abelman v. Booth.*

1862

Union forces commanded by General Samuel Curtis repulse a Confederate attack at the Battle of Pea Ridge, Arkansas, during the Civil War.

1876

Alexander Graham Bell is awarded a patent for the telephone.

1911

Twenty thousand United States troops are sent to the Mexican border as the Mexican Revolution continues.

1917

The Original Dixieland Jazz Band records the first jazz record, for the Victor Company in Camden, New Jersey.

1927

The Supreme Court rules that a Texas law prohibiting Blacks from voting in primary elections is unconstitutional.

1945

The United States First Army crosses the Remagen Bridge over the Rhine River, during World War II.

1946

The Lost Weekend wins the Academy Award for Best Picture of 1945.

1974

The Civil War ironclad ship, *Monitor,* which sank in 1862, is discovered off the coast of Hatteras, North Carolina.

The Battle of Pea Ridge

March

1822

The United States recognizes the independence of Argentina, Brazil, Chile, Columbia, Peru, and Mexico.

1862

The Confederate ironclad ship, *Virginia*, sinks the Union ship, *Cumberland*, and destroys the *Congress* at Hampton Roads, Virginia, during the Civil War.

1862

Captain Nathaniel Gordon becomes the last pirate to be hanged in the United States.

1874

Millard Fillmore, thirteenth President of the United States, dies in Buffalo, New York.

1881

The Southern Pacific and Atchison, Topeka & Sante Fe railroads join in Deming, New Mexico, completing the second transcontinental railroad.

1925

As the worst tornado in the United States sweeps through the midwest, 689 people are killed.

1930

William H. Taft, twenty-seventh President of the United States, dies in Washington, D.C.

1948

The United States Supreme Court rules that religious education in public schools is unconstitutional.

1962

The United States and the Soviet Union sign a two-year cultural exchange agreement.

1965

A force of 3500 United States Marines land in Danang, becoming the first American combat troops in Vietnam.

United States Marines landing in Vietnam

1847
In the first major amphibious operation undertaken by United States forces, General Winfield Scott lands 10,000 troops near Vera Cruz, Mexico, during the Mexican War.

1862
In a landmark naval battle between two ironclad warships, the Confederate, *Virginia*, and the Union, *Monitor*, fight to a standoff at Hampton Roads, Virginia, during the Civil War.

1864
In a ceremony at the White House, Ulysses S. Grant is given his commission as Lieutenant General and becomes Commander in Chief of the Union Army, during the Civil War.

1893
President Cleveland withdraws the Hawaiian Annexation Treaty pending an investigation of the overthrow of the monarchy in January.

1916
Mexican revolutionary, "Pancho" Villa, leads a band of 1500 guerrillas into New Mexico, killing 17 Americans.

1941
The Italians launch an offensive into Albania, personally supervised by Benito Mussolini, during World War II.

1942
The Japanese take complete control of Java, after the Dutch government evacuates, during World War II.

1961
The Devil's Advocate by Dory Schary opens at the Billy Rose Theater in New York.

1975
The first International Women's Art Festival is held in New York.

The *Monitor* driving off the *Merrimac*

1629

King Charles I of England dissolves Parliament, encouraging immigration to the American Colonies.

1785

Congress appoints Thomas Jefferson Minister to France.

1849

The Missouri Legislature rules that the right to prohibit slavery in any territory belongs to the people.

1876

The first coherent message is transmitted on the telephone by its inventor, Alexander Graham Bell, who says: "Come here Watson, I want you."

1933

One hundred eighteen people are killed in an earthquake centered in Long Beach, California, the second most destructive earthquake in the United States.

1938

The Life of Emile Zola wins the Academy Award for Best Picture of 1937.

1944

American forces take Talasea in New Britain, during World War II.

1966

Two thousand North Vietnamese troops attack a Green Beret camp in the Ashau Valley, killing 200 soldiers, during the Vietnam War.

1982

The United States imposes economic sanctions against Libya for its role in international terrorism.

Demonstrating the telephone

1861
The Confederate Constitution, declaring sovereignty of states and allowing slavery, passes the Confederate Congress.

1863
Federal gunboats on the Yazoo Pass off the Mississippi River are repelled by the Confederates at the hastily built Fort Pemberton, forcing them to withdraw, during the Civil War.

1865
Union troops commanded by General William T. Sherman occupy Fayetteville, North Carolina, during the Civil War.

1940
The Soviet Union and Finland sign an armistice, with Finland giving up the Karelian Isthmus, during World War II.

1941
President Roosevelt signs the Lend-Lease Bill, providing a system under which the United States can lend military equipment to democratic nations, during World War II.

1942
General Douglas MacArthur leaves the Philippines declaring, "I shall return," during World War II.

1959
A Raisin in the Sun by Lorraine H. Hansberry opens at the Ethel Barrymore Theater in New York.

1974
Candide, by Leonard Bernstein and Hugh Wheeler, opens at the Broadway Theater in New York.

Union gunboats on the Yazoo River

March

1862
Union troops occupy Winchester, Virginia, after its evacuation by the Confederates commanded by Stonewall Jackson, during the Civil War.

1864
The Red River Campaign begins with Union forces commanded by General Nathaniel Banks heading up the Red River on gunboats into Louisiana, during the Civil War.

1877
John Wanamaker of Philadelphia opens the first major department store in the United States.

1888
The Blizzard of '88 strikes the Atlantic Seaboard, killing 400 people and cutting off New York from the rest of the country for 36 hours.

1889
Almon B. Strowger of Kansas City is awarded a patent for the first automatic telephone exchange.

1912
The Girl Guides, the forerunner of the Girl Scouts, is established by Daisy Gordon.

1933
President Roosevelt broadcasts his first "Fireside Chat" radio address to the Nation.

1942
The first American "Seabees" see action as they land and build a base in New Caledonia, during World War II.

1966
Bobby Hull of the Chicago Blacks becomes the first hockey player to score 50 goals in one season.

Fighting the blizzard in New York

March

1862

Union troops commanded by General Ambrose Burnside land in North Carolina, during the Civil War.

1865

Confederate President Jefferson Davis signs a bill making slaves subject to military service, during the Civil War.

1901

Benjamin Harrison, twenty-third President of the United States, dies in Indianapolis, Indiana.

1928

When the St. Francis Dam, outside Los Angeles, California, collapses, 451 people are killed.

1930

The planet Pluto is identified, from a photograph taken at the Lowell Observatory in Flagstaff, Arizona.

1944

An American landing force overruns Hauwei in the Admiralty Islands, during World War II.

1947

The Best Years of Our Lives wins the Academy Award for Best Picture of 1946.

1950

General Motors Corporation announces earnings of over $656 million, a record for a corporation.

1963

Soviet reconnaissance planes fly over Alaskan airspace, becoming the first established Soviet overflight of the United States.

1981

The Star of Peace diamond, at 170.45 carats, is sold for a record $20 million.

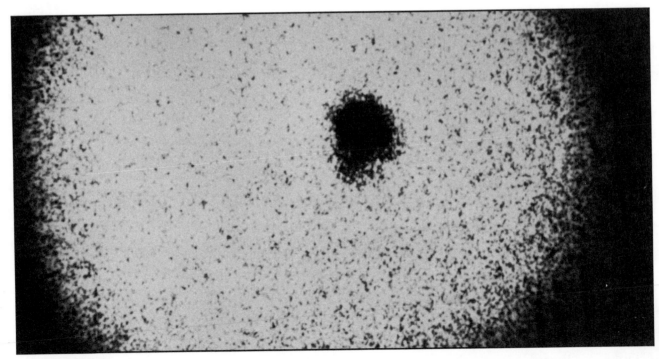

The planet Pluto

March

1780
The Spanish Governor of Louisiana captures the port of Mobile, Alabama.

1794
Eli Whitney of Mulberry Grove, Georgia, is awarded a patent for his cotton gin.

1812
Congress authorizes the first war bonds, to help finance the War of 1812.

1893
The Waldorf Hotel opens on Park Avenue in New York.

1900
Congress passes the Currency Act, establishing a gold standard for United States currency.

1904
The Supreme Court orders the Northern Securities Company dissolved in a landmark antitrust decision.

1907
President Roosevelt appoints an Inland Waterways Commission to study the problems of forest preservation and commercial waterways.

1936
Bury the Dead by Irwin Shaw opens at the Forty-Sixth Street Theater in New York.

1951
United States forces recapture Seoul, during the Korean War.

1961
The Rise and Fall of the Third Reich by William L. Shirer, wins the National Book Award for Non-Fiction.

Eli Whitney's Cotton Gin

March

1729
Sister St. Stanislaus Hachard of the Ursuline Convent in New Orleans becomes the first Catholic nun in America.

1767
Andrew Jackson, seventh President of the United States, is born in Cureton's Pond, South Carolina.

1781
The British led by General Cornwallis defeat the Americans at the Battle of Guilford Court House, North Carolina, during the Revolutionary War.

1820
Maine joins the Union as the twenty-third state.

1836
Roger B. Taney is confirmed by the Senate as Chief Justice of the Supreme Court.

1862
President Lincoln approves an act of Congress calling for the United States, England, and France to consider ways of preserving Atlantic fisheries.

1869
The Cincinnati Red Stockings becomes the first professional baseball team in the United States.

1875
Archbishop John McCloskey of Chicago becomes the first American cardinal.

1892
Jesse W. Reno of New York is awarded a patent for the first escalator.

1916
An American expeditionary force commanded by General John J. Pershing crosses into Mexico in pursuit of revolutionary "Pancho" Villa.

1917
Czar Nicholas II of Russia abdicates his throne as a popular revolution sweeps through the country protesting food shortages and the continuation of World War I.

1919
The American Legion is formed by delegates representing veterans of the American Expeditionary Force in Europe.

1941
President Roosevelt promises that the United States will supply England and the Allies with military aid.

1943
The United States Seventh Fleet is formed to organize naval operations around New Guinea, during World War II.

1945
Going My Way wins the Academy Award for Best Picture of 1944.

1956
My Fair Lady, by Lerner and Loewe, opens at the Mark Hellinger Theater in New York.

1964
Elizabeth Taylor and Richard Burton are married in Montreal, Canada.

1980
The Penobscot Indians in Maine settle a claim for land taken in a violation of the Indian Nonintercourse Act of 1790.

1988
Eugene A. Marino of Atlanta, Georgia, becomes the first Black Catholic Archbishop in the United States.

March

1751
James Madison, fourth President of the United States, is born in Port Conway, Virginia.

1802
Congress establishes the United States Military Academy at West Point, New York.

1827
Freedom's Journal, the first newspaper for Blacks, begins publication.

1910
Barney Oldfield sets a new land speed record of 133 mph, in Daytona, Florida.

1926
Robert H. Goddard of Auburn, Massachusetts, launches the first liquid fuel rocket.

1934
Cavalcade wins the Academy Award for Best Picture of 1932-1933.

1950
The Man with the Golden Arm by Nelson Algren wins the first National Book Award for Fiction.

1955
President Eisenhower issues a statement affirming the United States' intention to use nuclear weapons in the event of a war.

1966
Gemini 8 makes the first successful space docking.

1968
United States troops kill 300 civilians, including children, in the South Vietnamese hamlet of My Lai, during the Vietnam War.

1968
(Sittin' On) The Dock of the Bay by Otis Redding becomes the number one record in the United States.

The United States Military Academy

March

1737
The first celebration of St. Patrick's Day is held in Boston.

1775
The Cherokee Indians sign the Treaty of Sycamore Shoals, selling their land in Kentucky to the Transylvania Company.

1776
The British are forced to evacuate Boston after American forces occupy Dorcester Heights overlooking the city.

1811
The *New Orleans* becomes the first practical sidewheel steamboat in the United States.

1863
A Union cavalry force, commanded by General William Wood, attacks the Confederates, commanded by General Fitz Lee, but are forced to withdraw, at the Battle of Kelly's Ford in Virginia, during the Civil War.

1871
The National Association of Professional Baseball Players is formed.

1906
President Roosevelt uses the word ''muckraker'' to describe writers who expose social ills in the United States.

1910
The Camp Fire Girls is organized by Dr. and Mrs. Luther Halsey Gulick.

1941
The National Gallery of Art opens in Washington, D.C.

1953
The Office of Price Stabilization officially ends all price controls in the United States.

An early sidewheel steamboat

March

1766
The English Parliament passes the Declaratory Act giving England the power to pass laws binding on the Colonies.

1766
The English Parliament repeals the Stamp Act after intense opposition in the Colonies.

1837
Grover Cleveland, twenty-second and twenty-fourth President of the United States, is born in Caldwell, New Jersey.

1837
The University of Michigan is established in Ann Arbor.

1911
The Roosevelt Dam on the Salt River in Arizona opens.

1924
Congress passes the Soldier's Bonus Bill, providing most veterans with 20-year annuities.

1937
Two hundred ninety-four students are killed in New London, Texas, in the worst school fire in the United States.

1938
Mexico nationalizes all United States oil properties within her borders.

1940
Adolph Hitler meets Italian dictator Benito Mussolini at the Brenner Pass, agreeing to join forces, during World War II.

1970
The first major postal workers strike in the United States begins.

Adolph Hitler and Benito Mussolini

1524
Looking for a route to the East Indies, Giovanni de Verrazano sights land near the Carolinas.

1776
The Continental Congress authorizes raids on British shipping, during the Revolutionary War.

1831
During the first bank robbery in the United States, $245,000 is stolen from City Bank in New York.

1865
Union forces, commanded by General William T. Sherman, defeat the Confederates, under General William Hardee, at the Battle of Bentonville, North Carolina, during the Civil War.

1944
The Germans move into Hungary to ensure a continued supply of oil and a line of retreat, during World War II.

1953
The Greatest Show on Earth wins the Academy Award for Best Picture of 1952.

1965
The Indonesian government seizes three American oil companies and the Goodyear Tire and Rubber Company in a takeover of foreign properties.

1981
The Buffalo Sabres score an NHL record nine goals in one period in a game against the Toronto Maple Leafs.

1987
Television evangelist, Jim Bakker, resigns his ministry after the discovery of his extramarital affair with his church secretary.

Giovanni de Verrazano

1782

British Prime Minister, Lord North, resigns under pressure from the peace faction in Parliament.

1832

The United States signs a commercial treaty with the King of Siam, in Bangkok.

1896

United States Marines go to Corinto, Nicaragua, to protect American citizens after a revolution.

1940

Edouard Daladier, the French prime minister, is forced to resign, during World War II.

1948

Gentlemen's Agreement wins the Academy Award for Best Picture of 1947.

1952

An American in Paris wins the Academy Award for Best Picture of 1951.

1976

Patricia Hearst is convicted of taking part in a 1976 bank robbery along with Symbionese Liberation Army members, who had abducted her.

1986

The House of Representatives votes down a $100 million Contra aid bill for Nicaraguan rebel forces.

1987

The Federal Government approves the use of AZT, the first drug to be used in the treatment of AIDS patients.

Patty Hearst testifying in court

March

1868
Sorosis, in New York, becomes the first professional club for women in the United States.

1907
United States Marines land in Honduras to protect American interests during political disturbances.

1913
More than 600 people are killed in floods along the Ohio and Indiana Rivers.

1941
British troops attack Italian positions in the Marda Pass, west of Jijiga, in West Africa and force them to withdraw, during World War II.

1945
Eight hundred thirty-two sailors are killed on the USS *Franklin* during a series of Japanese Kamikaze attacks, the highest casualties ever suffered by an American aircraft carrier, during World War II.

1956
Marty wins the Academy Award for Best Picture of 1955.

1964
UCLA wins the NCAA basketball championship, becoming the first college basketball team to go undefeated in a season since 1957.

1965
Dr. Martin Luther King, Jr. leads a civil rights march from Selma, Alabama, to Montgomery, the State Capital.

1965
Ranger 9 is launched, becoming the last moon probe of the Ranger series.

1970
UCLA wins its fourth consecutive NCAA basketball championship.

Dr. Martin Luther King, Jr. leading a march

March

1622
The first Indian massacre in America almost wipes out settlements near Jamestown, Virginia.

1765
The English Parliament passes the Stamp Act, a tax on newspapers, legal documents, and pamphlets.

1774
Spanish explorers arrive at Mission San Gabriel, California.

1794
Congress passes a bill banning slave trade with other nations.

1865
Union forces commanded by General James Wilson advance from the Tennessee River to Selma, Alabama, in conjunction with an attack south of Selma, during the Civil War.

1874
The Young Men's Hebrew Association is formed in New York.

1917
The United States recognizes the Russian Government headed by Aleksandr Kerenski, after the Russian Revolution.

1936
On Your Toes, by Richard Rodgers and Lorenz Hart, opens at the Shubert Theater in New York.

1941
The Grand Coulee Dam in Washington begins operations.

1947
President Truman orders all Federal employees to undergo loyalty investigations.

1960
Charles H. Townes and Arthur L. Schawlow are awarded a patent for the laser.

1968
General William Westmoreland is named Army Chief of Staff during the Vietnam War.

1972
The Twenty-Seventh Amendment is passed by the Senate, prohibiting discrimination based on sex.

1988
The Civil Rights Restoration Act becomes law, over President Reagan's veto.

Cartoon depicting the repeal of the Stamp Act

1713
The Tuscarora Indian War ends with the Indians fleeing after the capture of their fort in South Carolina.

1775
Patrick Henry of Virginia declares in a speech, "Give me liberty or give me death."

1857
Elisha Graves Otis installs the first passenger elevator in a department store, the E.V. Haughwout Co., in New York.

1867
Congress passes the second Reconstruction Act over President Johnson's veto, providing for registration of voters readmitted to the Union.

1868
The University of California is established in Berkeley.

1901
Emilio Aguinaldo, the leader of the Philippine rebellion against the United States, is captured in Luzon.

1932
Congress passes the Norris-La Guardia Anti-Injunction Act, prohibiting injunctions that block strikes or boycotts.

1965
Gemini 3, with astronauts Virgil Grissom and John Young aboard, becomes the first manned Gemini flight.

1988
Janet Evans sets a world record of 8:17.20 for the 800 meter freestyle.

Patrick Henry addressing an assembly

1661
William Leddra becomes the last Quaker to be executed in the United States, in Boston.

1663
King Charles I of England creates the Carolina Colony, based on the English estate system.

1825
The new Mexican state of Texas-Coahuila authorizes American settlement of Texas.

1900
The Carnegie Steel Company is incorporated in New Jersey.

1916
Three Americans are killed when German submarines sink the French ship, *Sussex*, in the English Channel.

1934
Congress passes the Tydings-McDuffie Act, granting independence to the Philippines.

1941
Watch on the Rhine by Lillian Hellman opens at the Ford Theater in Baltimore, Maryland.

1949
Hamlet wins the Academy Award for Best Picture of 1948.

1957
Forty people are killed in a blizzard that strikes the Midwest and Southwest.

1986
Out of Africa wins the Academy Award for Best Picture of 1985.

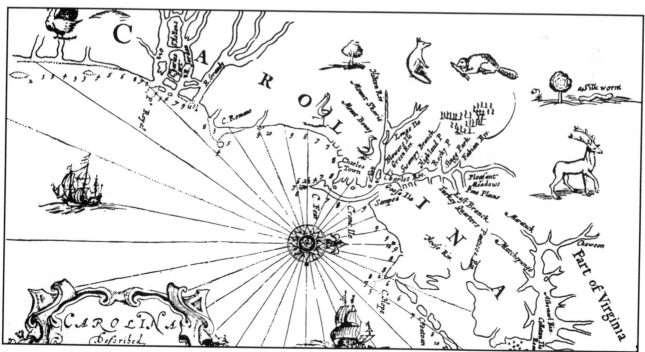

An early map of Carolina

1655
A civil war between Catholics and Puritans in Maryland comes to an end.

1863
The first Army Medal of Honor is awarded.

1865
Confederate forces commanded by General Robert E. Lee unsuccessfully attempt to break through Union lines at the siege of Petersburg, Virginia, during the Civil War.

1911
One hundred forty-six people are killed in a fire at the Triangle Waist Company, a sweatshop in New York.

1934
Horton Smith wins the first Masters golf tournament held in Augusta, Georgia.

1951
The Rose Tattoo by Tennessee Williams wins the Tony Award for Best Play of 1951.

1954
From Here to Eternity wins the Academy Award for Best Picture of 1953.

1960
The United States Circuit Court of Appeals rules that *Lady Chatterley's Lover* by D.H. Lawrence is not obscene.

1978
The longest coal miners strike in United States ends after 110 days.

1984
The world's largest active volcano, Mauna Loa in Hawaii, erupts, spewing lava 150 feet into the air.

Union soldiers in the trenches at Petersburg

1790
Congress passes the first Naturalization Act.

1862
A Confederate force commanded by major General John Chivington defeats Union volunteers from Colorado at Apache Canyon in the New Mexico Territory, during the Civil War.

1883
Mrs. William K. Vanderbilt inaugurates her Fifth Avenue mansion with a ball conspicuous even for the gilded age.

1889
The *Kansas Times and Star* refers to followers of baseball as "fans" for the first time.

1958
The Bridge on the River Kwai wins the Academy Award for Best Picture of 1957.

1967
Cabaret, by John Kander and Fred Ebb, wins the Tony Award for Best Musical of 1966-1967.

1973
UCLA defeats Memphis State 87-66 to win its record seventh straight NCAA basketball championship.

1976
The United States and Turkey sign a four-year military pact, reopening United States military bases in Turkey.

1987
Nick Thometz sets a world record of 36.23 for 500 meters in speed skating.

1988
Janet Evans sets a world record of 15:52.10 for the 1500 meter freestyle.

Action in the West during the Civil War

March

1935
It Happened one Night wins the Academy Award for Best Picture of 1934.

1945
The Germans launch the last V-2 rocket at England, during World War II.

1952
The Grass Harp, Truman Capote's first play, opens at the Martin Beck Theater in New York.

1955
The Pajama Game wins the Tony Award for Best Musical of 1954.

1956
Internal Revenue Service agents seize the Communist newspaper, the *Daily Worker*, for non-payment of income taxes.

1957
Around the World in 80 Days wins the Academy Award for Best Picture of 1956.

1958
Nikita Khrushchev becomes Premier of the Soviet Union, returning Russia to one-man rule.

1964
One hundred seventeen people are killed as an earthquake strikes Anchorage, Alaska.

1972
Gerry Cheevers of the Boston Bruins ends his NHL record streak of 32 consecutive games in goal without a loss.

1973
The Godfather wins the Academy Award for Best Picture of 1972.

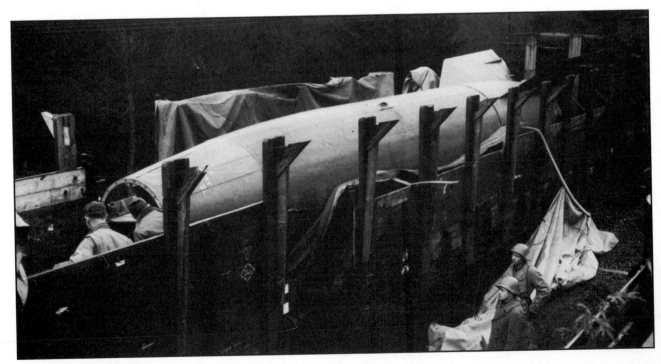

A captured V-2 rocket

1814
The British ships, *Phoebe* and *Cherub*, capture the American frigate, *Essex*, in a naval battle off the coast of Valparaiso, Chile, during the War of 1812.

1845
Mexico breaks off diplomatic relations with the United States.

1846
American troops commanded by General Zachary Taylor move onto the left bank of the Rio Grande River, considered Mexican territory.

1862
In the last Confederate threat to Union control in the Southwest, General R.S. Canby's Union troops defeat the Confederates at the Battle of Glorietta Pass, New Mexico, during Civil War.

1881
P.T. Barnum and James A. Bailey form the Barnum and Bailey Circus.

1932
Confidential Service by George M. Cohan opens in New York.

1969
Dwight D. Eisenhower, thirty-fourth President of the United States, dies in Washington, D.C.

1971
Sleuth by Anthony Shaffer wins the Tony Award for Best Play of 1970-1971.

1977
Rocky wins the Academy Award for Best Picture of 1976.

1979
A power plant malfunctions at the Three Mile Island nuclear power plant near Harrisburg, Pennsylvania, causing a near-disaster.

A trick rider performing at the circus

1790

John Tyler, tenth President of the United States, is born in Greenway, Virginia.

1814

An American force commanded by General Andrew Jackson defeats the Creek Indians at the Battle of Horseshoe Bend, Alabama, ending the Creek War.

1847

United States forces commanded by General Winfield Scott occupy the fortress at Vera Cruz, Mexico, during the Mexican War.

1942

British forces attack the Japanese at Boungde in Burma, during World War II.

1951

The King and I, by Richard Rodgers and Oscar Hammerstein, opens at the St. James Theater in New York.

1967

The U.S. Court of Appeals for the Fifth Circuit, orders Alabama, Florida, Georgia, Louisiana, Mississippi, and Texas to complete school desegregation by the fall term.

1971

Lieutenant William L. Calley, Jr. is convicted of murdering 22 innocent civilians in My Lai, South Vietnam, during the Vietnam War.

1976

One Flew Over the Cuckoo's Nest wins the Academy Award for Best Picture of 1975.

1982

Chariots Of Fire wins the Academy Award for Best Picture of 1981.

General Scott entering Mexico City, during The Mexican War

March

1743
French explorer Pierre de la Verendrye reaches South Dakota.

1791
Construction begins on the Knoxville Road, linking the Wilderness Road with Knoxville, south of the Ohio River.

1855
Armed violence mars the Kansas Territory's first election, with a pro-slavery legislature being voted in.

1867
Secretary of State, William H. Seward, negotiates the purchase of Alaska from Russia.

1870
Texas is readmitted to the Union.

1909
The Queensboro Bridge, connecting Queens with Manhattan, opens in New York.

1955
On the Waterfront wins the Academy Award for Best Picture of 1954.

1965
The Los Angeles County Art Museum becomes the largest museum west of the Mississippi River.

1972
North Vietnamese forces launch a massive attack across the Demilitarized Zone, during the Vietnam War.

1981
President Reagan is shot outside the Washington Hilton Hotel by John W. Hinckley.

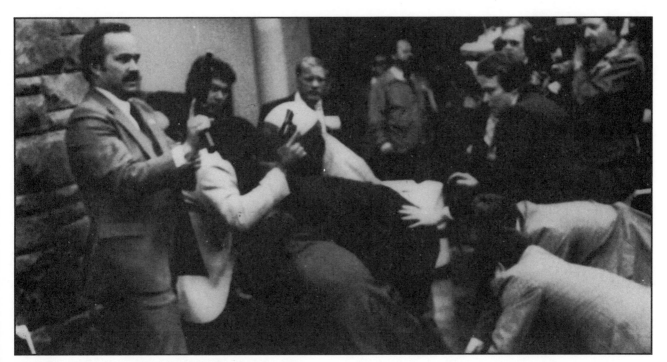

Secret Service Agents surround John W. Hinckley

March

1774
The English Parliament passes the first Intolerable Act, punishing colonists for dumping tea into Boston Harbor.

1840
The United States establishes a ten-hour workday for all Federal employees.

1854
The United States and Japan sign the Treaty of Kanagawa, opening some Japanese ports to trade.

1861
Texas troops seize Fort Bliss, a Union military outpost.

1863
Union troops evacuate Jacksonville, Florida, during the Civil War.

Commodore Perry in the Bay of Yedo

1880
Wabash, Indiana, becomes the first United States city to be totally lit by electricity.

1882
Congress votes to extend pensions to widows of presidents.

1918
President Wilson signs a bill establishing Daylight Savings Time.

1933
The Civilian Conservation Corps is established to create jobs through a reforestation program.

1943
Oklahoma!, by Richard Rodgers and Oscar Hammerstein, II, opens at the St. James Theater in New York.

1960
The Best Man by Gore Vidal opens at the Morosco Theater in New York.

1967
The United States and the Soviet Union sign the first consular treaty since the Russian Revolution.

1968
President Johnson announces he will not seek reelection.

1980
President Carter signs a bill deregulating the banking industry, raising the limit on federally insured accounts to $100,000.

1981
Ordinary People wins the Academy Award for Best Picture of 1980.

The original production of *Oklahoma*

April

1775
Explorer Daniel Boone establishes the settlement of Boonesborough on the Kentucky River.

1826
Samuel Mory of Orford, New Hampshire, is awarded a patent for the two-cylinder engine.

1856
The Western Union Telegraph Company is founded by Ezra Cornell.

1865
Union forces, commanded by General Philip Sheridan, rout the Confederate Army of Northern Virginia, commanded by General George E. Pickett, at the Battle of Five Forks, Virginia, during the Civil War.

1866
Western Union becomes the first monopoly by absorbing U.S. Telegraph.

1913
Henry Ford installs the first moving assembly line in Detroit, Michigan.

1920
Five members of the New York legislature are expelled for being members of the Socialist Party.

1925
Dillon, Read & Company purchases the Dodge Brothers Automobile Company for a record $146 million.

1939
The United States recognizes the Spanish Government headed by General Francisco Franco.

1942
The British cruiser, *Bande Nere*, is sunk by the German U-boat, *Urge*, in the Mediterranean, during World War II.

1944
German forces are surrounded near Skala in the Soviet Union, during World War II.

1945
United States forces invade Okinawa, during World War II.

1954
Congress establishes the United States Air Force Academy in Colorado.

1956
The Diary of Anne Frank wins the Tony Award for Best Play of 1955.

1960
The United States launches *Tiros I*, the first weather satellite.

1970
President Nixon signs a bill banning cigarette advertising on television.

1972
The first major league baseball strike begins, delaying the start of the season by 10 days.

1976
Pianist Arthur Rubinstein is awarded the Presidential Medal of Freedom.

1976
Conrail begins operations as a federally funded corporation to manage six bankrupt Northeastern railroads.

1513
Spanish explorer, Juan Ponce de Leon, discovers Florida, claiming the territory for the King of Spain.

1842
The New York Philharmonic Society is established, with Ureli Corelli Hill as its first conductor.

1865
Confederate General Robert E. Lee urges President Jefferson Davis to evacuate Richmond, Virginia, during the Civil War.

1866
President Johnson declares the state of insurrection over in Georgia, South Carolina, North Carolina, Virginia, Tennessee, Alabama, Louisiana, Florida, Mississippi, and Arkansas.

1876
Boston beats Philadelphia 6-5 in the first official National League baseball game.

1917
Jeannette Rankin of Montana becomes the first woman in the House of Representatives.

1974
The Sting wins the Academy Award for Best Picture of 1973.

1980
President Carter signs the Crude Oil Windfall Profits Tax Bill.

1986
Four Americans are killed in a terrorist bombing aboard a TWA jet flying from Rome, Italy, to Athens, Greece.

The landing of Ponce de Leon

1860
The Pony Express mail service begins, between Sacramento, California, and St. Joseph, Missouri.

1860
The Pony Express mail service leaves St. Joseph, Missouri, on its first run to California.

1865
Union forces occupy Petersburg, Virginia, after the Confederates commanded by General Robert E. Lee evacuate, during the Civil War.

1882
Outlaw Jesse James is shot and killed by Robert Ford.

1891
An organized group of cattlemen kill a suspected rustler in northern Wyoming, beginning the Johnson County War.

1930
Broadway Melody wins the Academy Award for Best Picture of 1928-1929.

1948
President Truman signs the Foreign Assistance Act of 1948, providing over $5 billion for a European Recovery Program.

1974
Three hundred fifty people are killed as tornadoes strike from Georgia to Canada.

1975
Anatoly Karpov becomes world chess champion when Bobby Fischer defaults by refusing to accept a match with the Soviet challenger.

1978
Annie Hall wins the Academy Award for Best Picture of 1977.

A Pony Express rider

April

4

1775
The Pennsylvania *Mercury* becomes the first newspaper to be set in type manufactured in America.

1790
Congress establishes the Revenue Marine Service, the forerunner of the Coast Guard.

1800
Congress passes the first Federal Bankruptcy Act, applying to merchants and traders.

1818
Congress limits the number of stripes on the American flag to thirteen, providing that a new star be added for each new state.

1841
William Henry Harrison, ninth President of the United States, dies after only 31 days in office, of pneumonia.

1854
An American commission to Hawaii attempts to meet with King Kamehameha to discuss annexation by the United States.

1859
The song, *Dixie*, written by Dan D. Emmet, has its first performance, at Mechanics Hall in New York.

1862
Union forces commanded by General George B. McClellan advance on Yorktown, Virginia, at the beginning of the Peninsular Campaign, during the Civil War.

1865
President Lincoln is cheered as he enters Richmond, Virginia, evacuated the day before by the Confederate Government, during the Civil War.

1877
The first telephone installed in a private home is put in Charles Williams, Jr.'s house in Sommerville, Massachusetts.

1887
Susanna Medora of Argonia, Kansas, becomes the first woman mayor in the United States.

1917
The United States Senate votes to declare war on Germany.

1921
The United States Navy Department completes the first helium production plant, in Fort Worth, Texas.

1949
The North Atlantic Treaty Organization is formed, in Washington, D.C.

1951
Supreme Headquarters of the Allied Powers in Europe is established, with General Dwight D. Eisenhower in command.

1960
Ben Hur wins the Academy Award for Best Picture of 1959.

1964
Can't Buy Me Love by the Beatles becomes the number one record in the United States.

1968
Dr. Martin Luther King is shot and killed by a sniper in Memphis, Tennessee.

1975
Two hundred Vietnamese refugees are killed when a United States C-5A transport plane crashes in Saigon, South Vietnam.

April

1614
Indian Chief Powhatan's daughter Pocahontas marries Jamestown colony tobacco planter John Rolfe.

1863
In a change of policy, England detains the Confederate ship, *Alexandria*, undergoing repairs in the port of Liverpool, during the Civil War.

1915
Jess Willard knocks out Jack Johnson in the 26th round, to win the heavyweight boxing championship.

1941
Yugoslavia and the Soviet Union sign a Nonaggression Pact, attempting to halt the imminent German attack, during World War II.

1942
The United States Task Force 39 arrives in Scapa Flow to aid British squadrons, during World War II.

1958
Fidel Castro proclaims a total war against the Cuban regime of President Fulgencio Batista.

1965
My Fair Lady wins the Academy Award for Best Picture of 1964.

1968
The siege at the United States Marine base in Khe Sanh is lifted, during the Vietnam War.

1986
A United States soldier is killed in a terrorist bombing at a discotheque in West Berlin.

Pocahontas and John Rolfe

April

1789
The first Congress is officially organized.

1808
John Jacob Astor establishes the American Fur Company.

1814
Napoleon Bonaparte is deposed in France, freeing the British to concentrate on the War of 1812 with the United States.

1830
Mexico forbids further colonization by Americans in Texas.

1830
Joseph Smith founds the Church of Jesus Christ of the Latter Day Saints, in Fayette, New York.

1832
The Sauk Indians, led by Chief Black Hawk, begin killing white settlers after two Indians are killed seeking a meeting, beginning the Black Hawk War.

1865
Eight thousand Confederate soldiers are captured at the Battle of Saylers Creek, Virginia, during the Civil War.

1896
The United States team dominates at the first modern Olympic Games, held in Athens, Greece.

1909
Robert Peary becomes the first person to reach the North Pole.

1926
Varney Air lines becomes the first air mail contractor in the United States, establishing a route between Nevada and Washington.

1942
A Japanese naval force sinks over 83,000 tons of shipping in a series of attacks in the Bay of Bengal, during World War II.

1959
Gigi wins the Academy Award for Best Picture of 1958.

1965
NASA launches *Early Bird*, the first commercial communications satellite in space.

Commander Robert E. Peary

April

1788
Rufus Putnam founds Muskingum, near present-day Marietta, Ohio, the first step in the settlement of the Northwest Territory.

1798
Congress creates the Mississippi Territory from land ceded from Spain.

1862
In the largest battle to date in the Western Hemisphere, Confederate General Albert Sydney Johnston is killed as Union forces commanded by General Ulysses S. Grant repulse an attack at the Battle of Shiloh, near Pittsburg Landing, Tennessee, during the Civil War.

1865
Union General Ulysses S. Grant sends Confederate General Robert E. Lee a message asking under what terms he would surrender his army, during the Civil War.

1891
Nebraska passes the first law limiting the work day to eight hours.

1922
Secretary of the Interior, Albert Fall, leases the Teapot Dome Oil Reserve in Wyoming to the Marathon Oil Company in exchange for a secret interest free loan.

1927
Bell Telephone Laboratories in New York conducts the first public demonstration of television.

1941
The United States opens naval and air bases in Bermuda, basing the aircraft carrier, *Ranger*, there, during World War II.

1943
Japanese Admiral Yamamoto launches an offensive against Allied positions on Guadalcanal, sinking a destroyer, during World War II.

1945
The Japanese battleship, *Yamato*, is sunk by the United States Navy near Okinawa, during World War II.

1947
The first annual Antoinette Perry (Tony) Awards, for contributions to the American Theater, are presented.

1949
South Pacific, by Richard Rodgers and Oscar Hammerstein, II, opens at the Majestic Theater in New York.

1959
Oklahoma repeals prohibition, making Mississippi the only dry state in the Union.

1962
Johnny Angel by Shelley Fabares becomes the number one record in the United States.

1970
Midnight Cowboy wins the Academy Award for Best Picture of 1969.

1972
Congress passes the Federal Election Campaign Act, setting limits on the financing of election campaigns.

1980
The United States breaks off diplomatic relations with Iran as a result of the hostage crisis.

April

1788
Maryland becomes the seventh state to ratify the Constitution.

1789
The raising of revenue for the Government becomes the first item on the agenda of the House of Representatives.

1864
The Confederates, commanded by General Richard Taylor, turn back the Union advance, led by General Nathaniel Banks, at the Battle of Sabine Crossroads, Louisiana during the Civil War.

1864
The Senate passes the Thirteenth Amendment, abolishing slavery in the United States.

1913
President Wilson becomes the first President to address Congress since John Adams in 1800.

1940
The British destroyer, *Glowworm*, is sunk by German warships of the coast of Norway during World War II.

1942
The Americans prepare to surrender to the Japanese on Bataan after severe losses, during World War II.

1950
The Soviet Union shoots down a United States Navy patrol plane over Latvia, killing all 10 crew members.

1952
President Truman orders the nation's steel mills seized to prevent a strike.

1954
The United States and Canada announce the establishment of an early warning radar network across the Canadian north.

1960
The Senate passes the first civil rights bill to survive Southern filibustering.

1963
Lawrence of Arabia wins the Academy Award for Best Picture of 1962.

1968
One hundred thousand Allied troops launch Operation Complete Victory, designed to drive North Vietnamese forces from the Saigon area, during the Vietnam War.

1971
The OTB system in New York becomes the first legal off track betting system in the United States.

1974
Atlanta Braves outfielder Hank Aaron hits his 715th home run to surpass Babe Ruth on the all-time home run list.

1975
The Godfather, Part II wins the Academy Award for Best Picture of 1974.

1986
Actor Clint Eastwood is elected Mayor of Carmel, California.

April

1682
French explorer La Salle reaches the mouth of the Mississippi River and claims the territory for King Louis IV.

1772
An interpretation of English law allows the colonists to purchase Indian lands without patents from the Crown.

1865
The Confederate Army of Northern Virginia, commanded by General Robert E. Lee, surrenders to Union forces, commanded by General Ulysses S. Grant, at Appomattox Court House, Virginia, during the Civil War.

1866
Congress passes a Civil Rights Act over President Johnson's veto, granting citizenship to all people born in the United States, except Indians.

Lee surrendering to Grant

1924
The Dawes Plan is formulated to reorganize German war debt and help stabilize its economy.

1942
The Japanese take Bataan as the American defenders withdraw to Corregidor, during World War II.

1950
South Pacific by Richard Rodgers wins the Tony Award for Best Musical of 1949.

1959
The first seven astronauts are picked by NASA.

1962
West Side Story wins the Academy Award for Best Picture of 1961.

1963
The United States grants Winston Churchill honorary citizenship.

1965
The Houston Astrodome opens, becoming the first major enclosed stadium in the United States.

1972
The French Connection wins the Academy Award for Best Picture of 1971.

1978
George Gervin of the San Antonio Spurs scores an NBA record 33 points in one quarter in a game against the New Orleans Jazz.

1984
Terms Of Endearment wins the Academy Award for Best Picture of 1983.

April

1790
Captain Robert Gray docks his ship, *Columbia*, in Boston, becoming the first American to circumnavigate the globe.

1830
The first wagon train to travel the Oregon Trail leaves from St. Louis.

1841
The New York *Tribune*, edited by Horace Greeley, begins publication.

1849
Walter Hunt is awarded a patent for the safety pin.

1865
Applauding their courage and valor, Confederate General Robert E. Lee gives his formal farewell to the Army of Northern Virginia, during the Civil War.

1866
The American Society for the Prevention of Cruelty to Animals is founded.

1869
Georgia, Mississippi, Texas, and Virginia ratify the Fifteenth Amendment, providing for suffrage regardless of race or color.

1916
The first professional golf tournament in the United States is held at the Siwanoy Golf Course in Bronxville, New York.

1942
The Bataan Death March begins as the Japanese force American and Philippine prisoners to march 85 miles in 6 days, resulting in over 5200 American deaths, during World War II.

1963
The nuclear submarine, *Thresher*, sinks during a test dive in the Atlantic Ocean, killing all 129 crew members.

1967
A Man for All Seasons wins the Academy Award for Best Picture of 1966.

1968
In the Heat of the Night wins the Academy Award for Best Picture of 1967.

1971
An American table tennis team begins its tour of the Peoples Republic of China, becoming the first American sports team to visit Communist China.

A wagon train heading west

April

1713
The Treaty of Utrecht ends the second French and Indian War.

1816
The African Methodist Church in Philadelphia becomes the first Black church in the United States.

1861
Union Major Robert Anderson refuses a Confederate demand to surrender his garrison at Fort Sumter, in Charleston Harbor.

1862
Union forces take Fort Pulaski, commanding the approaches to Savannah, along the coast of Georgia, during the Civil War.

1921
Iowa levies the first cigarette tax in the United States.

1921
The junior-lightweight fight between Johnny Dundee and Johnny Ray becomes the first boxing match in the United States broadcast over the radio.

1951
President Truman relieves General Douglas MacArthur of his command, because of his Korean policies.

1964
President Johnson signs the Agricultural Act of 1964, establishing price support programs for farmers.

1968
President Johnson signs the Civil Rights Act of 1968, making discrimination in housing illegal.

1983
Ghandi wins the Academy Award for Best Picture of 1982.

President Johnson signing the Civil Rights Act.

April

1764
Former supporters of Chief Pontiac sign the Treaty of Presque Isle with the English.

1776
North Carolina becomes the first Colony to propose independence from England.

1844
The United States and Texas sign the Texas Annexation Treaty, providing for the admission of Texas as a territory.

1846
Mexican General Pedro de Ampudia warns the American force commanded by General Zachary Taylor to retire beyond the Neuces River.

1858
Michael J. Phelan wins the first United States billiards championship, at Fireman's Hall in Detroit.

1861
The first shots of the Civil War are fired when Confederate shore batteries commanded by General P.G.T. Beauregard open fire on the Federal garrison at Fort Sumter, in Charleston Harbor.

1864
Confederate troops commanded by Major General Nathan Bedford Forrest massacre Black Union troops after capturing Fort Pillow, Tennessee, during the Civil War.

1865
Union forces commanded by General George Stoneman capture Salisbury, North Carolina, and take over 1700 Confederate prisoners, during the Civil War.

1900
Puerto Rico becomes an unconsolidated territory of the United States with the signing of the Foraker Act.

1929
Mexican rebel General, F.R. Manzo, and his staff are interned after crossing into Arizona.

1943
The Germans announce the discovery of a mass grave in the Katyn Forest in Poland, where over 4000 Polish officers were killed by the Soviets.

1945
Franklin D. Roosevelt, thirty-second President of the United States, dies in office, in Warm Springs, Georgia.

1959
Redhead by Herbert and Dorothy Fields wins the Tony Award for Best Musical of 1958.

1963
The Reverend Martin Luther King, Jr. is arrested in Birmingham, Alabama during a desegregation drive.

1981
NASA successfully launches *Columbia*, the first space shuttle.

1983
Harold Washington becomes the first Black mayor of Chicago.

1988
Harvard University is awarded a patent for the first higher form of life, a genetically altered mouse.

April

1743
Thomas Jefferson, third President of the United States, is born in Shadwell, Virginia.

1830
President Jackson, at a White House dinner, proposes a toast, stating, "Our Federal Union—it must be preserved!"

1846
The Pennsylvania Railroad is founded.

1861
The Union garrison at Fort Sumter in Charleston Harbor, commanded by Major Robert Anderson, surrenders to the Confederates, during the Civil War.

1869
George Westinghouse, Jr. is awarded a patent for the air brake.

1908
The New England Methodist Episcopal Conference ends a ban on dancing, card playing, and theater going.

1943
The Jefferson Memorial is dedicated, in Washington, D.C.

1945
British and American forces liberate the German extermination camps, Belsen and Buchenwald, during World War II.

1958
The Music Man by Meredith Wilson wins the Tony Award for Best Musical of 1957.

1964
Tom Jones wins the Academy Award for Best Picture of 1963.

Prisoners freed at Buchenwald

April

1775
The Society for the Relief of Free Negroes in Philadelphia becomes the first abolition society in America.

1789
The Secretary of the new Congress informs George Washington of his election as first President of the United States.

1813
American forces commanded by General Jàmes Wilkinson capture Mobile, Alabama, from the British, during the War of 1812.

1834
The "Whig" party is established by opponents of Andrew Jackson.

1860
Mormons establish the first permanent settlement in Idaho.

1863
William Bullock of Pittsburgh is awarded a patent for his continuous roll printing press.

1865
President Abraham Lincoln is shot by actor, John Wilkes Booth, while attending a performance at Ford's Theater in Washington, D.C.

1894
The first commercial showing of a film takes place at the Kinetoscope Parlor in New York.

1917
President Wilson orders the establishment of the Committee on Public Information in order to control censorship of the news.

1918
Lt. Douglas Campbell becomes the first American air ace after shooting down his fifth German aircraft.

1957
The United States moves the Sixth Fleet to the Eastern Mediterranean to support King Hussein of Jordan after an attempted revolt.

1960
Bye Bye Birdie, by Charles Strouse and Lee Adams, opens at the Martin Beck Theater in New York.

1960
A Polaris missile becomes the first to be fired from under water, in a test near San Clemente Island, California.

1969
Oliver! wins the Academy Award for Best Picture of 1968.

1971
President Nixon announces the lifting of a trade embargo with the Peoples Republic of China.

1971
Patton wins the Academy Award for Best Picture of 1970.

1971
President Nixon announces the lifting of the 20-year-old trade embargo with the Peoples Republic of China.

1980
Kramer vs. Kramer wins the Academy Award for Best Picture of 1979.

April

1715
The Yamassee Indians attack and kill several hundred Carolina settlers.

1789
William L. Smith of South Carolina becomes the first person to be elected to the House of Representatives.

1861
Declaring a state of "insurrection," President Lincoln issues a call for 75,000 volunteers for three months service.

1865
Abraham Lincoln, sixteenth President of the United States, dies of a gunshot wound inflicted by assassin, John Wilkes Booth, in Washington, D.C.

1893
The gold reserve falls below $100 million, causing runs on the Federal Treasury.

1912
The British steamship, *Titanic*, sinks after hitting an iceberg off the coast of Newfoundland, killing 1500 people.

1921
At a lecture at Columbia University, Albert Einstein describes time as the fourth dimension.

1929
New York police raid the Birth Control Clinical Research Center, acting on a complaint by the Daughters of the American Revolution.

1952
The Franklin National Bank of New York issues the first bank credit card.

1964
The Chesapeake Bay Bridge-Tunnel opens, at 17.65 miles, the longest in the world.

The *Titanic* sailing from England

April

1863
Union Admiral David Porter successfully runs his 12-ship fleet past the batteries at Vicksburg, Mississippi, during the Civil War.

1900
The United States Post Office issues the first stamp books.

1926
The Book-of-the-Month Club begins operations with 4750 charter members.

1940
The British land at Namsos, Norway, during World War II.

1947
Five hundred people are killed in Texas City, Texas, when a nitrate laden French ship explodes, followed by several other explosions, annihilating the entire city.

1961
Bye Bye Birdie, by Charles Strouse and Lee Adams, wins the Tony Award for Best Musical of 1960-1961.

1965
The *Saturn S-1C* rocket is launched at Cape Kennedy, Florida, becoming the United States' largest booster.

1970
The second round of the Strategic Arms Limitations Talks begins, in Vienna, Austria.

1986
Mount Sinai Hospital in Cleveland, Ohio, announces the first surrogate birth of a test-tube baby in the United States.

1987
The Federal Government announces that new forms of animal life created through gene splicing are patentable.

Admiral Porter running the Vicksburg batteries

1524
Giovanni de Verrazano discovers the Hudson River and New York harbor.

1702
The colonies of East and West Jersey are designated the royal province of New Jersey.

1754
The French capture the strategic forks of the Ohio River, during the French and Indian War.

1808
Napoleon Bonaparte orders the French seizure of American shipping.

1824
The United States and Russia sign a treaty giving the United States the rights to all land along the Pacific coast below the 54th parallel.

1861
Virginia secedes from the Union.

1864
General Ulysses S. Grant discontinues the exchanging of prisoners of war, during the Civil War.

1894
The Lowell Observatory near Flagstaff, Arizona, becomes the first astronomical observatory in the United States.

1905
The Supreme Court rules that state laws limiting working hours are unconstitutional.

1961
Fifteen hundred anti-Castro Cuban exiles, supported by President Kennedy, conduct an unsuccessful landing in Cuba in the Bay of Pigs Invasion.

1961
The Apartment wins the Academy Award for Best Picture of 1960.

Cuban soldiers at the Bay of Pigs

April

1796
Congress passes an act, establishing trading houses with Indian tribes.

1842
Dorr's Rebellion occurs in Rhode Island when voters disgruntled by property-owning requirements hold their own elections and elect Thomas W. Dorr as Governor.

1847
American forces commanded by General Winfield Scott defeat the Mexicans at the Battle of Cerro Gordo, Mexico, during the Mexican War.

1906
The most extensive earthquake in the United States hits San Francisco, killing 450 people and destroying 25,000 buildings.

1923
Babe Ruth of the New York Yankees hits a home run in the first game played at Yankee Stadium.

1934
The Washateria becomes the first launderette in the United States, opening in Fort Worth, Texas.

1942
United States bombers, commanded by Major General Doolittle, launch the first American bombing raid over Tokyo, Japan, during World War II.

1945
German Field Marshal Model commits suicide after the last of 350,000 German troops in the Ruhr surrender to the Allies, during World War II.

1950
The first jet airmail service is inaugurated, between Toronto and New York.

1963
Dr. James B. Campbell, of the New York University Medical Center, announces the first successful human nerve transplant.

1966
The Sound of Music wins the Academy Award for Best Picture of 1965.

1976
A Chorus Line, by James Kirkwood and Marvin Hamlisch, wins the Tony Award for Best Musical of 1975-1976.

1983
The United States Embassy in Beirut, Lebanon, is destroyed by a car-bomb, killing 17 Americans.

San Francisco after the earthquake

April

1775
Seventy Minute Men engage British troops at Lexington, Massachusetts, in the first battle of the Revolutionary War.

1782
The Netherlands recognizes the independence of the United States.

1850
The United States and England sign the Clayton-Bulwer Treaty, providing for the neutrality of a canal to be built across Central America.

1861
President Lincoln orders a blockade of Confederate ports, during the Civil War.

1861
Four soldiers are killed in Baltimore when troops of the Sixth Massachusetts Regiment are stoned by mobs, during the Civil War.

1865
Funeral services for assassinated President Abraham Lincoln are held in the East Room of the White House.

1897
John J. McDermott wins the first Boston Marathon in 2 hours, 55 minutes, and 10 seconds.

1901
The United States proclaims the rebellion in the Philippines at an end.

1911
Kismet opens at the Knickerbocker Theater in New York.

1945
Carousel, by Richard Rodgers and Oscar Hammerstein II, opens at the Majestic Theater in New York.

1956
American actress Grace Kelly marries Prince Rainier III of Monaco.

1962
Skybolt is launched from a jet, becoming the United States' first airborne ballistic missile.

1970
Applause by Betty Comden and Adolph Green, wins the Tony Award for Best Musical of 1969-1970.

The Battle of Lexington

April

1836
Congress establishes the Wisconsin Territory.

1861
Union forces evacuate the Norfolk Navy Yard after its destruction by the Confederates, during the Civil War.

1871
Congress passes the Klu Klux Klan Act to provide legislation to support the Fourteenth Amendment granting citizenship to people born in the United States.

1953
The Justice Department orders the American Communist Party to register as an organization controlled by the Soviet Union.

1967
Two power plants are destroyed by United States bombers in the port city of Haiphong during the Vietnam War.

1969
The Great White Hope by Howard Sackler wins the Tony Award for Best Play of 1968-1969.

1970
President Nixon announces a troop level reduction of 150,000, during the Vietnam War.

1971
The Supreme Court rules that the use of busing to end racial segregation in public schools is constitutional.

1983
President Reagan signs a bill making changes in the Social Security System, which are designed to raise additional revenues to make the system solvent.

1988
Jack Clark hits a home run making the New York Yankees the first major league team to reach the 10,000 home run mark.

The burning of the Norfolk Navy Yard

April

1789
Vice President John Adams takes his seat as the first presiding officer of the Senate.

1828
Noah Webster publishes his *American Dictionary of the English Language*, containing over 70,000 definitions.

1836
The Texas Army under General Sam Houston defeats the Mexicans at the Battle of San Jacinto, Texas.

1856
The first railroad bridge over the Mississippi River opens between Rock Island, Illinois, and Davenport, Iowa.

1898
Spain breaks diplomatic relations with the United States.

1914
United States forces take Veracruz, Mexico, after a dispute with Mexican dictator, General Victoriano Huerta.

1956
Heartbreak Hotel by Elvis Presley becomes the number one record in the United States.

1957
My Fair Lady by Alan Jay Lerner and Frederick Loewe wins the Tony Award for Best Musical of 1956.

1967
Twenty-one people are killed and over 1000 injured, as a tornado strikes northern Illinois.

1968
Rosenkranz and Guildenstern Are Dead by Tom Stoppard wins the Tony Award for Best Play of 1967-1968.

1975
Equus by Peter Shaffer wins the Tony Award for Best Play of 1974-1975.

1976
Convertible production ceases in the United States as the last Cadillac Eldorado rolls off the assembly line.

1977
Annie, by Thomas Meehan and Charles Strouse, opens at the Alvin Theater in New York.

Texas troops in action

1793
President Washington affirms United States neutrality in the war between France and England.

1861
North Carolina state troops seize the Federal arsenal at Fayetteville, Arkansas, during the Civil War.

1864
The phrase "In God We Trust" begins to be incorporated on United States currency.

1889
The Oklahoma Land Rush begins as Congress opens up 1.9 million acres to settlement.

1898
President McKinley orders a blockade of Cuban ports, during the Spanish-American War.

1903
Jack Root outpoints Charles "Kid" McCoy, to win the first light-heavyweight boxing championship.

1904
The Panama Canal property is formally transferred to the United States.

1914
Mexico severs diplomatic relations with the United States.

1930
The United States, England, and Japan sign the London Naval Treaty, limiting the number and size of ships each country is allowed.

1944
United States forces invade Netherlands New Guinea, during World War II.

1964
The New York World's Fair opens in Flushing Meadow, New York.

1970
Dramatizing America's concern about the environment, Earth Day is observed.

1976
Barbara Walters of ABC Television becomes the first woman anchor of a network television news program.

1986
The Department of Agriculture approves the first genetically altered virus to be released into the environment.

The Oklahoma Land Rush

April

1791
James Buchanan, fifteenth President of the United States, is born in Mercersburg, Pennsylvania.

1838
The steamer, *Great Western*, arrives in New York from England to begin the first transatlantic steamship service.

1898
President McKinley calls for 125,000 volunteers to fight the war with Spain.

1945
The United States Fifth and Eighth Armies reach the Po River in Italy, during World War II.

1950
The Minneapolis Lakers defeat the Syracuse Nationals in the first National Basketball Association championship.

1954
The Army-McCarthy hearings open in Washington to investigate charges that the Army was hampering efforts to uncover Communists in the military.

1968
Students begin a sit-in protest at Columbia University in New York, which leads to the closing of the University.

1969
Sirhan Sirhan is given the death penalty for the murder of Senator Robert F. Kennedy.

1985
The Coca Cola Company announces it's changing the 99-year-old recipe for its soft drink.

Minneapolis Laker star George Mikan in action

April

1800
The Library of Congress is founded in Washington, D.C.

1833
A patent is awarded for the soda fountain.

1846
Mexican forces attack American troops in the first military action of the Mexican War.

1877
Louisiana becomes the last state to regain control of its local government when Federal troops are withdrawn.

1878
The Edison Speaking Phonograph Company is formed in New York, to manufacture the first phonographs.

1898
Spain declares war on the United States.

1913
The Woolworth Building opens in New York and is the tallest building in the world.

1949
Death of a Salesman by Arthur Miller wins the Tony Award for Best Play of 1948-1949.

1960
The Miracle Worker by William Gibson wins the Tony Award for Best Play of 1959-1960.

1964
The New York City Ballet, formed in 1948 and directed by George Balanchine, opens its first season at Lincoln Center for the Performing Arts in New York.

1969
United States B-52 bombers drop over 3000 tons of bombs northwest of Saigon, during the Vietnam War.

1980
A mission to rescue the American hostages in Iran ends in disaster as three of the eight helicopters to be used fail.

1981
President Reagan lifts the grain embargo imposed on the Soviet Union.

1985
The Good War: An Oral History of World War II by Studs Terkel wins the Pulitzer Prize for general non-fiction.

The Library of Congress

1507
In his book *Cosmographiae Introductio*, geographer Martin Waldseemuller uses the name "America" for the New World.

1838
One hundred people are killed as the steamer, *Moselle*, explodes on the Ohio River.

1861
The Seventh New York Regiment arrives in Washington, D.C. to help protect the Capital, during the Civil War.

1927
Hit the Deck opens at the Belasco Theater in New York.

1945
United States and Soviet forces meet at the Elbe River in Germany, during World War II.

1953
Senator Wayne Morse of Oregon sets a filibustering record, holding the floor of the Senate for over 22 hours.

1959
The St. Lawrence Seaway opens, connecting the Great Lakes with the Atlantic Ocean through the Eastern border of the United States and Canada.

1962
The United States resumes nuclear testing in the atmosphere after a three-year moratorium.

1963
Who's Afraid of Virginia Woolf? wins the Tony Award for Best Play of 1962-1963.

American and Soviet forces at the Elbe River

1791

The Cherokee Indians cede the majority of their land to the United States, in the Treaty of Holston.

1805

The Lewis and Clark Expedition reaches the mouth of the Yellowstone River.

1854

The Emigrant Aid Society is organized in Worcester, Massachusetts, to encourage anti-slavery supporters to settle in the Kansas Territory.

1862

The Confederate garrison at Fort Macon, North Carolina surrenders, during the Civil War.

1865

John Wilkes Booth is shot to death by Union soldiers in a barn near Bowling Green, Virginia.

1865

Confederate General Joseph E. Johnston surrenders the Army of Tennessee to Union forces commanded by General William T. Sherman, near Durham Station, North Carolina, during the Civil War.

1942

Hitler's absolute power is extended after a speech in the Reichstag predicts major victories for German armies in the field, during World War II.

1945

French Vichy Government leader Marshal Petain is arrested after crossing into Switzerland, during World War II.

1962

Ariel is launched from Cape Canaveral, becoming the first international satellite.

The Lewis and Clark Expedition

1773

The English Parliament passes the Tea Act, severely hurting American tea merchants.

1805

A force of United States Marines captures Derna, on the coast of Tripoli, during the Tripolitan War.

1813

American General Zebulon Pike is killed as the Americans force the British to surrender York, Canada, during the War of 1812.

1822

Ulysses S. Grant, eighteenth President of the United States, is born in Point Pleasant, Ohio.

1846

President Polk signs a resolution to end the joint American-English occupation of the Oregon Territory.

1865

Seventeen hundred people are killed when the steamer, *Sultana*, explodes on the Mississippi River, the worst maritime disaster in the United States.

1887

George Thomas Morton performs the first appendix operation in the United States, at a hospital in Philadelphia.

1941

The German army enters Athens, Greece, during World War II.

1987

Former United Nations Secretary General and President of Austria, Kurt Waldheim, becomes the first head of state to be excluded from the United States, for hiding his activities with the Nazis during World War II.

The German Army entering Athens

April

1758
James Monroe, fifth President of the United States, is born in Virginia.

1818
The United States and Canada sign the Rush-Bagot Agreement, making the Great Lakes neutral.

1862
The Confederates surrender Forts Jackson and St. Philip, opening up the Mississippi River to New Orleans, during the Civil War.

1865
Over 50,000 people view Abraham Lincoln's coffin in Cleveland, Ohio.

1897
The Choctaw and Chickasaw Indian Nations agree to give their lands to the Federal Government and dissolve their tribal governments.

1945
Italian dictator Benito Mussolini is killed by partisans and hung in the main square in Milan, during World War II.

1956
The New York Coliseum opens, becoming the largest exhibition building in the world.

1965
United States Marines are sent to the Dominican Republic after a military coup threatens American citizens.

1986
General Motors becomes the largest corporation in the United States, with sales of over $96 billion.

1988
The Baltimore Orioles start the season with a record 21 consecutive losses.

Government officials addressing the Indians

1861
The Maryland Legislature votes to remain in the Union.

1913
Gideon Sundback of Hoboken, New Jersey, is awarded a patent for the first zipper.

1926
The United States and France sign a debt funding agreement, providing for the repayment of France's World War I debts.

1940
The Government of King Hakkon is evacuated from Norway aboard the British cruiser, *Glasgow*, during World War II.

1945
The German concentration camp at Dachau is liberated by United States troops, during World War II.

1962
A Man for All Seasons by Robert Bolt wins the Tony Award for Best Play of 1961-1962.

1969
President Nixon awards the Presidential Medal of Freedom to composer "Duke" Ellington at a White House ceremony.

1970
Fifty thousand United States and South Vietnamese troops launch an invasion into Cambodia, during the Vietnam War.

1986
Boston Red Sox pitcher Roger Clemens strikes out a record 20 batters in one game.

United States troops invading Cambodia

April

30

1492
Christopher Columbus is appointed Admiral of the Ocean Sea and governor of any land he discovers.

1562
Port Royal, off the coast of South Carolina, becomes the first French colony in America.

1789
George Washington is inaugurated as the first President of the United States, at a ceremony in New York.

1802
Congress passes the Enabling Act, authorizing territories organized under the Northwest Ordinance to prepare for statehood.

1803
The United States acquires from France 828,000 square miles of land between the Mississippi River and the Rocky Mountains, in the Louisiana Purchase.

1812
Louisiana joins the Union as the eighteenth state.

1846
The Mexican Army crosses the Rio Grande River, during the Mexican War.

1855
The College of California in Oakland becomes the first institution in the West to offer a curriculum comparable to Eastern colleges.

1865
Union General E. R. S. Canby and Confederate General Richard Taylor agree to a truce in Alabama and Mississippi, during the Civil War.

1871
One hundred Apache Indians are killed at Camp Grant, Arizona, beginning the Apache War.

1894
Jacob Coxey begins his march from Ohio to Washington, D.C., with 400 people in order to protest the Government's inability to deal with unemployment.

1900
Congress passes an act establishing the Territory of Hawaii.

1900
Railroad engineer, John "Casey" Jones, dies as the *Cannon Ball* express train slams into the rear of another train.

1908
Worcester, Massachusetts, becomes the largest city in the United States to prohibit liquor.

1939
President Roosevelt opens the New York World's Fair.

1939
New York Yankees first baseman Lou Gehrig's record-consecutive-game playing streak ends at 2,130.

1945
Adolph Hitler commits suicide in his bunker in Berlin, during World War II.

1961
The New York Giants centerfielder Willie Mays hits a record-tying four home runs in one game.

May

1740
French explorers Pierre and Paul Mallet begin their exploration of New Mexico.

1811
The American ship, *Spitfire*, is stopped by the British frigate, *Guerriere*, off Sandy Hook, New York, where an American seaman is seized.

1847
The Smithsonian Institution officially opens in Washington, D.C.

1861
Confederate troops commanded by Colonel Thomas J. Jackson are sent to occupy Harpers Ferry, Virginia, during the Civil War.

1862
Union forces commanded by Captain David Farragut capture New Orleans, during the Civil War.

1873
The United States Postal Service issues the first penny postcards.

1890
The Bank of America in Philadelphia fails, causing the failure of several other companies, including the American Life Insurance Company of Philadelphia.

1898
The United States fleet, commanded by Admiral George Dewey, destroys the Spanish fleet in Manila Bay, Philippines, in the first naval battle of the Spanish-American War.

1912
The Federal Government issues stricter ship safety regulations as a result of the *Titanic* disaster.

1915
The American tanker, *Gulflight*, is sunk by a German submarine.

1916
The *Chicago Herald* uses the word "jazz" to describe that form of music for the first time.

1920
The Brooklyn Dodgers and the Boston Red Sox play a record 26-inning game, which ends in a tie.

1931
The Empire State Building opens in New York, becoming the world's tallest building.

1939
Abe Lincoln in Illinois by Robert E. Sherwood wins the Pulitzer Prize for Drama.

1941
United States Defense Savings Bonds go on sale to raise funds for the war effort.

1944
Oklahoma!, by Richard Rodgers and Oscar Hammerstein II, wins the Pulitzer Prize for Theater.

1960
The Soviet Union shoots down a United States U-2 spy plane, piloted by Francis Gary Powers, over the Soviet Union.

1971
The National Railroad Passenger Corporation, known as Amtrak, begins service.

1776
France consigns one million dollars worth of military supplies to the American colonists.

1861
Union General George B. McClellan is given the comand of the newly formed Department of the Ohio, during the Civil War.

1865
The first professional fire department in the United States is created in New York.

1865
President Johnson offers a $100,000 reward for the capture of Confederate President Jefferson Davis.

1890
Congress establishes the Oklahoma Territory.

1913
The United States recognizes the Republic of China.

1932
Of Thee I Sing, by George and Ira Gershwin, becomes the first musical to win the Pulitzer Prize for Drama.

1938
Our Town by Thorton Wilder wins the Pulitzer Prize for Drama.

1945
Soviet troops capture Berlin, Germany, during World War II.

1954
St. Louis Cardinals outfielder Stan Musial hits a record five home runs in a doubleheader.

1955
Cat on a Hot Tin Roof by Tennessee Williams wins the Pulitzer Prize for Fiction.

1956
The General Conference of the Methodist Church abolishes racial segregation.

1960
Caryl Chessman is executed in the gas chamber at San Quentin Prison in California after a 12-year legal battle.

1972
Ninety-one miners are killed in a fire in the Sunshine Silver Mine near Kellogg, Idaho.

Russian soldiers on a balcony in Berlin

May

1765
The College of Philadelphia opens the first medical school in the Colonies.

1845
Macon B. Allen of Massachusetts becomes the first Black lawyer admitted to the bar.

1846
The Mexican Army places Fort Texas under siege, during the Mexican War.

1861
President Lincoln calls for 42,000 Army volunteers and 18,000 sailors, during the Civil War.

1864
The Union Army of the Potomac, commanded by Generals Ulysses S. Grant and George G. Mead, crosses the Rapidan River in Virginia with 100,000 men, during the Civil War.

1934
Famous Funnies becomes the first comic book published in the United States.

1937
Gone With The Wind by Margaret Mitchell wins the Pulitzer Prize for Fiction.

1943
Dragon's Teeth by Upton Sinclair wins the Pulitzer Prize for Fiction.

1973
The Sears Tower in Chicago becomes the tallest building in the world.

1988
Ninety-two hundred pounds of cocaine, valued at $2 billion, is seized by drug enforcement officials in Tarpon Springs, Florida.

The siege of Fort Texas

May

4

1702
Queen Anne's War, the second French and Indian War, begins in Europe, soon spreading to North America.

1846
The Michigan Legislature becomes the first in the United States to ban capital punishment.

1862
Union forces commanded by General George B. McClellan occupy Yorktown, Virginia, during the Civil War.

1863
Confederate General Stonewall Jackson is mortally wounded as the Union Army of the Potomac, commanded by General Joseph Hooker, is defeated at the Battle of Chancellorsville, Virginia, during the Civil War.

1865
Confederate General Richard Taylor surrenders the last major Confederate Army to Union forces commanded by General Edward Canby, in Citronelle, Alabama, during the Civil War.

1886
A bomb explodes at a labor rally in Chicago's Haymarket Square, wounding 60 people.

1923
The New York Legislature repeals the New York State Prohibition Enforcement Act, marking the beginning of the end of prohibition in the United States.

1942
Reveille in Washington by Margaret Leech wins the Pulitzer Prize in History.

1953
The Old Man and the Sea by Ernest Hemingway wins the Pulitzer Prize for Fiction.

1959
The Music From Peter Gunn by Henry Mancini wins Best Album at the first Grammy Awards.

1961
Bus trips called Freedom Rides begin in order to challenge Southern segregationist practices.

1961
Two Navy scientists set a balloon altitude record of 113,500 feet aboard the *Stratolab High No. 5*.

1970
National Guard troops shoot and kill four students during antiwar demonstrations on the Kent State University campus.

National Guardsman at Kent State

May

5

1682
William Penn's liberal *Frame of Government* goes into effect in Pennsylvania.

1862
The Union Army of the Potomac commanded by General George McClellan occupies Williamsburg, Virginia, during the Civil War.

1865
An Ohio & Mississippi railroad train becomes the first to be robbed, by a gang in North Bend, Ohio.

1891
Carnegie Hall opens in New York, with a performance of works by Tchaikovsky.

1892
Congress passes the Geary Chinese Exclusion Act, making it mandatory for Chinese to register or face deportation.

1904
Cy Young of the Boston Americans pitches the first perfect game, retiring all 27 Philadelphia Phillies batters.

1920
The War Department adopts the shoulder patch to identify members of Army units.

1925
John T. Scopes is arrested for teaching Darwin's theory of evolution in a Tennessee public school.

1926
Sinclair Lewis refuses to accept the Pulitzer Prize for his novel *Arrowsmith*, declaring that prizes make writers "sterile."

1936
Mutiny on the Bounty wins the Academy Award for Best Picture of 1935.

1943
The Postmaster General introduces the first system of postal zones in the United States.

1947
All The Kings Men by Robert Penn Warren wins the Pulitzer Prize for Fiction.

1952
The Caine Mutiny by Herman Wouk wins the Pulitzer Prize for Fiction.

1955
Damn Yankees by George Abbot opens at the Forty-Sixth Street Theater in New York.

1958
George Washington by Douglas Southall Freeman wins the Pulitzer Prize for Biography.

1961
President Kennedy signs the Fair Labor Standards Act, increasing the minimum wage to $1.25.

1961
Navy Commander Alan Shepard, Jr. makes a suborbital flight aboard the Mercury Capsule, *Freedom 7*, becoming the first American in space.

1963
Doctors in Denver, Colorado, perform the first successful liver transplant.

1975
The Killer Angels by Michael Shaara wins the Pulitzer Prize for Fiction.

1985
President Reagan lays a wreath at the military cemetery in Bitburg, West Germany, causing worldwide controversy because of the Nazi Waffen SS graves there.

May

6

1780
Fort Moultrie in Charleston, South Carolina, falls to the British, during the Revolutionary War.

1851
Linus Yale of New York is awarded a patent for the first drum and pin lock.

1851
John Gorrie is awarded a patent for the first ice-making machine.

1859
John H. Gregory discovers gold at Gregory's Gulch in present-day Colorado.

1861
Arkansas secedes from the Union.

1864
The Union Army of the Potomac, commanded by General Ulysses S. Grant, sustains over 17,000 casualties at the Battle of the Wilderness in Virginia, during the Civil War.

1935
R.E. Lee by Douglas Southall Freeman wins the Pulitzer Prize for Biography.

1935
The Works Progress Administration is established, providing millions of unemployed Americans with work.

1937
The German dirigible, *Hindenburg*, is destroyed by fire as it approaches its mast in Lakehurst, New Jersey.

1940
The Grapes of Wrath by John Steinbeck wins the Pulitzer Prize in Fiction.

1942
The Japanese take Corregidor after American forces, commanded by General Jonathan M. Wainwright, surrender, during World War II.

1957
Profiles in Courage by John F. Kennedy wins the Pulitzer Prize for Biography.

1963
The Guns of August by Barbara Tuchman wins the Pulitzer Prize for Non-Fiction.

1986
Reverend Donald E. Pelotte of Gallup, New Mexico, becomes the first Indian to become a Roman Catholic Bishop.

The Battle of the Wilderness

May

1763
Ottawa Indians led by Chief Pontiac attack the fort at Detroit.

1789
President Washington attends the first inaugural ball in New York.

1871
The United States and England sign the Treaty of Washington, settling fishing and boundary disputes off the Pacific Coast.

1906
Congress passes the Alaska Delegate Bill, allowing Alaska to send a non-voting member to Congress.

1914
Congress passes a resolution establishing Mother's Day on the second Sunday in May.

1915
The British steamship, *Lusitania*, is sunk by a German submarine off the coast of Ireland, killing 1198 people, including 114 Americans.

1928
The Bridge of San Luis Rey by Thornton Wilder is awarded the Pulitzer Prize for Fiction.

1943
American forces capture Bizerte, Tunisia, during World War II.

1945
A Bell for Adano by John Hersey wins the Pulitzer Prize for Fiction.

1945
German General Jodl signs the unconditional surrender of Germany at General Eisenhower's headquarters in Reims, France, during World War II.

1951
Complete Poems by Carl Sandburg wins the Pulitzer Prize for Poetry.

1954
The French are defeated by the North Vietnamese at Dien Ben Phu, forcing the withdrawal of French troops from Vietnam.

1956
The Diary of Anne Frank, by Francis Goodrich and Albert Hackett, wins the Pulitzer Prize for Drama.

German Gen. Jodl signs the unconditional surrender

May

1541
Spanish explorer, Fernando de Soto, and his expedition become the first Europeans to reach the Mississippi River.

1785
Congress passes the Land Ordinance of 1785, calling for the northwestern territories to be divided into six-mile-square townships.

1792
Congress passes the Militia Act, allowing the states to draft able-bodied men to counter Indian hostilities.

1846
The United States Army defeats the Mexicans at the Battle of Palo Alto, the first major engagement of the Mexican War.

1871
The United States and England sign the Treaty of Washington, providing for damages to United States shipping by Confederate vessels built in England during the Civil War.

1884
Harry S. Truman, thirty-third President of the United States, is born in Lamar, Missouri.

1886
Dr. John Styth perfects the syrup for Coca Cola.

1914
Congress passes the Smith-Lever Act, providing Federal funds for state agricultural colleges.

1915
Regret becomes the first filly to win the Kentucky Derby.

1942
The Battle of the Coral Sea ends with seven Japanese warships sunk by United States carrier-based airplanes, during World War II.

1950
The United States decides to offer military and economic aid to the former French colony of South Vietnam.

1952
Army Secretary Frank C. Pace announces the development of an atomic cannon.

1972
President Nixon orders the mining of Haiphong Harbor, during the Vietnam War.

De Soto at the Mississippi River

1712
The Carolina Territory is separated into two colonies, North Carolina and South Carolina.

1781
The British surrender Pensacola, Florida, leaving the Spanish to conquer all of West Florida.

1832
The Seminole Indians sign the Treaty of Payne's Landing, accepting resettlement west of the Mississippi River.

1846
United States forces commanded by General Zachary Taylor force the Mexican Army back across the Rio Grande River at the Battle of Resaca de la Palma, during the Mexican War.

1926
Rear Admiral Richard E. Byrd makes the first successful flight over the North Pole.

1936
The German dirigible, *Hindenburg*, lands in Lakehurst, New Jersey, completing its first transatlantic flight.

1941
The Allies capture the *Enigma*, the German's master coding machine, allowing the intercepting of secret messages, during World War II.

1960
The United States announces the suspension of all U-2 spy flights over the Soviet Union.

1978
Ain't Misbehavin' by Richard Maltby, Jr. opens at the Longacre Theater in New York.

1984
Alexander Calder's *Big Crinkly* sells for $852,000, a record for an American sculpture.

An American officer shot during the Mexican War

May

1775

American forces under Colonel Ethan Allen take Fort Ticonderoga, New York, during the Revolutionary War.

1779

The British capture and burn Portsmouth and Norfolk, Virginia, during the Revolutionary War.

1797

The *United States* becomes the first ship of the United States Navy.

1837

The financial panic of 1837 occurs when New York banks cease making specie payments.

1860

Congress passes the Morrill Tariff Bill to regulate imports.

1863

Confederate General Stonewall Jackson dies of wounds suffered at the Battle of Chancellorsville, Virginia, during the Civil War.

1865

Confederate President Jefferson Davis is captured by a cavalry detachment commanded by General James H. Wilson, in Irwinville, Georgia.

1869

The Central Pacific and Union Pacific railroads link up in Promontory Point, Utah, to complete the first transcontinental railroad in the United States.

1926

The United States Marines land in Nicaragua following civil unrest.

1934

A severe dust storm blows 300 million tons of topsoil from Texas, Oklahoma, Arkansas, and Colorado, causing the abandonment of hundreds of farms.

1939

After a division lasting 109 years, the Methodist Church is reunited when the Methodist Protestant Church and the Methodist Episcopal Church sign a Declaration of Union.

1940

The German Army invades Belgium and Luxembourg, during World War II.

1960

The U.S.S. *Triton* becomes the first submarine to make an undersea voyage around the world.

Completing the transcontinental railroad

May

1647
Peter Stuyvesant assumes the leadership of
New Amsterdam in the New Netherland
Colony.

1690
English forces capture Port Royal, Nova Scotia,
during King William's War.

1792
American explorer Captain Robert Gray discovers the Columbia River, in Washington.

1816
The American Bible Society is formed in New
York.

1858
Minnesota joins the Union as the thirty-second
state.

1862
The Confederate ironclad, *Virginia*, is scuttled,
as the naval yard at Norfolk, Virginia, is evacuated, during the Civil War.

1864
Confederate cavalry commander J.E.B. Stuart is
mortally wounded at Yellow Tavern, Virginia,
during the Civil War.

1928
Station WGY in Schenectady, New York,
becomes the first station to inaugurate television service in the United States.

1930
The Adler Planetarium in Chicago becomes the
first planetarium in the United States.

1935
President Roosevelt establishes the Rural Elec-
trification Administration to build power lines
and bring electric service into rural areas.

Peter Stuyvesant arriving in New Amsterdam

1780

The Americans under General Benjamin Lincoln surrender their 5400-man garrison at Charleston, South Carolina, during the Revolutionary War.

1859

The Vicksburg Commercial Convention urges the reopening of the African slave trade.

1864

Union forces commanded by General Winfield Scott Hancock capture 4000 Confederate troops at the Battle of Spotsylvania, Virginia, during the Civil War.

1898

A United States naval fleet commanded by Admiral Sampson bombards San Juan, Puerto Rico, during the Spanish-American War.

1902

After management refuses to negotiate with United Mine Worker's President John Mitchell, 140,000 coal miners go on strike in Pennsylvania.

1922

A 500-square-foot hole is created when a meteor strikes near Blackstone, Virginia.

1929

John Brown's Body by Stephen Vincent Benet wins the Pulitzer Prize for Poetry.

1933

Congress passes the Agricultural Adjustment Act, restricting the production of certain crops and offering to pay farmers for uncultivated acreage.

1937

The coronation of King George VI of England is heard over the radio, becoming the first worldwide radio broadcast.

1958

The United States and Canada establish the North American Air Defense Command.

1975

The United States ship, *Mayaguez*, is seized by Cambodian forces and charged with spying.

1985

Amy Eilberg becomes the first woman Conservative rabbi in the United States.

1987

The first three-way heart and lung transplant is performed by doctors in Baltimore, Maryland.

The Battle of Spotsylvania

1607
Jamestown, Virginia, becomes the first permanent English colony in America.

1792
The Democratic-Republican Party is formed by Thomas Jefferson.

1846
Congress authorizes $10 million for the recruitment of 50,000 soldiers to serve in the Mexican War.

1861
Union General Benjamin Butler moves Federal troops into Baltimore after several demonstrations there, during the Civil War.

1861
England declares its neutrality in the Civil War.

Settlers landing in Jamestown

1865
Confederate forces commanded by Colonel John S. Ford attack Union troops at the Battle of Palmitto Ranch, Texas, the last battle of the Civil War.

1915
The United States sends a note to Germany protesting the sinking of the *Lusitania* and demanding reparations.

1918
The United States Post Office issues the first airmail stamps.

1922
Otto I. Wiedfeldt, the first German Ambassador to the United States since World War I, arrives in Washington, D.C.

1925
The Florida Legislature passes a bill requiring daily Bible readings in public schools.

1943
The Germans and Italians surrender, ending the Axis campaign in North Africa, during World War II.

1954
President Eisenhower signs the St. Lawrence Seaway Bill, authorizing construction of the St. Lawrence Seaway to connect the Great Lakes with the Atlantic Ocean.

1958
A hostile mob in Caracas, Venezuela, attacks Vice President Nixon's motorcade with rocks and bottles.

1982
Braniff International Corporation becomes the first major United States airline to declare bankruptcy.

May

1801
The Tripolitan War begins with the Pasha of Tripoli's soldiers cutting down the flagpole at the United States Consulate.

1804
The Lewis and Clark expedition leaves St. Louis to explore the new territory acquired by the United States in the Louisiana Purchase.

1863
Union forces commanded by General Ulysses S. Grant attack and occupy Jackson, Mississippi, during the Civil War.

1901
The California Development Company completes a canal, bringing water from the Colorado River to California.

1904
The American team wins the unofficial championship at the first Olympics held in the United States, in St. Louis.

1908
Mechanic Charles Furnas becomes the first passenger on an airplane, on a flight with Orville Wright in Dayton, Ohio.

1913
John D. Rockefeller donates a record $100 million to the Rockefeller Foundation.

1942
Congress establishes the Women's Army Auxiliary Corps.

1948
The United States becomes the first country to recognize Israel as an independent nation.

1973
The United States successfully launches the *Skylab* orbital space station.

Tripolitan pirates attacking a U.S. ship

May

15

1602
Captain Bartholomew Gosnold becomes the first Englishman to land on the New England Coast, near Cape Cod, Massachusetts.

1672
The Massachusetts General Court enacts the first copyright law in the colonies.

1685
Chief Justice Nicolas More of Pennsylvania becomes the first official to be impeached in America.

1797
The first special session of Congress convenes, to debate a crisis in French-American relations.

1862
The Department of Agriculture is created by act of Congress.

1864
The Confederates, commanded by General Jubal A. Early, defeat a Union force, commanded by General Franz Sigel, in the Shenandoah Valley in Virginia, during the Civil War.

1869
Elizabeth Cady Stanton forms the National Woman Suffrage Association, along with Susan B. Anthony.

1911
The Supreme Court orders the Standard Oil Company of New Jersey dissolved because of antitrust violations.

1916
United States marines land in Santo Domingo to quell disorder.

1924
All God's Children Got Wings by Eugene O'Neill opens at the Provincetown Playhouse in New York.

1928
Congress passes the Flood Control Act, providing Federal funds for the controlling of the Mississippi River.

1930
Miss Ellen Church becomes the first stewardess, aboard a United Airlines flight from Oakland, California, to Cheyenne, Wyoming.

1940
The Dutch Army surrenders to the Germans as the French withdraw, during World War II.

1941
A Sikorsky VS-300 makes the first successful helicopter flight in the United States.

1942
Gas rationing begins in 17 states in the United States, during World War II.

1951
The American Telephone & Telegraph Company becomes the first corporation to have one million stockholders.

1955
The United States, England, France, and the Soviet Union sign the Austrian State Treaty, returning sovereignty to the Republic of Austria.

1982
Ebony and Ivory by Paul McCartney and Stevie Wonder becomes the number one record in the United States.

1832

The United States signs a treaty of peace and commerce with Chile, in Santiago.

1861

The Kentucky Legislature declares its intentions to remain neutral in the Civil War.

1863

Confederate forces, commanded by General John Pemberton, are forced to retreat after an attack by Union troops, commanded by General Ulysses S. Grant, at the Battle of Champion Hill, Virginia, during the Civil War.

1864

Confederate troops, commanded by General P.G.T. Beauregard, attack a Union force, commanded by General Benjamin Butler, at the Battle of Drewry's Bluff, Virginia, during the Civil War.

1866

Congress authorizes the issuance of the nickel.

1874

One hundred people are killed when the Ashfield Reservoir Dam near Williamsburg, Massachusetts, collapses.

1910

The United States Bureau of Mines is established.

1918

Congress passes the Sedition Act, providing heavy penalties for anyone hindering the war effort.

1929

Wings wins the first Academy Award for Best Picture of 1928.

1946

Annie Get Your Gun by Irving Berlin opens in New York.

1958

United States Air Force Captain, Walter Irwin, sets a new jet speed record of 1404.1 mph in an F-101A Starfighter.

1960

Soviet Premier Khrushchev cancels the Paris summit conference due to the downing of an American U-2 spy plane over the Soviet Union.

1981

Bette Davis Eyes by Kim Carnes becomes the number one record in the United States.

A scene from *Wings*

1733
England passes the Molasses Act, placing a high duty on rum and molasses imported from the French and Spanish West Indies.

1768
The British frigate, *Romney*, arrives in Boston Harbor after customs officials call for protection.

1774
Rhode Island calls for the first intercolonial congress.

1792
The New York Stock Exchange is organized.

1875
Aristedes wins the first Kentucky Derby, at Churchill Downs, Kentucky.

The first Kentucky Derby

1877
The first telephone switchboard is put into operation at the Holmes Burglar Alarm Company in Boston.

1929
Al Capone is sentenced to one year in prison in Chicago for carrying a concealed weapon.

1938
Congress passes the Naval Expansion Act of 1938, authorizing one billion dollars for the production of capital ships.

1940
The Belgian Government flees as the German Army enters Brussels, during World War II.

1954
The Supreme Court declares racial segregation in public schools unconstitutional.

1971
Godspell by Stephen Schwartz opens at the Cherry Lane Theatre in New York.

1974
Six members of the Symbionese Liberation Army are killed in a shootout with Los Angeles police.

1980
Fourteen people are killed in race riots in Miami, which erupt as a result of the acquittal of four white policemen charged with the fatal beating of a Black man.

1987
Thirty-seven United States sailors aboard the U.S.S. *Stark* are killed when an Iraqi warplane mistakenly fires missiles at the ship, in the Persian Gulf.

May

1652
Rhode Island becomes the first colony to abolish slavery.

1804
Napoleon Bonaparte becomes Emperor of France.

1846
United States forces commanded by General Zachary Taylor cross the Rio Grande River and occupy Matamoros, Mexico, during the Mexican War.

1861
Union forces seal off the Rappahannock River in Virginia, completing the Federal blockade, during the Civil War.

1863
The Union siege of Vicksburg, Mississippi, begins, as the Union army commanded by General Ulysses S. Grant surrounds the city, during the Civil War.

1899
The Permanent Court of International Arbitration is established at the First Hague Peace Conference.

1917
Congress passes the Selective Service Act, authorizing conscription for the armed forces.

1926
A Disarmament Conference opens in Geneva, Switzerland.

1933
Congress passes the Tennessee Valley Act, establishing the Tennessee Valley Authority.

1934
Congress passes the Lindbergh Act, calling for the death penalty in kidnapping cases.

1944
Allied forces enter Rome, during World War II.

1980
Mt. St. Helens in southern Washington erupts, spewing volcanic ash over 120 square miles.

1988
Howard Nemerov is named the third poet laureate of the United States.

Mt. St. Helens erupting

May

1643
Representatives of four New England colonies confederate as the United Colonies of New England.

1863
Union forces commanded by General William T. Sherman unsuccessfully attack Confederate positions in the first major attack against Vicksburg, Mississippi, during the Civil War.

1864
Confederate forces commanded by General Richard S. Ewell withdraw, ending the Battles of Spotsylvania, Virginia, during the Civil War.

1921
President Harding signs the first generally restrictive immigration act in the United States, initiating a quota system.

1928
The first frog jumping contest, in Calaveras County, California, is held.

1940
German Panzer forces advance to St. Quentin in the Western Front, beginning the encirclement of the British Expeditionary Force, during World II.

1941
The last Italian troops in North Africa, commanded by the Duke of Aosta, surrender to the British, during World War II.

1942
The German Army mounts a major attack near Kharkov in the Soviet Union, during World War II.

1960
Disc jockey Alan Freed is arrested on commercial bribery charges stemming from the payola scandal in the radio industry.

The siege of Vicksburg, Mississippi

1639
The Council of Dorchester, Massachusetts, establishes the first school in America maintained by community taxes.

1690
A combined French and Indian force destroy a settlement at Casco, Maine, during King William's War.

1777
The Cherokee Indians give up all of their territory in South Carolina, signing the Treaty of DeWitts Corner.

1861
North Carolina secedes from the Union.

1865
Confederate General Kirby Smith surrenders all forces west of the Mississippi River, during the Civil War.

1873
Jacob Davis and Levi Strauss are awarded a patent for riveted pocket denim pants.

1902
Cuba becomes an independent nation.

1926
President Coolidge signs the Civilian Aviation Act, giving the Federal Government jurisdiction over civil aviation.

1932
Amelia Earhart becomes the first woman to fly across the Atlantic Ocean, landing near Londonderry, Ireland.

1959
Forty-nine hundred seventy-eight Japanese-Americans, who renounced their citizenship during World War II, are restored to citizenship.

1960
An Atlas intercontinental ballistic missile flies a record 9,000 miles, from Cape Canaveral, Florida, to the tip of Africa.

1967
Groovin' by the Young Rascals becomes the number one record in the United States.

1969
United States and South Vietnamese troops take Hamburger Hill after a 10-day battle, during the Vietnam War.

Indians attacking Casco, Maine

May

1832
The Democratic Party formally adopts its name and nominates Andrew Jackson for a second term at its convention in Baltimore.

1861
Richmond, Virginia, becomes the capital of the Confederate States of America.

1878
D.A. Buck is awarded a patent for the first mass-produced watch.

1881
The American branch of the International Red Cross is founded by Clara Barton.

1906
The United States and Mexico sign an agreement over the distribution of the waters of the Rio Grande River for irrigation.

1940
British tank forces attack the Germans commanded by Field Marshall Irwin Rommel on the Western Front, during World War II.

1959
Gypsy, by Jule Stein and Stephen Sondheim, opens at the Broadway Theatre in New York.

1973
Lynn Genesko of Woodbridge, New Jersey, becomes the first woman to receive an athletic scholarship, from the University of Miami.

1975
A Chorus Line, by James Kirkwood and Marvin Hamlisch, opens at the New York Shakespeare Festival's Newman Theater.

Clara Barton

1843

The first pioneers bound for the Oregon Territory leave Elm Grove, Missouri.

1856

Representative Preston Brooks of South Carolina severely beats Senator Charles Sumner of Massachusetts at his Capital Hill office, in a dispute over the slavery issue.

1863

Union forces commanded by General Ulysses S. Grant sustain heavy losses in an unsuccessful attack on Vicksburg, Mississippi, during the Civil War.

1865

Confederate soldier A. Bordunix becomes the last man killed in action during the Civil War.

1882

The United States recognizes the independence of Korea.

1891

Representatives of the National Federation of Women's Clubs see the first public display of a film at the Edison Laboratories in West Orange, New Jersey.

1909

Seven hundred thousand acres of land in Washington, Montana, and Idaho are opened up to settlement.

1928

Congress passes the Jones-White Act, providing Government subsidies for American shipping.

1947

The United States successfully launches the Corporal, the first ballistic missile, at the White Sands Proving Grounds, in New Mexico.

1947

President Truman signs the Greek-Turkish Aid Bill, authorizing $400 million in aid to Greece and Turkey.

1972

President Nixon becomes the first American president to visit Moscow, meeting with Soviet Premier Brezhnev.

1984

The Supreme Court rules that law firms may not discriminate on the basis of sex, race, or religion in awarding partnerships.

The Corporal missile

1788

South Carolina becomes the eighth state to ratify the Constitution.

1814

Andrew Jackson becomes Major General of the United States Army, during the War of 1812.

1865

American flags fly at full mast for the first time in four years as the victorious Army of the Potomac passes in grand review in Washington, D.C.

1876

Joe Borden of Boston pitches the first no-hitter in the National League.

1922

Abie's Irish Rose by Anne Nichols opens at the Fulton Theater in New York.

1923

Twelve members of the cast of the play, *God of Vengeance*, presented at the Apollo Theater in New York, are convicted of immoral behavior.

1934

Outlaws Bonnie Parker and Clyde Barrow are shot and killed in Plain Dealing, Louisiana, by a group of Texas Rangers led by Frank Hamer.

1955

The General Assembly of the Presbyterian Church approves the ordination of women ministers.

1962

Doctors at the Massachusetts General Hospital in Boston perform the first successful reimplantation of a human limb.

1988

Maryland becomes the first state to ban the sale of cheap hand guns.

Outlaw Clyde Barrow's bullet ridden car

1818

American troops commanded by General Andrew Jackson capture Pensacola, Florida, during the First Seminole War.

1819

The *Savannah* becomes the first steamship to cross the Atlantic Ocean, sailing from Savannah, Georgia, to Liverpool, England, in 27 days.

1844

Samuel F.B. Morse sends the first telegraph message, from Washington, D.C. to Baltimore.

1856

Abolitionist John Brown kills five pro-slavery Kansans in retaliation for the sacking of Lawrence, Kansas.

1861

Elmer Ellsworth becomes the first Union battle casualty as Federal troops occupy Alexandria, Virginia, during the Civil War.

1869

Major John Wesley Powell begins the first exploration of the Grand Canyon.

1883

The Brooklyn Bridge, designed by John A. Roebling, opens, with a ceremony attended by Presidents Chester A. Arthur and Grover Cleveland.

1915

Thomas A. Edison announces the invention of the telescribe for recording telephone conversations.

1935

The Cincinnati Reds defeat the Philadelphia Phillies in major league baseball's first night game.

1959

The Obie Construction Company in Pittsburgh installs the first fallout shelter.

1962

Astronaut Scott M. Carpenter becomes the second American in orbit, aboard the Mercury capsule *Aurora 7*.

1964

Hello Dolly, by Michael Stewart and Jerry Herman, wins the Tony Award for Best Musical of 1963-1964.

1966

Mame, by Jerome Lawrence and Jerry Herman, opens at the Winter Garden in New York.

President Arthur at the Brooklyn Bridge

1775

British reinforcements under the commands of Generals William Howe, Henry Clinton, and John Burgoyne arrive in Boston.

1787

The Constitutional Convention convenes in Philadelphia.

1850

New Mexico forms its own state government and applies for statehood.

1928

Amelia Earhart takes off from Boston, becoming the first woman to fly across the Atlantic Ocean.

The Constitutional Convention

1935

Jesse Owens achieves a record of six world records in one day at a track meet in Ann Arbor, Michigan.

1950

The Brooklyn-Battery Tunnel opens, becoming the longest vehicular tunnel in the United States.

1953

The first atomic-powered artillery shell is successfully fired, at a test range in Nevada.

1959

The Supreme Court rules that a Louisiana law banning boxing matches between Blacks and whites is illegal.

1961

In a speech before Congress, President Kennedy commits the United States to a manned landing on the Moon before the end of the decade.

1964

The United States Supreme Court declares the closing of schools to avoid segregation to be unconstitutional.

1968

The Gateway Arch in St. Louis, Missouri, opens.

1979

Two hundred seventy-two people are killed when an American Airlines DC-10 crashes after takeoff from O'Hare International Airport in Chicago.

1986

Six million people link hands to make a chain across the United States in an event called Hands Across America, an effort to raise money for the homeless.

May

1637
New Englanders attack the Pequot Indian stronghold near New Haven, Connecticut, in the first battle of the Pequot War.

1790
Congress establishes a government for Tennessee, part of which was formerly the state of Franklin.

1805
The Lewis and Clark Expedition sights the Rocky Mountains.

1864
Congress forms the Montana Territory.

1868
The impeachment trial of President Johnson ends with the Senate failing by one vote to convict.

1922
President Harding signs a bill establishing a Federal narcotics control board.

1928
Andrew Payne reaches New York, winning the first cross-country foot race in the United States, with a time of 573 hours.

1938
The House Committee to Investigate Un-American Activities is formed.

1959
Pittsburgh Pirates pitcher Harvey Haddix pitches a record 12 perfect innings before losing the game in the 13th inning.

1977
Daredevil George Willig climbs up the World Trade Center in New York and is fined $1.10.

Pequot Indians attacking New Haven, Connecticut

1813

The Americans commanded by Lieutenant General Winfield Scott capture a 1600-man British garrison near the mouth of the Niagara River, during the War of 1812.

1863

The Union siege of Port Hudson, Louisiana, begins as Union forces, commanded by General Nathaniel Banks, attack Confederate forces, commanded by General Franklin Gardner, during the Civil War.

1873

Survivor wins the first Preakness Stakes in Pimlico, Maryland.

1896

Five hundred people are killed as a tornado strikes St. Louis, Missouri.

The Siege of Port Hudson

1901

The Supreme Court rules that territories acquired in the Spanish-American War are not part of the United States *or* a foreign country.

1924

The Methodist Episcopal Church lifts its ban on dancing and theater going.

1929

The Supreme Court upholds the President's use of the pocket veto to prevent the enactment of legislation.

1933

Congress passes the Federal Securities Act, requiring registration of all issues of stocks and bonds.

1935

The Supreme Court rules that the National Industrial Recovery Act is unconstitutional.

1937

The Golden Gate Bridge opens in San Francisco.

1943

Congress establishes the Office of War Mobilization, to direct the conduct of the war on the home front.

1953

Frank Lloyd Wright wins the Gold Medal for Architecture from the National Institute for Arts and Letters.

1985

Spend a Buck wins a record $2.6 million dollars in a race at Garden State Park in Cherry Hill, New Jersey.

1754

A force led by George Washington defeats the French near Fort Duquesne, in the first action of the French and Indian War.

1773

The first Jewish service in America is held at the Touro Synagogue, Newport, Rhode Island.

1798

Congress authorizes President Adams to order American warships to seize French ships interfering with American shipping.

1830

President Jackson signs the Removal Act, calling for all Indians to be resettled west of the Mississippi River.

1908

The District of Columbia passes the first child labor law in the United States.

1915

Germany replies to the United States protest about the sinking of the *Lusitania* by asserting that the ship was armed and carrying munitions.

1918

The United States First Division helps win the Battle of Cantigny, France, in its first independent action of World War I.

1918

The American Railroad Express Company is formed, when the Adams, American, Wells-Fargo, and Southern Express companies are merged.

1956

Pittsburgh Pirates first baseman Dale Long hits his record eighth home run in as many consecutive games.

1959

The United States Army launches two monkeys into space from Cape Canaveral, Florida.

1976

The United States and the Soviet Union sign a nuclear test pact, permitting examination of Soviet test sites.

1980

The first women graduate from the United States Military Academy at West Point, New York.

1985

Ninety-nine people are killed as tornadoes sweep through parts of Pennsylvania, Ohio, and New York.

The Battle of Cantigny

May

1658

The Massachusetts General Court bans the holding of Quaker meetings in the colony.

1790

Rhode Island becomes the thirteenth state to ratify the Constitution.

1843

The John C. Fremont Expedition leaves Kansas City to make the first accurate survey of the route to the Oregon Territory.

1848

Wisconsin joins the Union as the thirtieth state.

1911

The Supreme Court orders the American Tobacco Company dissolved because of anti-trust violations.

1917

John F. Kennedy, thirty-fifth President of the United States, is born in Brookline, Massachusetts.

1942

Bing Crosby records *White Christmas*, which becomes the best-selling record in the United States.

1944

The United States escort carrier *Block Island* is sunk by a German submarine, during World War II.

1968

The United States nuclear submarine, *Scorpion*, and its crew of 99 is reported missing in the Atlantic Ocean.

1982

Little Shop of Horrors opens at the WPA Theatre in New York.

John Fremont entering Oregon

May

1539
Spanish explorer, Fernando de Soto, lands in Florida, consolidating Spanish dominion over the territory.

1783
The *Pennsylvania Evening Post* becomes the first daily newspaper in the United States.

1854
President Pierce signs the Kansas-Nebraska Act, creating two new territories and allowing settlers to decide whether they will enter the Union as free or slave states.

1868
Decoration Day is celebrated for the first time in the United States.

1908
Congress passes the Aldrich-Vreeland Act, freeing banks to issue commercial paper.

1911
Ray Harroun wins the first Indianapolis 500 auto race, averaging 74.5 mph.

1914
Lassen Peak in the Sierra Nevada Mountains in California erupts, spewing steam and ash 10,000 feet into the air.

1922
The Lincoln Memorial is dedicated in Washington, D.C.

1943
United States forces recapture Attu in the Aleutian Islands, during World War II.

1952
Twenty-two-year-old Troy Ruttman becomes the youngest person to win the Indianapolis 500 auto race.

John Harroun's winning car

May

1647
The Rhode Island General Assembly drafts a constitution calling for separation of church and state.

1790
President Washington signs the first United States copyright act.

1821
The Cathedral of the Assumption of the Blessed Virgin Mary, in Baltimore, becomes the first Catholic cathedral in the United States.

1861
General P.G.T. Beauregard becomes commander of the Confederate Army of the Potomac, during the Civil War.

1862
Confederate forces commanded by General Joseph E. Johnston attack part of the Union Army at the Battle of Seven Pines, Virginia, during the Civil War.

1884
Dr. John H. Kellog of Battle Creek, Michigan, applies for a patent for a process to manufacture corn flakes.

1889
When the dam above Johnstown, Pennsylvania, breaks after heavy rains, 2295 people are killed.

1894
Congress declares that the Monroe Doctrine applies to Hawaii, stating that any foreign interference will be considered a hostile act against United States.

1913
The Seventeenth Amendment goes into effect, providing for the popular election of United States senators.

1925
The United States and England ratify a treaty to preserve fisheries in the northern Pacific Ocean.

1938
Henry Armstrong outpoints Barney Ross, to win the welterweight boxing championship.

1955
The Supreme Court bans racial segregation in United States public schools.

1962
Convicted Nazi Adolf Eichmann is executed in Israel.

The Battle of Seven Pines

Johnstown, Pennsylvania after the flood

June

1792
Kentucky joins the Union as the fifteenth state.

1796
Tennessee joins the Union as the sixteenth state.

1813
Lying mortally wounded aboard the United States ship, *Chesapeake*, Captain James Lawrence cries, "Don't give up the ship."

1862
Confederate General Joseph E. Johnston is seriously wounded when Union reinforcements arrive to repel the Confederate attack at the Battle of Seven Pines, Virginia, during the Civil War.

The death of Captain Lawrence

1862
Robert E. Lee is appointed commander of the Confederate Army of Northern Virginia, during the Civil War.

1868
James Buchanan, fifteenth President of the United States, dies in Lancaster, Pennsylvania.

1880
The first public telephone booth goes into operation in New Haven, Connecticut.

1909
The National Association for the Advancement of Colored People is founded by W.E.B. Du Bois.

1924
Congress establishes the Border Patrol, under the jurisdiction of the Immigration and Naturalization Service.

1936
The British liner, *Queen Mary*, arrives in New York Harbor on her maiden voyage.

1946
Assault becomes the seventh horse to win racing's Triple Crown.

1967
Sgt. Pepper's Lonely Hearts Club Band by the Beatles is released by Capitol Records.

1975
California Angels pitcher Nolan Ryan pitches his record fourth no-hitter.

1986
The Metropolitan Opera's last tour ends with a performance of *La Traviata* in Minneapolis, Minnesota.

June

1784

North Carolina cedes its western territories to the United States.

1862

President Lincoln signs the Morrill Land Grant Act, providing 30,000 acres for every loyal state, to endow agricultural and engineering colleges.

1862

Congress passes an act forbidding slavery in all Federal territories.

1865

The last naval action of the Civil War takes place as Confederate forces surrender the port of Galveston, Texas, to Union troops.

1883

Fort Wayne beats Quincy 19-11 in the first baseball game played under electric lights.

1899

A gang led by Butch Cassidy and the Sundance Kid rob a Union Pacific train in Wilcox, Wyoming.

1924

Congress passes the Snyder Act, giving citizenship to all Indians born within the borders of the United States.

1944

The Provisional Governor of the French Republic is formed by members of the resistance, during World War II.

1952

The United States Supreme Court rules that the seizure of steel mills by the Federal Government is unconstitutional.

1966

Surveyor I becomes the first American spacecraft to make a soft landing on the Moon, after a flight of over 231,000 miles.

Butch Cassidy robbing a train

June

1621
The Dutch West India Company is formed with the right to colonize the New World.

1848
The United States and New Grenada sign the Treaty of New Grenada, providing the United States with a right of way across the Isthmus of Panama.

1851
The New York Knickerbockers wear the first baseball uniforms.

1861
A Union force commanded by General George B. McClellan defeats the Confederates at Phillipi, Virginia, during the Civil War.

1864
The Union Army of the Potomac, commanded by General George G. Meade, loses over 7000 men at the Battle of Cold Harbor, Virginia, during the Civil War.

1916
Congress passes the National Defense Act, increasing the standing army to 175,000 men.

1921
Fifteen hundred people are killed in Colorado as the Arkansas River floods its banks after a cloudburst.

1948
The 200-inch Hale telescope at the Palomar Mountain Observatory begins operating, becoming the largest reflector telescope in the world.

1957
The United States joins the Baghdad Pact, reaffirming its support for Turkey, Iraq, Iran, Pakistan, and England against Communist aggression.

1972
Sally J. Priesand of Cincinnati becomes the first woman rabbi in the United States.

The New York Knickerbocker baseball team

1805

A peace treaty is signed ending the Tripolitan War, with Tripoli agreeing to stop menacing United States shipping.

1845

Leonora by William Henry Fry becomes the first American grand opera to be performed, at the Chestnut Theater in Philadelphia.

1896

The first Ford automobile is completed, in a brick worked in Detroit, Michigan.

1917

Laura E. Richards and Maude H. Elliott win the first Pulitzer Prize for their biography, *Julia Ward Howe.*

1917

The first Pulitzer Prizes are awarded.

1918

The United States Second Division halts the German advance at Chateau-Thierry, France, during World War I.

1919

Congress passes a proposal for the Nineteenth Amendment, enfranchising American women.

1920

Congress passes the Army Reorganization Act, establishing a peacetime force of 300,000 men.

1931

William G. Swan flies the first rocket-powered glider in the United States in Atlantic City, New Jersey.

1937

The first supermarket carts are put into service, at the Humpty Dumpty store in Oklahoma City.

1940

British and French troops complete an evacuation from Dunkirk, after being trapped by German forces, during World War II.

1975

Paleontologists in North Carolina discover animal fossils over 620 million years old.

1987

Edwin Moses' record 122 consecutive 400-meter-hurdles victories end.

The Battle of Chateau-Thierry

1806

Race horse, Yankee, becomes the first trotter to break the three minute mile, at a race track in New York.

1851

Harriet Beecher Stowe's *Uncle Tom's Cabin* appears as a serial in an anti-slavery newspaper in Washington, D.C.

1854

The United States and Canada sign the Canadian Reciprocity Treaty, opening trade in agricultural products and giving American fishermen rights on the Great Lakes.

1912

United States Marines land in Cuba to protect American interests.

1920

Congress passes the Merchant Marine Act as an incentive to United States shipping.

1937

War Admiral becomes the fourth horse to win racing's Triple Crown.

1940

The German Army invades France, during World War II.

1943

Count Fleet becomes the sixth horse to win racing's Triple Crown.

1947

Secretary of State, George Marshall, proposes the Marshal Plan for the reconstruction of Europe.

1967

The Six-Day War begins as the Israeli Air Force conducts raids, destroying most of Egypt's, Jordan's, and Syria's air forces.

Detail from the cover of *Uncle Tom's Cabin*

June

1716

The first Black slaves arrive in the French territory of Louisiana.

1778

British peace commissioners arrive in Philadelphia.

1798

Congress passes a bill abolishing debtors' prisons in the United States.

1846

The American Flag becomes the first publication for troops on active duty, during the Mexican War.

1847

British Minister, Charles Bankhead, initiates peace negotiations between the United States and Mexico, during the Mexican War.

1865

Missouri is readmitted to the Union.

1884

The roller coaster opens at Coney Island, New York.

1918

The United States Second Division, along with the Fourth Marine Brigade, halt the Germans and recapture the area, as the Battle of Belleau Wood begins, during World War I.

1933

The first drive-in cinema in the United States opens in Camden, New Jersey.

1934

President Roosevelt signs the Securities Exchange Act, creating the Securities and Exchange Commission.

1942

The Battle of Midway ends with the United States fleet sinking four Japanese aircraft carriers and 13 other ships, during World War II.

1944

The Normandy Invasion, designated D-Day, begins, with 4000 ships of all kinds eventually landing over 4 million Allied troops on the beaches at Normandy, France.

1968

Democratic Presidential Candidate Robert F. Kennedy is shot and killed after winning the California primary.

Allied assualt troops landing in Normandy

June

1494
Spain and Portugal sign the Treaty of Tordesillas, dividing up lands discovered in the new world.

1712
The Pennsylvania Assembly bans slavery in the colony.

1769
Daniel Boone sees Kentucky for the first time after traveling through the Cumberland Gap.

1864
President Lincoln is nominated for a second term at the Republican National Convention in Baltimore.

1905
A 1250-square-foot plot in lower Manhattan sells for a record $700,000.

1915
William Jennings Byran resigns as Secretary of State in a disagreement over the sinking of the *Lusitania* by a German submarine.

1930
Gallant Fox becomes the second horse to win racing's Triple Crown.

1934
Congress passes the Corporate Bankruptcy Act, allowing a corporation to reorganize itself with the agreement of its creditors.

1939
King George VI visits Niagara Falls to become the first British monarch to come to the United States.

1941
Whirlaway becomes the fifth horse to win racing's Triple Crown.

Daniel Boone in the wilderness

June

8

1778
The United States Secret Service is organized with Aaron Burr as its director.

1793
England orders the seizure of neutral vessels carrying provisions to France, including the United States'.

1845
Andrew Jackson, seventh President of the United States, dies in Tennessee.

1861
Tennessee secedes from the Union.

1861
President Lincoln establishes the United States Sanitary Commission to aid in maintaining healthful conditions for Union troops, during the Civil War.

1869
Ives W. McGaffey of Chicago is awarded a patent for the first vacuum cleaner.

1908
The National Conservation Commission is established.

1935
Omaha becomes the third horse to win racing's Triple Crown.

1937
An 8½ foot giant callalily flower blooms at the New York Botanical Gardens, becoming the largest flower in the world.

1953
As a tornado cuts through Ohio and Michigan, 139 people are killed.

1962
President Kennedy establishes the Office of Science and Technology.

1967
Thirty-four sailors are killed when Israeli torpedo boats mistakenly attack the United States communications ship, *Liberty*, off the Sinai Peninsula.

1980
Evita wins the Tony Award for Best Musical of 1979.

1986
The Baltimore Orioles beat the New York Yankees in an American League record 4 hour, 16 minute baseball game.

Aaron Burr on a secret mission

1742

The Spanish are repulsed by the English in the Battle of Bloody Marsh off the coast of Georgia, during the War of Jenkins' Ear.

1767

British customs officials seize John Hancock's sloop, *Liberty*, falsely accusing him of smuggling.

1860

Malaeska: The Indian Wife of the White Hunter, written by Ann S. Stephens, becomes the first dime novel published in the United States.

1863

In the largest cavalry battle of the Civil War, a Union force, commanded by General Alfred Pleasonton, defeats the Confederates, commanded by General J.E.B. Stuart, at the Battle of Brandy Station, Virginia.

1899

James J. Jeffries knocks out Bob Fitzimmons in the 11th round, to win the heavyweight boxing championship.

1942

The Germans murder over 2000 people in the village of Lidice in Czechoslovakia, during World War II.

1972

In flash floods around Rapid City, South Dakota, 239 people are killed.

1973

Secretariat becomes the ninth horse to win racing's Triple Crown, winning the Belmont Stakes with a record 30 length, 2:24 performance.

1984

Disneyland, in California, celebrates Donald Duck's fiftieth birthday.

Secretariat winning the Kentucky Derby

June

1652

The first mint in America is established by John Hull, in Boston.

1772

Colonists set fire to the British customs schooner, *Gaspe*, near Providence, Rhode Island.

1779

Spain declares war on England, without making any alliances with the United States.

1809

The *Phoenix* becomes the first steamboat to navigate in the open sea, making a 13-day voyage from Philadelphia to New York.

1837

Connecticut passes the first law in the United States providing for general incorporation.

1859

Peter O'Riley and Patrick McLaughlin discover the Comstock Lode in the Utah Territory, the richest mining discovery in the United States.

1861

A Union force is defeated by the Confederates at Bethel Church, Virginia, during the Civil War.

1864

A Confederate force, commanded by General Nathan B. Forrest, routs Union troops, commanded by General S.D. Sturgis, at Brice's Crossroads, Mississippi, during the Civil War.

1898

The United States Marines invade Cuba, landing at Guantanamo Bay, during the Spanish-American War.

1920

Congress passes the Water Power Act, creating the Federal Power Commission to regulate power plants.

1921

Congress establishes the Bureau of the Budget and the office of Comptroller General.

1935

Alcoholics Anonymous is organized in New York.

1940

Italy declares war on England and France, during World War II.

1978

Affirmed becomes the eleventh horse to win racing's Triple Crown.

Union troops in action during The Civil War

June

1776

John Adams, Benjamin Franklin, Thomas Jefferson, and others are appointed to draft a declaration of independence.

1782

British forces evacuate Savannah, Georgia.

1895

Charles E. Duryea is awarded a patent for the first gasoline driven automobile in the United States.

1905

The Pennsylvania Railroad is established.

1906

Congress passes the Forest Homestead Act, opening up forest land for agricultural use.

1919

Sir Barton becomes the first horse to win racing's Triple Crown.

1927

Charles A. Lindbergh becomes the first recipient of the Distinguished Flying Cross.

1959

D.H. Lawrence's novel, *Lady Chatterley's Lover*, is banned from the United States mails for obscenity.

1963

Governor George C. Wallace steps aside, allowing two Black students escorted by National Guard troops to enroll at the University of Alabama.

1977

Seattle Slew becomes the tenth horse to win racing's Triple Crown.

1986

The Supreme Court reaffirms Constitutional protection for the right to abortion, by a narrow margin.

Duryea's first gasoline automobile

June

1676
Connecticut colonists, led by Captain John Talcott, defeat the Wampanoag Indians, led by King Philip, near Hadley.

1836
Arkansas joins the Union as the twenty-fifth state.

1838
Congress establishes the Iowa Territory.

1864
The Union Army of the Potomac crosses the James River in Virginia with over 100,000 men, one of the great army movements in military history, during the Civil War.

1908
The steamship, *Lusitania*, sets a transatlantic speed record of 4 days and 15 hours, from Queenstown, Ireland, to New York.

1915
William Johnson wins United States Lawn Tennis Association singles championship, the first time the tournament is held at Forest Hills, in New York.

1948
Citation becomes the eighth horse to win racing's Triple Crown.

1963
NAACP field secretary, Medgar Evers, is shot and killed by a sniper in Jackson, Mississippi.

1963
Cleopatra, the most expensive movie ever made—costing over $37 million—opens in the United States.

1988
Andy Hampsten becomes the first American to win the Tour of Italy bicycle race.

The shooting of King Philip

1862
Confederate cavalry commanded by Jeb Stuart continue their raid around the Union Army of the Potomac, during the Civil War.

1935
James J. Braddock outpoints Max Baer, to win the heavyweight boxing championship.

1940
The first shipment of American military supplies leaves the United States bound for England aboard the *Eastern Prince*, during World War II.

1941
The French Vichy government arrests more than 12,000 Jews and places them in concentration camps, during World War II.

1942
President Roosevelt establishes the Office of War Information to control official news and propaganda, during World War II.

1965
Fiddler on the Roof, by Joseph Stein, Sheldon Harnick and Jerry Bock, wins the Tony Award for Best Musical of 1964-1965.

1966
In *Miranda v. Arizona*, the Supreme Court rules that a suspect must be read his rights by police before interrogation.

1979
The Sioux Indian Nation is granted an award of $17.5 million for land taken from them by the United States in the Black Hills of South Dakota in 1877.

1988
The Liggett Group becomes the first cigarette manufacturer to be found guilty and liable for the death of a smoker.

Jeb Stuart's cavalry attacking Union troops

June

1777
Congress adopts the official American flag.

1838
One hundred forty people are killed as the steamer, *Pulaski*, explodes off the coast of North Carolina.

1846
A group of settlers proclaim California a republic, during the Bear Flag Revolt.

1864
Union engineers construct the James River Bridge, the longest pontoon bridge to be used in warfare, during the Civil War.

1922
President Harding dedicates the Francis Scott Key Memorial in Baltimore, becoming the first President to be heard over the radio.

1934
Max Baer knocks out Primo Carnera in the 11th round, to win the heavyweight boxing championship.

1940
France surrenders to the Germany Army, during World War II.

1941
The United States freezes the assets of Germany and Italy, during World War II.

1947
President Truman signs peace treaties with Italy, Bulgaria, Rumania, and Hungary.

1951
The first Universal Automatic Computer (UNIVAC) is installed, in the United States Office of Census Taking.

California in the early 1840 s

1775
George Washington is chosen commander in chief of the Continental Army.

1834
Fort Hall becomes the first settlement in Idaho.

1843
The Republics of Texas and Mexico declare a truce in their hostilities.

1844
Charles Goodyear is awarded a patent for the vulcanization process to prevent rubber from sticking in warm weather.

1846
The United States and England sign the Oregon Treaty, establishing the 49th parallel as the boundary between the United States and western Canada.

General George Washington

1849
James Polk, eleventh President of the United States, dies in Nashville, Tennessee.

1877
Henry O. Flipper becomes the first Black to graduate from the United States Military Academy at West Point, New York.

1904
One thousand thirty people are killed when the excursion ship, *General Slocum*, catches fire on the Hudson River, the worst maritime disaster in the United States.

1907
The Second Hague Peace Conference meets to deliberate international regulations.

1916
President Wilson signs a bill establishing the Boy Scouts of America.

1917
Congress passes the Espionage Act, making it illegal to engage in disloyal acts against the United States.

1924
The Ford Motor Company manufactures its 10 millionth automobile.

1929
President Hoover signs the Agricultural Marketing Act, authorizing the establishment of the Federal Farm Board.

1938
Cincinnati Reds pitcher Johnny Vander Meer pitches his record second consecutive no hit game.

June

1755
The University of Pennsylvania is founded as the College, Academy and Charitable School, becoming the first non-sectarian college in America.

1858
In a speech accepting the Republican nomination for the Senate, Abraham Lincoln declares, "A house divided against itself cannot stand."

1879
H.M.S. Pinafore becomes the first Gilbert & Sullivan play presented in the United States, opening at the Bowery Theater in New York.

1894
George Case of the Yale baseball team uses the squeeze play, for the first time, scoring from third base on a bunt with two outs.

1897
The United States and Hawaii sign a treaty of annexation.

1933
Congress passes the Banking Act of 1933, establishing the Federal Bank Deposit Insurance Corporation.

1933
Congress passes the National Industrial Recovery Act, establishing the National Recovery Administration.

1938
Boston Braves outfielder Jimmy Foxx walks a record six times in one game.

1940
The United States orders all German consulates closed, during World War II.

1966
Man of La Mancha, by Dale Wasserman, Mitch Lee, and Joe Darion, wins the Tony Award for Best Musical of 1965-1966.

1976
Frances E. Meloy, Jr., the United States Ambassador to Lebanon, is killed by an unidentified gunman, in Beirut.

1985
Willie Banks sets a world outdoor record of 58' 11½ " for the triple jump.

1987
Carl Lewis wins the long jump with a leap of 28' 4½ ", his record fiftieth consecutive victory in that event.

A performance of *H.M.S. Pinafore*

June

1579
English explorer, Francis Drake, sails into San Francisco Bay, claiming the region for Queen Elizabeth.

1775
Colonel William Prescott says, "Don't fire until you see the whites of their eyes," at the Battle of Bunker Hill, during the Revolutionary War.

1824
Congress establishes the Bureau of Indian Affairs.

1850
The steamship, *Griffith*, catches fire on Lake Erie, killing 300 people.

1876
Army units, commanded by General George Crook, repel an attack by Sioux Indians, led by Chief Crazy Horse, on the Rosebud River in the Montana Territory.

1903
Babes in Toyland by Victor Herbert opens in Chicago.

1930
President Hoover signs the Smoot-Hawley Act, raising duties on 890 articles to high levels.

1942
Eight Germans are caught after landing on the coast of Long Island, New York, and in Florida, to conduct sabotage operations, during World War II.

1955
Disneyland opens in Anaheim, California.

1965
A squadron of B-52's conducts the first full scale bombing raid of the Vietnam War.

1971
The United States and Japan sign a treaty returning Okinawa to Japanese rule.

The Battle of Bunker Hill

June

1778
Threatened by a French blockade, the British evacuate Philadelphia, during the Revolutionary War.

1798
Congress passes the first of the Alien and Sedition Acts, amending the Naturalization Act of 1795.

1812
President Madison declares war on England, beginning the War of 1812.

1864
Union forces, commanded by General Ulysses S. Grant, are repulsed by the Confederates, commanded by General Robert E. Lee, and suffer heavy casualties at Petersburg, Virginia, during the Civil War.

1905
The New York Central Railroad is established.

1910
Congress passes the Mann-Elkins Act, increasing the authority of the Interstate Commerce Commission.

1953
The Boston Braves score a record 17 runs in one inning.

1959
A Federal court rules that the Arkansas state law used to close public schools to prevent integration is unconstitutional.

1979
The United States and the Soviet Union sign the SALT 2 strategic arms limitation treaty in Vienna, Austria.

1983
Sally K. Ride becomes the first United States woman in space, aboard the space shuttle, *Challenger*.

Astronaut Sally K. Ride

June

1846
The first recorded baseball game is won by the New York Club, beating the Knickerbockers 23-1 at the Elysian Field in Hoboken, New Jersey.

1862
President Lincoln signs a bill prohibiting slavery in the territories of the United States, during the Civil War.

1864
The Union ship, U.S.S. *Kearsarge*, sinks the Confederate cruiser, *Alabama*, in a naval battle off the coast of France, during the Civil War.

1867
Ruthless wins the first Belmont Stakes, in Jerome Park, New York.

1890
The North American Phonograph Company produces the first cylinder recordings.

1910
The first Father's Day is celebrated, in Spokane, Washington.

1934
President Roosevelt signs the Communications Act, establishing the Federal Communications Commission.

1934
Congress passes the Silver Purchase Act, allowing an increase in the monetary value of the Treasury's silver holdings.

1953
Julius and Ethel Rosenberg are executed at Sing Sing Prison in Ossining, New York, becoming the first people in the United States to be executed for espionage.

The *Kearsage* in action against the *Alabama*

June

20

1632
Cecilius Calvert is granted a charter for the settlement of Maryland.

1863
The Confederate Army of Northern Virginia commanded by General Robert E. Lee, crosses the Potomac River to invade Pennsylvania, during the Civil War.

1863
West Virginia joins the Union as the thirty-fifth state.

1898
An American force commanded by Captain Henry Glass captures the island of Guam, during the Spanish-American War.

1921
Alice Robertson of Oklahoma becomes the first woman to preside over the House of Representatives.

1944
The Japanese lose 400 planes and 3 aircraft carriers as the Battle of the Philippine Sea ends, during World War II.

1960
Floyd Patterson becomes the first man to regain the heavyweight boxing championship, knocking out Ingemar Johansson in the fifth round.

1967
Heavyweight champion Muhammad Ali is given a five year sentence for refusing to be drafted into the army.

1988
The Supreme Court upholds a law forcing the admission of women to private clubs.

The Battle of the Philippine Sea

1684
King Charles II of England revokes the Massachusetts Bay Colony's charter, accusing the colony of discriminating against the Church of England.

1788
New Hampshire becomes the ninth state to ratify the Constitution.

1834
Cyrus McCormick is awarded a patent for an improved version of the reaper.

1900
Filipino insurgents are granted amnesty by American military Governor, General Arthur MacArthur.

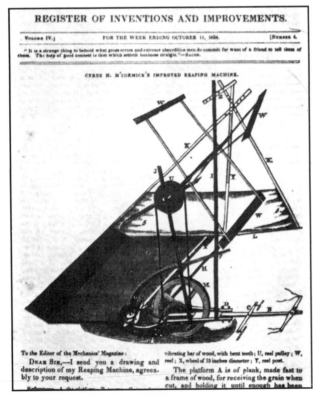

Patent drawing of the reaper

1916
United States troops are attacked by a Mexican force commanded by General Jacinto Trevino in Carrizal, Mexico.

1932
Jack Sharkey outpoints Max Schmeling, to win the heavyweight boxing championship.

1942
No one is hurt as a Japanese submarine shells the coast of Oregon, during World War II.

1942
German General Irwin Rommel's Africa Corps captures Tobruk, along with 30,000 British soldiers, during World War II.

1945
Japanese forces on Okinawa surrender after losing over 100,000 soldiers, during World War II.

1946
Frederick Moore Vinson becomes Chief Justice of the Supreme Court.

1948
The 33⅓ RPM long-playing record is introduced by Columbia Records.

1969
John Pennel sets a new pole vault record, vaulting 17' 10½ " at a track meet in Sacramento, California.

1975
Love Will Keep Us Together by the Captain and Tennile becomes the number one record in the United States.

1981
The longest strike in sports history is begun by Major League baseball players.

June

1807
The British frigate, *Leopard*, searching for British deserters, stops the United States warship, *Chesapeake*, off Norfolk, Virginia.

1848
A progressive faction of the Democratic party called the Barnburners withdraws from the national convention in Baltimore.

1864
Confederates commanded by General A.P. Hill attack Union positions south of Petersburg, Virginia, taking over 1700 prisoners, during the Civil War.

1868
Arkansas is readmitted to the Union.

1933
The Illinois Ship Canal, completing a link between the Gulf of Mexico and the Great Lakes, opens.

1936
Congress passes an act granting the Virgin Islands the right to elect their own legislature.

1937
Joe Louis knocks out James J. Braddock in the eighth round, to win the heavyweight boxing championship.

1941
The German Army launches Operation Barbarossa, the invasion of the Soviet Union, during World War II.

1949
Ezzard Charles outpoints Jersey Joe Walcott, to win the heavyweight boxing championship.

1972
Man of La Mancha by Dale Wasserman opens at the Vivian Beaumont Theater in New York.

Joe Louis knocking out James Braddock

1780

American forces led by General Nathaniel Greene defeat the British at the Battle of Springfield, New Jersey, during the Revolutionary War.

1836

Congress passes the Deposit Act, calling for one or more banks in each state to hold public deposits.

1845

The Texas Congress accepts annexation by the United States.

1860

Congress establishes the Government Printing Office.

1865

Cherokee Indian General Watie surrenders the last remaining Confederate force, in the Oklahoma Territory, ending hostilities during the Civil War.

1938

Congress passes the Civil Aeronautics Act, creating the Civil Aeronautics Authority.

1947

Congress passes the Taft-Hartley Act, reducing many advantages of the labor unions.

1967

President Johnson and Soviet Premier Aleksei Kosygin meet in Glassboro, New Jersey.

1968

The Vietnam War becomes the longest war in American history.

1969

Warren Burger becomes Chief Justice of the Supreme Court.

1982

Congress passes an extension of the Voting Rights Act of 1965.

American troops in action during the Revolutionary War

1497

English explorer, John Cabot, discovers Newfoundland.

1675

A massacre of Plymouth colonists by Wampanoag Indians led by King Philip, sets off King Philip's War.

1770

Father Sebastien Louis Meurin blesses the first log cabin church in North America in St. Louis, Missouri.

1879

A crew from the University of Pennsylvania wins the first Childs Cup, the oldest trophy in sprint racing.

1898

A United States force defeats the Spaniards at Las Guasimas, Cuba, in the first land battle of the Spanish-American War.

1908

Grover Cleveland, twenty-second and twenty-fourth President of the United States, dies in Princeton, New Jersey.

1936

Mary McLeod Bethune is appointed director of Negro affairs for the National Youth Administration, becoming the first Black woman to hold a major Federal office.

1936

New York Yankees outfielder Joe DiMaggio hits two home runs in one inning.

1948

President Truman signs the Selective Service Act, providing for the registration of all men between the ages of 18 and 25.

1964

The Federal Trade Commission announces that health warnings must appear on all cigarette packages.

John Cabot in Newfoundland

June

1610
English explorer Henry Hudson enters the strait leading to the Bay named after him, while searching for a Northwest Passage.

1788
Virginia becomes the tenth state to ratify the Constitution.

1862
Confederate troops, commanded by General Robert E. Lee, attack the Union Army of the Potomac, commanded by General George B. McClellan, at the Battle of Oak Grove, Virginia, the first of the Seven Days' Battles, during the Civil War.

1867
Lucien B. Smith of Kent, Ohio, is awarded a patent for barbed wire.

Custer at the Little Big Horn

1876
General George A. Custer is killed, along with all 265 of his men, by Sioux Indians led by Chief Sitting Bull at the Battle of Little Big Horn in Montana.

1906
Architect Stanford White is shot and killed by socialite Harry K. Thaw, at the roof garden of Madison Square Garden in New York.

1910
Congress passes the Mann Act, prohibiting the interstate transport of women for "immoral purposes."

1910
Congress establishes the Postal Savings System in response to America's lack of faith in savings banks.

1921
Oil is discovered at Signal hill in Long Beach, California.

1921
Samuel Gompers becomes President of the American Federation of Labor for the fortieth time.

1925
Santa Barbara, California, is partially destroyed by an earthquake, felt as far away as Wyoming and Montana.

1950
North Korean forces invade South Korea, beginning the Korean War.

1962
The Supreme Court rules that the reading of prayers in New York's public schools is unconstitutional.

June

1721
The first smallpox inoculations are administered, at a hospital in Boston.

1844
President John Tyler becomes the first president to marry while in office.

1896
The Vitascope Hall of New Orleans becomes the first permanent cinema in the United States.

1917
The first United States troops arrive in Europe during World War I, landing at St.-Nazaire, France.

1923
The first in-flight refueling connecting two airplanes takes place, over San Diego, California.

1927
Radio communication is established between the United States and the Philippines.

1936
Congress passes the Merchant Marine Act, establishing the United States Maritime Commission.

1945
Fifty countries sign the United Nations Charter in San Francisco, California.

1958
Rebel forces led by Fidel Castro kidnap 47 Americans in the Guantanamo Bay area in order to focus worldwide attention on their cause.

1983
Twelve hundred people are forced to evacuate their homes when the Colorado River bursts through a dike in Grand Junction, Colorado.

Administering smallpox shots

June

1542
Spanish explorer, Juan Rodriguez Cabrillo, sails up the California coast, claiming the territory for Spain.

1629
John Winthrop leads the first settlers of the Massachusetts Bay Company into Salem Harbor.

1776
Thomas Hickey becomes the first American soldier to be executed, for treason.

1844
Brigham Young becomes head of the Mormon Church after its leader, Joseph Smith, is killed by a mob in Nauvoo, Illinois.

1862
Confederate troops commanded by General Robert E. Lee break through Union lines at the Battle of Gaines' Mill, Virginia, during the Civil War.

1863
Major General George Gordon Meade replaces Major General Joseph Hooker as Commander of the Union Army of the Potomac, during the Civil War.

1864
Union forces, commanded by General William T. Sherman sustain heavy casualties in an unsuccessful assault on Confederate positions at the Battle of Kennesaw Mountain, Georgia, during the Civil War.

1893
Silver hits an all-time low of $.77 per ounce, prompting Colorado producers to shut down their mines.

1893
The New York Stock Market crashes, beginning four years of deep depression in the United States.

1938
Congress establishes Olympic National Park in Washington.

1939
Pan American becomes the first airline to offer transatlantic service, with a flight from Botwood, Newfoundland, to Southampton, England.

1940
The British ask for help in standing up to Japan at a secret meeting with United States Secretary of State, Cordell Hull, during World War II.

1944
Cherbourg falls to United States forces, the first major French port to come under Allied control, during World War II.

1950
President Truman orders United States combat troops to help South Korea, during the Korean War.

1957
As Hurricane Audrey hits the Louisiana and Texas coasts, 531 people are killed.

1958
Colonel Harry Burrell of the USAF sets a transatlantic speed record of 5 hrs., 27 min., and 42 sec. in an Air Force KC-135.

1986
Betsy Mitchell sets a world record of 2:08.60 for the 200 meter backstroke.

June

June

28

1687
William Phipps becomes the first native American to be knighted in England.

1778
General George Washington defeats the British at the Battle of Monmouth, New Jersey, during the Revolutionary War.

1832
The first epidemic of Asiatic cholera appears in New York, eventually killing over 2200 people and rapidly spreading across the United States.

1834
The Second Coinage Act establishes a 16-1 ratio between gold and silver.

1836
James Madison, fourth President of the United States, dies in Montpelier, Virginia.

1862
A Union naval fleet commanded by Admiral David Farragut passes the land batteries at Vicksburg, Mississippi, beginning the campaign to take the city, during the Civil War.

1863
President Lincoln appoints General George Meade to replace General Joseph Hooker as commander of the Union Army of the Potomac, during the Civil War.

1894
During a period of intense labor unrest, Congress establishes Labor Day as a national holiday.

1902
Congress passes the Isthmian Canal Act, authorizing the financing for the construction of a canal across the Isthmus of Panama.

1914
Archduke Francis Ferdinand of Austria is assassinated in Sarajevo, Yugoslavia, precipitating World War I.

1919
The Treaty of Versailles is signed in France, officially ending World War I.

1927
Lieutenants Lester J. Maitland and Albert F. Hegenberger complete the first successful flight from San Francisco to Hawaii.

1934
President Roosevelt signs the Federal Farm Bankruptcy Act, establishing a moratorium on farm mortgage foreclosures.

1939
Pan American begins the first regular transatlantic air service.

1940
Congress passes the Alien Registration Act, requiring registration of all aliens in the United States.

1942
The German 90th Light Division takes Mersa Matruh in North Africa, during World War II.

1944
The Russians reach Petrozavodsk in Finland, crossing the Murmansk rail line, during World War II.

1976
Captain Eldon W. Joersz attains a world record speed of 2193.1 mph in a Lockheed SR-71A, near Beale Air Force Base in California.

1767

The English Parliament passes the Townshend Revenue Act, requiring colonists to pay an import duty on tea and other goods.

1854

Andrew Reeder is appointed the first territorial Governor of Kansas.

1862

Union troops commanded by General George B. McClellan withdraw towards the James River after an attack by the Confederates at Savage Station, Virginia, during the Civil War.

1906

Congress passes the Railroad Rate Act, giving the Federal Government authority to set rates for interstate shipments.

1933

Primo Carnera knocks out Jack Sharkey in the sixth round, to win the heavyweight boxing championship.

1949

The United States withdraws its last forces from Korea.

1966

Most of North Vietnam's oil supply is destroyed in the first bombing raids over Hanoi, during the Vietnam War.

1972

The Supreme Court rules that the death penalty can constitute cruel and unusual punishment.

1973

President Nixon signs a bill establishing a Federal Energy Office.

Union cavalry attacking at Savage Station

June

1815
A treaty ends the United States war with Algeria and the Barbary Coast pirates.

1831
The 1st Division of the Maryland Guards becomes the first military unit to travel by railroad.

1834
Congress establishes the Department of Indian Affairs.

1835
A Texas force commanded by Colonel William B. Travis captures the Mexican garrison at Anahuac.

1859
Charles Blondin becomes the first man to cross over Niagara Falls on a tightrope.

1862
Union troops regroup to defensive positions after attacks by the Confederates commanded by Generals James Longstreet and Stonewall Jackson at the Battle of White Oak Swamp, Virginia, during the Civil War.

1864
Congress establishes Yosemite Valley Park as the first state park in the United States.

1900
More than 325 people are killed in a pier and steamship fire in Hoboken, New Jersey.

1906
Congress passes the Pure Food and Drug Act, calling for a statement of contents on food and drug labels.

1921
Former President, William H. Taft, is appointed Chief Justice of the Supreme Court.

1924
Former Secretary of the Interior, Albert B. Fall, is indicted by a Federal grand jury on charges of bribery in connection with his leasing of the Teapot Dome Oil Reserve in Wyoming.

1944
The last German forces surrender in the Cotentin in France, during World War II.

1956
One hundred twenty-eight people are killed when two airliners crash into the Grand Canyon.

1958
The development of the transistor is announced by researchers at Bell Laboratories.

1971
The Twenty-Sixth Amendment is ratified, lowering the voting age for all elections in the United States to 18.

1973
The 230,000-ton supertanker, *Brooklyn*, is launched, becoming the largest merchant ship built in the United States.

1975
Astronomers at the University of California announce the discovery of Galaxy 3C123, 8 billion light-years from Earth.

1976
Swan Lake becomes the first full-length ballet to be performed on television.

1982
The Equal Rights Amendment fails to achieve ratification.

July

1

1656
The first Quakers arrive in America in Boston.

1850
The first regular overland mail service west of the Missouri River begins, between Independance, Missouri, and Salt Lake City, Utah.

1859
Amherst defeats Williams in the first intercollegiate baseball game in the United States.

1862
The public debt exceeds $500 million for the first time.

1862
The Seven Days' Campaign ends as the Confederates are defeated at the Battle of Malvern Hill, Virginia, during the Civil War.

1863
Union General John Reynolds is killed on the first day of the Battle of Gettysburg, Pennsylvania, during the Civil War.

1898
Theodore Roosevelt, commanding the last United States cavalry unit, the Rough Riders, leads a charge up Kettle Hill in Cuba, during the Spanish-American War.

1902
Congress passes the Philippine Government Act, declaring the Philippine Islands an unorganized territory.

1930
The United States Navy's first streamlined submarine, the *Nautilus*, is commissioned at the Mare Island Navy Yard in Vallejo, California.

1931
The National Council of Congregational and Christian Churches is established in Seattle, Washington.

1936
The International Bridge between Texas and Mexico opens, completing the highway linking Texas with Mexico City.

1941
Station WCBS in New York becomes the first television station to broadcast a regularly scheduled news program.

1946
The United States drops an atomic bomb in a test at Bikini Atoll in the Pacific Ocean.

1950
The first United States combat troops land in Korea.

1957
The International Geophysical Year launches its first scientific project, the study of the sun's effect on communications.

1964
The Census Bureau reports that California has surpassed New York in population.

1966
France withdraws its armed forces from NATO.

1966
Medicare, an insurance program for the elderly, is inaugurated.

1968
The United States, the Soviet Union, and 59 other nations sign the Nuclear Nonproliferation Treaty.

July

1776
New Jersey becomes the first Colony to grant women's suffrage.

1788
Cyrus Griffin, President of the Congress, formally announces the Constitution of the United States to be in effect.

1807
President Jefferson issues a proclamation calling for all British warships to leave the territorial waters of the United States.

1861
President Lincoln authorizes the suspension of the writ of *habeas corpus* in cases of national security.

1863
The Union Army of the Potomac assumes a strong defensive position along Cemetery Ridge at the end of the second day of the battle of Gettysburg, Pennsylvania, during the Civil War.

1881
President James A. Garfield is shot by Charles J. Guiteau at a railroad station in Washington, D.C.

1890
Congress passes the Sherman Anti-trust Act, putting restraints on monopolies.

1894
Congress issues an injunction against railroad strikers on the grounds of "interference with interstate commerce," the first use of a Government injunction during a strike.

1897
Seventy-five thousand coal miners go on strike in Pennsylvania, Ohio, and West Virginia.

1915
The United States Senate reception room is destroyed by a bomb placed there by a German professor.

1921
A joint resolution of Congress declares the state of war with Germany at an end.

1926
Congress establishes the United States Army Air Corps.

1932
Franklin Delano Roosevelt, the Democratic nominee for president, introduces the term "New Deal."

1937
Amelia Earhart vanishes over the Pacific Ocean during her attempt to become the first woman to fly around the world.

1940
The Lake Washington Floating Bridge opens in Seattle, Washington, becoming the largest floating structure in the world.

1964
President Johnson signs the Civil Rights Act of 1964 in a televised ceremony.

1972
Bob Seagren sets a new pole vault record of 18′ 5¼″ at a track meet in Eugene, Oregon.

1976
North and South Vietnam are officially reunited as one nation after 20 years of continuous warfare.

July

1608
French explorer, Samuel de Champlain, founds Quebec.

1775
General George Washington assumes command of American troops at Cambridge, Massachusetts.

1844
The United States and China sign the Treaty of Wang Hiya, providing for the opening of five Chinese ports to American merchants.

1852
Congress establishes a branch of the United States Mint in San Francisco.

1863
The Union Army of the Potomac, commanded by General George Meade, defeats the Confederate Army of Northern Virginia after a charge by 15,000 Confederates, led by General George Pickett, fails to break the Union lines on the final day of the Battle of Gettysburg, Pennsylvania, during the Civil War.

1886
The New York *Tribune* puts the first linotype machines into use.

1890
Idaho joins the Union as the forty-third state.

1898
The American fleet, commanded by Commodore Schley, destroys the Spanish fleet, commanded by Admiral Cerva, near Santiago Harbor, during the Spanish-American War.

1905
Marvin Hart stops Jack Root in the 12th round, to win the heavyweight boxing championship.

1930
President Hoover signs the Veterans Administration Act, establishing the Veterans Administration.

1944
The First and Third Russian Armies take Minsk, isolating units from the German Fourth Army, during World War II.

1988
The United States missile cruiser, *Vincennes*, mistakenly shoots down an Iranian jetliner over the Persian Gulf, killing all 290 people aboard.

The Battle of Gettysburg

July

1754
George Washington's force is defeated by the French near Fort Duquesne, leaving the Ohio Valley under French control.

1776
The Declaration of Independence is approved by the Continental Congress.

1789
Congress passes the first Tariff Act, setting a protective tariff on several imported items.

1798
Congress enacts the first tariff bill, putting protective duties on several commodities.

1826
John Adams, second President of the United States and Thomas Jefferson, third President of the United States, both die.

1831
James Monroe, fifth President of the United States, dies in New York.

1831
The song, "America," is sung for the first time, at a church in Boston.

1863
The Confederates formally surrender Vicksburg, Mississippi, to the Union Army commanded by General Ulysses S. Grant, during the Civil War.

1872
Calvin Coolidge, thirtieth President of the United States, is born in Plymouth, Vermont.

1883
The first "Buffalo Bill's Wild West Show" is performed in North Platte, Nebraska.

1888
The first rodeo is held in Prescott, Arizona Territory.

1894
Hawaii declares itself a republic, under a new constitution.

1895
Katherine Lee Bates' poem, *America The Beautiful*, is published.

1898
American troops raise the American flag over an unoccupied Wake Island in the Pacific, during the Spanish-American War.

1901
William Howard Taft becomes the first Governor-General of the Philippines.

1903
President Roosevelt sends a message around the world after the first Pacific communications cable opens.

1908
The Socialist Labor Party nominates Martin B. Preston of Nevada, who is serving a prison sentence for murder, for the presidency.

1960
The 50-star American flag, reflecting the admission of Hawaii, is flown for the first time, in Washington, D.C.

1964
I Get Around by the Beach Boys becomes the number one record in the United States.

1775
The Continental Congress adopts the Olive Branch Petition, hoping for a reconciliation with England.

1814
American forces commanded by General Winfield Scott defeat the British at the Battle of Chippewa, north of Fort Erie, during the War of 1812.

1861
Confederate troops defeat a Union force commanded by General Franz Sigel in Carthage, Missouri, during the Civil War.

1862
Union General David Hunter organizes the First Carolina Regiment, the first Black military unit in the United States, during the Civil War.

1864
A Confederate force commanded by General Jubal A. Early crosses the Potomac River into Maryland, during the Civil War.

1920
Franklin D. Roosevelt is nominated for vice president at the Democratic National Convention in San Francisco.

1935
President Roosevelt signs the National Labor Relations Act, empowering the National Labor Relations Board to oversee elections and collective bargaining.

1940
The French Government of Marshall Petain in Vichy breaks off diplomatic relations with England, during World War II.

1943
The Battle of Kursk in the Soviet Union begins, with over 2 million men and 6000 tanks, the largest tank battle of World War II.

Jubal Early crossing into Maryland

1699
Pirate Captain Kidd is captured in Boston and extradited to England to stand trial.

1777
American forces abandon Fort Ticonderoga, New York, after an attack by a superior British army under General Burgoyne, during the Revolutionary War.

1854
The Republican Party is formed in Jackson, Michigan.

1892
Twenty people are killed in Pennsylvania when striking Homestead Steel employees battle Pinkerton detectives brought in by management to break the strike.

1928
The Lights of New York premieres at the Strand Theater in New York, becoming the first full-length feature film.

1929
The St. Louis Cardinals score a record 28 runs in one game.

1933
The American League defeats the National League in Baseball's first all-star game.

1935
Helen Wills Moody wins her seventh Wimbledon tennis championship.

1944
American forces take over the Namber airstrip after landing in New Guinea, during World War II.

1954
Elvis Presley makes his first record at Sun Studios, Memphis, Tennessee.

Elvis Presley's first public appearance

1540
Spanish explorer, Francisco Vasquez de Coronado, captures the first of the seven cities of Cibola in New Mexico.

1846
American Commodore John Sloat lands at Monterey and claims possession of California for the United States.

1862
President Lincoln visits the Army of the Potomac encamped at Harrison's Landing, Virginia, during the Civil War.

1865
Four alleged conspirators in the assassination of President Lincoln are hanged at the Old Penitentiary in Washington, D.C.

1905
The Industrial Workers of the World is established in Chicago.

1927
The Moffatt Tunnel opens under the Continental Divide in Colorado, providing improved railroad service.

1941
United States forces land on Iceland, to relieve the British, during World War II.

1946
Mother Frances Xavier Cabrini becomes the first woman to be canonized by the Catholic Church.

1952
The SS *United States* sets a transatlantic speed record of 3 days, 10 hours, and 40 minutes.

1959
The American Lutheran Church is established with the merger of the Evangelical Lutherans and the United Evangelical Lutherans.

Commodore Sloat's squadron off Monterey, California

July

1654
Jacob Barsimson becomes the first Jew to settle in North America, in New York.

1670
England and Spain sign the Treaty of Madrid, agreeing to respect each nation's rights in the American territories they control.

1758
The British lose over 2000 men during an unsuccessful assault on Fort Ticonderoga on Lake George, during the French and Indian War.

1835
The Liberty Bell cracks while tolling the death of Chief Justice John Marshall.

1863
The Confederates surrender Port Hudson, Louisiana, leaving the Mississippi River under Union control, during the Civil War.

1889
The Wall Street Journal begins publication.

1898
American forces commanded by Admiral George Dewey occupy Isla Grande in Subic Bay, Philippines, during the Spanish-American War.

1923
Warren G. Harding becomes the first President to visit Alaska.

1944
British and Canadian forces mount an attack outside Caen, led by 450 RAF bombers, during World War II.

1950
General Douglas MacArthur is named Commander of all United Nations forces in Korea.

The capture of Fort Ticonderoga

1755
British General Edward Braddock is mortally wounded near Pittsburgh, during the French and Indian War.

1816
The Cherokee Indians cede their land in northern Maine to the United States.

1850
Zachary Taylor, twelfth President of the United States, dies in office, in Washington, D.C.

1862
Confederate cavalry commanded by John Hunt Morgan capture Tompkinsville, Kentucky, during the Civil War.

1863
Confederate forces, commanded by General Franklin Gardner, surrender Port Hudson, Louisiana, to Union troops, commanded by General Nathaniel Banks, during the Civil War.

1893
Dr. Daniel H. Williams of Chicago performs the first surgical closure of a heart wound.

1944
American forces reach Point Marpi in the Marinas, ending Japanese resistance there, during World War II.

1955
Rock Around the Clock by Bill Haley and the Comets becomes the number one record in the United States.

1959
Two United States soldiers are killed by Communist guerrillas in Bienhoa, South Vietnam.

1982
When a Pan American jet crashes in New Orleans, one of the worst single plane disasters in the United States, 154 people are killed.

General Braddock's retreat

July

1861

The Confederate Government signs a treaty with the Creek Indians, during the Civil War.

1863

Union troops land on Morris Island near Charleston, South Carolina, to begin the siege of Fort Wagner, during the Civil War.

1890

Wyoming joins the Union as the forty-fourth state.

1932

Cleveland Indians outfielder Johnny Burnett gets a record nine hits in one game.

1940

The German Air Force sends seventy planes to raid targets in South Wales, the beginning of the Battle of Britain, during World War II.

1943

The United States Seventh Army commanded by General George Patton invades Sicily, along with other Allied forces, during World War II.

1944

Twenty-five thousand Japanese soldiers are killed as Saipan falls to United States forces, during World War II.

1951

United Nations and Korean representatives hold the first peace talks during the Korean War.

1965

(I Can't Get No) Satisfaction by the Rolling Stones becomes the number one record in the United States.

1985

The Coca Cola Company reintroduces its original formula for "Coke" after a national outcry.

Allied forces landing in Sicily

1767

John Quincy Adams, sixth President of the United States, is born in Braintree, Massachusetts.

1789

The United States Marine Corps is formally established.

1804

Aaron Burr fatally shoots Alexander Hamilton in a duel in Weehawken, New Jersey.

1861

Union forces, commanded by General William S. Rosecrans, defeat the Confederates, commanded by Colonel John Pegram, at Rich Mountain in Virginia, during the Civil War.

Aaron Burr shooting Alexander Hamilton

1862

President Lincoln appoints Major General Henry W. Halleck commander in chief of the Union armies, during the Civil War.

1864

A Confederate force commanded by General Jubal A. Early breaks through Union lines and enters the District of Columbia, during the Civil War.

1869

The United States Fifth Cavalry attacks a Cheyenne Indian encampment at Summit Springs in the Colorado Territory, in the last Indian battle of the Great Plains.

1951

More than one million acres of farmland in Kansas, Oklahoma, Missouri, and Illinois are inundated when the Missouri River floods its banks.

1954

The United States Air Force Academy officially opens, at a base in Denver, Colorado.

1960

A United States RB-47 reconnaissance bomber is shot down over the Arctic Ocean by the Soviet Union, after allegedly flying over Soviet airspace.

1962

The American Telephone & Telegraph Company makes the first satellite transmission, from Andover, Maine, to Cornwall, England, via the *Telstar* satellite.

1979

The United States orbiting laboratory, *Skylab*, reenters the Earth's atmosphere and breaks up over the Indian Ocean.

1808

The Missouri *Gazette* becomes the first newspaper west of the Mississippi River.

1861

Confederate forces commanded by raider John Hunt Morgan capture Lebanon, Kentucky, during the Civil War.

1862

Congress authorizes the Medal of Honor to be awarded for battlefield bravery.

1864

Junior officer Oliver Wendell Holmes, Jr., shouts, "Get down, you fool" to President Lincoln, while the President is observing an attack at Fort Stevens, Washington, D.C., during the Civil War.

1909

Congress passes a resolution for the Sixteenth Amendment, authorizing the imposition of income taxes.

1912

French movie, *Queen Elizabeth*, starring Sarah Bernhardt, opens in the United States.

1941

The Germans bomb Moscow for the first time, during World War II.

1957

The Surgeon General announces that a scientific link between cigarette smoking and lung cancer has been established.

1963

Martial law is declared in Cambridge, Massachusetts, after the National Guard is called in to control racial violence.

John Hunt Morgan

July

1787
Congress passes the Northwest Ordinance to establish a government north of the Ohio River.

1832
An expedition led by Henry Schoolcraft discovers the source of the Mississippi River at Lake Itasca, Minnesota.

1857
President Buchanan appoints Alfred Cummings to replace Brigham Young as the governor of the Utah Territory.

1861
Confederate General Robert S. Garnett is killed as Union forces commanded by General George B. McClellan take control of Western Virginia, during the Civil War.

1862
Confederate forces commanded by General Nathan Bedford Forrest defeat the Union Army at Murfreesboro, Tennessee, during the Civil War.

1863
Antidraft riots break out in New York, quelled by Union troops after over 1000 civilian casualties, during the Civil War.

1940
Italian forces cross the border into Kenya and attack the town of Moyale, during World War II.

1944
The Germans launch the first V-I rocket, striking London, during World War II.

1954
A record six home runs is hit as the American League defeats the National League in the All-Star Game.

1973
The New Mexico Supreme Court rules that the state cannot impose taxes on Indians living on reservations, upholding the Federal Government's right of exclusive jurisdiction.

Anti-draft rioting in New York

July

1789
The American Minister to France, Thomas Jefferson, witnesses the beginning of the French Revolution.

1832
Congress passes the Tariff Act of 1832, requiring high duties on textiles and iron.

1881
William "Billy the Kid" Bonney is shot and killed by Sheriff Pat Garrett in Fort Sumner, New Mexico Territory.

1892
Congress authorizes a $50 per month pension for all Civil War veterans.

1938
Howard Hughes completes an around-the-world flight in a record 3 days, 19 hours, and 14 minutes.

1951
Citation becomes the first race horse to win over one million dollars.

1962
Roses Are Red by Bobby Vinton becomes the number one record in the United States.

1966
Eight student nurses are murdered in Chicago by Richard Speck, one of the worst crimes of the century.

1972
Jean Westwood is named head of the Democratic Party National Committee, becoming the first woman to head a major political party in the United States.

Pat Garrett shooting "Billy The Kid"

1779
American forces under General Anthony Wayne take the fort at Stony Point, New York, during the Revolutionary War.

1820
American explorer Edwin James becomes the first man to climb Pike's Peak.

1830
The Sauk and Fox Indians cede their land in Wisconsin and Illinois to the United States.

1862
The Confederate ironclad, *Arkansas*, attacks three Union ships on the Mississippi River, inflicting serious damage, during the Civil War.

1868
Mexican President Benito Juarez returns to restore republican government to Mexico, after a five year war against Archduke Maximilian of France.

1870
Georgia is readmitted to the Union.

1915
United States secret service agents discover a portfolio implicating Dr. Heinrich F. Albert in a German espionage network.

1918
Eighty-five thousand American troops are engaged in the Second Battle of the Marne in France, as the German forces attack but make no gains, during World War I.

1923
President Harding drives in the last spike, completing the Alaskan railroad, the first railroad operated by the Federal Government.

1949
President Truman signs the Housing Act, providing Federal aid for public housing.

The Second Battle of the Marne

1769

Father Junipero Serra founds the first permanent Spanish settlement on the West Coast, near San Diego.

1866

Sioux Indians drive off horses belonging to Colonel Henry Carrington's army regiment in Montana, beginning the First Sioux War.

1915

The *Missouri*, *Ohio*, and *Wisconsin* become the first warships to pass through the Panama Canal.

1934

Organized labor calls the first general strike in the United States, in support of 12,000 striking longshoremen in San Francisco.

1935

Oklahoma City installs the first parking meters.

1941

New York Yankees outfielder Joe DiMaggio's record 56-game hitting streak comes to an end.

1945

The United States explodes the first atomic bomb in a test at Alamagordo, New Mexico.

1946

Congress establishes the Bureau of Land Management to manage resources in public lands.

1952

President Truman signs a G.I. Bill of Rights, making soldiers who served in the Korean War eligible for veteran's benefits.

1956

The Ringling Brothers and Barnum and Bailey Circus performs its last show in a tent.

1957

Major John H. Glenn sets a transcontinental speed record of 3 hours, 23 minutes in a Navy F8U-1P jet.

1973

Former White House aide, Alexander P. Butterfield, reveals the existence of tapes of White House conversations, during the Watergate investigation.

1988

Florence Griffith-Joyner sets a world outdoor record of 10.49 for the 100 meter dash.

Joe DiMaggio at the end of his streak

July

1580

The Spanish defeat a French naval force off the coast of Florida, ending French influence in the area.

1862

President Lincoln signs the Second Confiscation Act, providing for the freedom of all slaves coming into Union lines, during the Civil War.

1876

Army units, commanded by General George Crook, repel an attack by Sioux Indians, led by Chief Crazy Horse, on the Rosebud River in the Montana Territory.

1877

Baltimore & Ohio Railroad workers go out on strike, beginning the first national strike necessitating a callout of Federal troops to restore order.

1898

An American force, commanded by General William Shafter, forces the surrender of Spanish troops, commanded by General Toral, in Santiago de Cuba, during the Spanish-American War.

1902

Congress passes the Newlands Reclamation Act, providing the construction of irrigation dams in 16 western states.

1916

President Wilson signs the Federal Farm Loan Act, establishing a banking system for loans to farmers.

1975

An Apollo space capsule completes the first docking with a Soviet Soyuz space capsule.

1981

One hundred eleven people are killed as an overhead walkway collapses in a hotel in Kansas City.

American and Soviet astronauts in the docking module.

July

1858

The Pennsylvania Railroad introduces the first smoking car.

1889

John L. Sullivan knocks out Jake Kilrain in the last bare knuckle boxing match in the United States.

1918

The Aisne-Marne offensive begins, as over 250,000 Americans launch an attack against German forces, during World War I.

1944

St. Lo, one of the key positions in the German defense of Normandy, falls to the United States First Army, during World War II.

1947

President Truman signs the Presidential Succession Act, designating the speaker of the house as next in succession after the vice president.

1951

Jersey Joe Walcott knocks out Ezzard Charles in the seventh round, to win the heavyweight boxing championship.

1960

I'm Sorry by Brenda Lee becomes the number one record in the United States.

1969

A car driven by Senator Edward M. Kennedy plunges off the Chappaquiddick Bridge near Edgartown, Massachusetts, drowning his passenger, Mary Jo Kopechne.

1975

Dave Forbes of the Boston Bruins becomes the first professional athlete to be indicted for assault during a game.

1976

Scientists at Yale University discover Lyme arthritis, a new strain of arthritis.

John L. Sullivan fighting Jake Kilrain

1754
Delegates from the English colonies approve Benjamin Franklin's "Plan of the Union," the first attempt to unite the colonies.

1812
The British attack the American naval base at Sacketts Harbor on Lake Ontario, during the War of 1812.

1867
Congress passes the third Reconstruction Act over President Johnson's veto, calling for the Southern States to ratify the Fifteenth Amendment before readmittance to the Union.

1943
The Big Inch oil pipeline opens, extending from Texas to Pennsylvania, becoming the longest oil pipeline in the world.

1943
Five hundred Allied planes bomb Rome for the first time, during World War II.

1957
Don Bowden becomes the first American to break the four-minute mile, in 3:58.7, at a meet in Stockton, California.

1961
TWA becomes the first airline to show regularly scheduled in-flight movies, on its New York to Los Angeles route.

1962
The United States suspends diplomatic relations with Peru, after a military coup.

1984
Geraldine Ferraro becomes the first woman to be nominated for vice president by a major party in the United States.

Geraldine Ferraro

July

1738

French explorer Pierre de la Verendrye reaches the western shore of Lake Michigan.

1858

The New York All Stars defeat Brooklyn 22-18 in the first baseball game with an admission charge.

1872

Mahlon Loomis of Washington, D.C., is awarded a patent for the first wireless telegraph.

1910

The Christian Endeavor Society of Missouri attempts to ban all motion pictures depicting kissing by people not related.

1944

Adolph Hitler survives an assassination attempt when a bomb explodes at his headquarters in East Prussia, during World War II.

1960

The submarine, U.S.S. *George Washington*, becomes the first to successfully launch a Polaris missile.

1963

Surf City by Jan and Dean becomes the number one record in the United States.

1969

Astronaut Neil Armstrong becomes the first human to walk on the moon.

1976

The *Viking I* becomes the first spacecraft to land on Mars.

1976

The United States removes its last forces from Thailand.

Men walking on the Moon

July

1667
English sovereignty is established over the former Dutch colony of New Amsterdam with the signing of the Peace of Breda, ending the Second Anglo-Dutch War.

1861
Inexperienced Union troops commanded by General Irvin McDowell are routed by the Confederates at the first Battle of Bull Run, near Manassas, Virginia, during the Civil War.

1873
Jesse and Frank James stage their first train robbery, on the Rock Island Line between Adair and Council Bluffs, Iowa.

1921
Colonel William Mitchell demonstrates the superiority of air power over sea power by sinking the captured German battleship, *Ostfriesland*, with bombs dropped from airplanes.

1946
Lt. James J. Davidson becomes the first man to take off from and land aboard a ship in a jet aircraft.

1955
The U.S.S. *Seawolf* is launched in Groton, Connecticut, becoming the second atomic submarine in the United States.

1961
Captain Virgil "Gus" Grissom, makes a suborbital flight aboard the Mercury capsule, *Liberty Bell Seven*, becoming the second American in space.

1971
Fiddler on the Roof becomes the longest-running musical on Broadway, with its 2845th performance.

1987
Lady's Secret wins a race at Monmouth Park race track in New Jersey to become the richest filly in thoroughbred history.

The Battle of Bull Run

1793
Canadian explorer Alexander MacKenzie reaches the Pacific Ocean, completing the first continental crossing.

1814
The Delaware, Miami, Seneca, and Wyandot Indians sign the Treaty of Grenville, making peace with the United States.

1861
Congress states that the Civil War is being fought to preserve the Union, not to end slavery.

1864
A Union force, commanded by General William T. Sherman, turns back an attack by the Confederate Army of Tennessee, commanded by General John Bell Hood, outside Atlanta, during the Civil War.

1905
A yellow fever epidemic begins in New Orleans, Louisiana, killing 400 people.

1931
Wheat prices collapse as Kansas begins harvesting a bumper crop of 240 million bushels, forcing many counties in Kansas to declare a tax moratorium.

1932
Congress passes the Federal Home Loan Bank Act, authorizing regional banks to provide discounted mortgage loans.

1934
Gangster John Dillinger is shot and killed outside a movie theater in Chicago, Illinois, by the FBI.

1937
Congress passes the Bankead-Jones Farm Tenant Act, which establishes a loan program to help tenant farmers and sharecroppers acquire their own farms.

Police surrounding the body of John Dillinger

July

1766
The first medical society in America is formed in New Brunswick, New Jersey.

1827
The first swimming pool in the United States opens, in Boston.

1851
The Sioux Indians sign the Treaty of Traverse des Sioux, giving up their land in Iowa and Minnesota to the United States.

1862
Major General Henry Wager Halleck assumes command of the Armies of the United States, during the Civil War.

1885
Ulysses S. Grant, eighteenth President of the United States, dies in Mt. McGregor, New York.

1892
Congress bans the sale of alcoholic beverages on all Indian lands.

1944
Soviet forces capture Pskov, the last major Russian town in German hands, during World War II.

1967
Forty-three people are killed in Detroit, Michigan, in the worst race riots in the United States.

1972
The first Earth Resources Technology Satellite is launched into orbit.

1984
Vanessa Williams becomes the first Miss America to resign.

The Sioux Indians signing a treaty

1701

Antoine de la Mothe Cadillac establishes a settlement at Detroit, an area of Michigan known to French trappers.

1824

The *Harrisburg Pennsylvanian* publishes the first public opinion poll in the United States, showing Andrew Jackson in the lead for the presidency.

1847

Brigham Young leads a group of Mormon emigrants to present-day Salt Lake City, in Utah.

1862

Martin Van Buren, eighth President of the United States, dies in Kinderhook, New York.

1864

A Confederate force, commanded by General Jubal A. Early, routs Union troops, commanded by General George Crook, in Kernstown, Virginia, during the Civil War.

1866

Tennessee is readmitted to the Union.

1915

The steamship, *Eastland*, capsizes at a pier in Chicago, killing 852 people.

1944

Napalm is used for the first time as American forces land in Tinian in the Marianas, during World War II.

1974

Fernando Bujones becomes the first American to win the international ballet competition.

1977

Two thousand people attend ceremonies in Ignacio, Colorado, marking the end of a 200-year-old feud between Commanche and Ute Indian tribes over hunting grounds.

Detroit in the early 1700 s

July

25

1775
Dr. Benjamin Church becomes the first surgeon general of the Continental Army.

1814
The Americans commanded by General Jacob Brown engage the British at the Battle of Lundy's Lane, near Niagara Falls, during the War of 1812.

1850
Gold is discovered in the Rogue River in the Oregon Territory.

1868
Congress establishes the Wyoming Territory.

1898
United States forces commanded by General Nelson Miles invade Puerto Rico, during the Spanish-American War.

1904
Twenty-five thousand textile workers go out on strike in Massachusetts, prompting a review of child labor laws in the United States.

1915
The American ship, *Leelanaw*, is sunk by a German submarine off the coast of Scotland.

1943
Italian dictator Benito Mussolini resigns.

1944
The United States First Army breaks out from its positions at St. Lo, leading to the collapse of the German defense in France, during World War II.

1947
Congress passes the National Security Act of 1947, unifying the armed forces and creating the United States Air Force.

The Battle of Lundy's Lane

1758

The British capture over 6000 French soldiers after taking the fortress of Louisbourg in Nova Scotia, during the French and Indian War.

1759

The French abandon Fort Ticonderoga on Lake George, withdrawing to Crown Point, New York, during the French and Indian War.

1775

Benjamin Franklin is chosen Postmaster General by the Continental Congress.

1788

New York becomes the eleventh state to ratify the Constitution.

1790

The House of Representatives votes to locate the new National Capital on a site along the Potomac River.

1790

The first commercial steamboat service is inaugurated, on the Delaware River, between Philadelphia and Camden, New Jersey.

1903

Nelson Jackson and Sewell Crocker arrive in New York, completing the first transcontinental automobile trip.

1926

The Sanctuary of Our Lady of Victory in Lackawanna, New York, becomes the first Roman Catholic Church consecrated a basilica in the United States.

1928

Lights of New York, the first all-talking feature film, opens in New York.

Washington, D.C.

July

1777
The Continental Congress commissions French-man Marquis de Lafayette a major general.

1789
The Department of Foreign Affairs is created by act of Congress.

1861
General George McClellan assumes command of the Union Division of the Potomac, during the Civil War.

1866
The laying of an Atlantic cable is completed between England and the United States.

1874
A group of buffalo hunters led by William Barclay "Bat" Masterson repel an attack by Kiowa, Comanche, and Cheyenne Indians at the Battle of Adobe Walls, Texas.

1909
Orville Wright sets a flight duration record of 1 hour, 1 minute, and 40 seconds.

1915
The United States establishes direct wireless service with Japan.

1953
An armistice is signed in Panmunjom, by the United States, North Korea, and Communist China, ending the Korean War.

1974
Mikhail Baryshnikov makes his American debut in *Giselle* with the American Ballet Theatre in New York.

1987
Greg LeMond becomes the first American to win the Tour de France bicycle race.

Greg LeMond (center) in the Tour de France

1864
The Confederates commanded by General Stephen D. Lee withdraw with heavy casualties after an attack on Union positions at Ezra Church, Georgia, during the Civil War.

1868
Congress adopts the Fourteenth Amendment, granting citizenship to people born or naturalized in the United States.

1898
Spanish forces at Ponce, Puerto Rico, surrender to United States troops commanded by General Nelson Miles, during the Spanish-American War.

1941
The Japanese freeze all of the United States' assets in Japan, during World War II.

1945
Thirteen people are killed when a B-52 bomber flies into the Empire State Building in New York, during a thick fog.

1965
President Johnson announces an increase in troop levels to 125,000, during the Vietnam War.

1971
The United States Army announces a military crackdown on narcotics use by troops in South Vietnam.

1977
The trans-Alaska pipeline stretching from Prudhoe Bay to Valdez, Alaska, opens.

1982
San Francisco becomes the first city in the United States to ban the sale and possession of hand guns.

The trans-Alaska pipeline

July

1776
Franciscan explorer Father Silvestre Velez de Escalante sets off on an expedition to map and explore what later became New Mexico, Utah, Colorado and Arizona.

1778
The French fleet commanded by Count d'Estaing arrives at Newport, Rhode Island, during the Revolutionary War.

1829
The Chippewa, Ottawa, and Potawatomi Indians cede their land in the Michigan Territory to the United States.

1844
The New York Yacht Club is formed, with John C. Stevens as its first commodore.

Washington visiting the French fleet

1862
United States attempts to prevent the Confederate ship, *Alabama*, from leaving the Port of Liverpool, England, are unsuccessful, during the Civil War.

1900
The White Pass and Yukon Railway is completed, linking Alaska with the Southern Yukon Territory of Canada.

1914
The Cape Cod Canal opens, cutting the travel distance between New York and Boston by 70 miles.

1915
United States marines land in Haiti after the assassination of Haitian President, Vilbrun Guillaume.

1921
Adolph Hitler becomes President of the National Socialist (Nazi) Party, in Germany.

1927
The first artificial respirator is installed at Bellevue Hospital in New York.

1953
The Soviet Union shoots down an American B-50 bomber off the coast of Vladivostok, Siberia.

1958
Congress establishes the National Aeronautics and Space Administration, launching the United States' space program.

1967
In a fire aboard the United States aircraft carrier, U.S.S. *Forestal*, in the Gulf of Tonkin, 134 sailors are killed.

1619

The House of Burgesses in Jamestown, Virginia, becomes the first legislative assembly in America.

1864

Union troops commanded by General Ulysses S. Grant are routed after storming into a gap created by an explosion set by a demolition team, at the Battle of the Crater in Petersburg, Virginia, during the Civil War.

1884

Jack Dempsey knocks out George Fulljames, to win the first middleweight boxing championship.

1916

German sabotage is suspected when an ammunition dump is destroyed in an explosion at a dock in Toms River, New Jersey.

1928

George Eastman of Rochester, New York, demonstrates the first color motion pictures.

1932

The tenth modern Olympic Games opens in Los Angeles, California.

1946

The United States joins the United Nations Educational, Scientific, and Cultural Organization.

1965

President Johnson signs the Medicare Bill, providing limited health care benefits to the elderly.

1966

United States planes bomb the demilitarized zone for the first time during the Vietnam War.

The Battle of the Crater

July

1790
The United States Patent Office is opened.

1861
President Lincoln appoints Ulysses S. Grant a General of Volunteers, in Illinois, during the Civil War.

1874
Patrick Francis Healy becomes the first Black to be president of a predominantly white university, becoming head of Georgetown University in Washington, D.C.

1875
Andrew Johnson, seventeenth President of the United States, dies.

1943
The United States Fourth Division takes Santo Stefano in Sicily, during World War II.

1948
Idlewild International Airport opens in New York, becoming the largest airport in the world.

1954
Milwaukees Braves outfielder Joe Adcock hits a double and four home runs for a record 18 total bases in one game.

1971
You've Got a Friend by James Taylor becomes the number one record in the United States.

1975
Former Teamsters Union President, James Hoffa, disappears outside a motel in Detroit, Michigan.

1988
The last Playboy Club, in Lansing, Michigan, closes.

General Ulysses S. Grant

Idlewild International Airport

August

1

1714
King George I becomes the King of England.

1768
Boston merchants sign a nonimportation pact, banning all English goods from the colonies.

1781
The British under General Cornwallis occupy Yorktown, Virginia, during the Revolutionary War.

1801
The United States ship, *Enterprise*, seizes the Tripolitan corsair *Tripoli*, during the Tripolitan War.

1876
Colorado joins the Union as the thirty-eighth state.

1906
John M. Huddleston discovers diamonds near Murfeesboro, Arkansas, establishing the only diamond mine in North America.

1914
Germany declares war on Russia and the French begin mobilization, during World War I.

1946
As a series of tidal waves strikes Hawaii, 113 people are killed.

1946
President Truman signs the McMahan Act, creating the Atomic Energy Commission.

1966
Police shoot and kill Charles Whitman after he kills 13 people and wounds 31 others, shooting from a tower at the University of Texas at Austin.

The siege of Yorktown, Virginia

August

1675
Brookfield, Massachusetts, is attacked by Wampanoag Indians, during King Philip's War.

1776
The Declaration of Independence is signed by members of the Continental Congress, in Philadelphia.

1793
The United States asks the Government of France to recall its Minister, Citizen Genet, who is compromising American neutrality in the war between France and England.

1832
An American force commanded by General Henry Atkinson defeats the Black Hawk Indians at Bad Axe River, Wisconsin, in the final battle of the Black Hawk War.

1832
Sauk Indians are massacred by Illinois militia led by General Henry Atkinson, during the Black Hawk War.

1876
James "Wild Bill" Hickok is shot and killed during a poker game in Deadwood, Dakota Territory.

1909
The Lincoln penny is issued by the Philadelphia Mint.

1914
Germany invades Luxembourg and demands passage through Belgium to launch an attack on France, during World War I.

1923
Warren G. Harding, twenty-ninth President of the United States, dies in office, in San Francisco.

"Wild Bill" Hickok

August

1780

Benedict Arnold is appointed commander of the military academy at West Point, New York.

1795

The Indians cede two thirds of Ohio and part of Indiana to the United States in the Treaty of Greenville.

1852

A Harvard crew defeats Yale on Lake Winnepesaukee, New Hampshire, in the first intercollegiate sporting event in the United States.

1854

Congress passes the Graduation Act, providing for the disposal of public lands that remain unsold for 20-30 years.

1882

Congress passes the first law to restrict immigration into the United States.

1914

Germany declares war on France, during World War I.

1921

Baseball Commissioner, Judge Kenesaw Mountain Landis, rules that the Chicago White Sox players charged with throwing the 1919 World Series are banned from baseball for life.

1922

The Wolf, broadcast by station WGY in Schenectady, New York, becomes the first play presented on radio.

1981

An illegal nationwide strike by air traffic controllers begins.

1984

The National Dance Hall of Fame is established in Saratoga, New York.

A collegiate crew practicing

1756
French General, Joseph de Montcalm, captures Fort Oswego in northern New York, during the French and Indian War.

1790
Congress passes the Funding Act, authorizing the issuing of bonds to finance the national debt.

1914
The United States declares its neutrality in World War I.

1916
The United States and Denmark sign a treaty for the United States' purchase of the Virgin Islands from Denmark for $25 million.

1944
Units of the British XII Corps take Florence and districts south of the Arno River in Italy, during World War II.

1960
Joseph A. Walker, a civilian test pilot, sets an air speed record of 2,196 mph, in the X-15 experimental rocket plane.

1964
James Chaney, Andrew Goodman, and Michael Schwerner, working in civil rights campaigns in the South, are found murdered in Philadelphia, Mississippi.

1977
The Department of Energy is created by act of Congress.

1988
Representative Mario Biaggi of New York is convicted of several counts of racketeering in connection with the Wedtech Corp. of the Bronx.

The X-15 experimental rocket plane

August

1583
Sir Humphrey Gilbert founds a colony at St. Johns, Newfoundland, the first English colony in North America.

1861
Congress enacts the first income tax as a measure to help finance the Civil War.

1864
Exclaiming, "Damn the torpedoes! Full speed ahead," Union Admiral David Farragut runs the minefield at the entrance to Mobile Bay, capturing the Confederate flotilla, during the Civil War.

1897
The first advertising film in the United States is made for Admiral Cigarettes at the Edison Company in West Orange, New Jersey.

1909
Congress passes the Payne-Aldrich Act, keeping tariff rates high.

1914
Cleveland, Ohio, installs the first electric traffic lights in the United States.

1917
The National Guard is taken into national service, as the United States mobilizes for its entry into World War I.

1933
President Roosevelt establishes the National Labor Board to mediate collective bargaining disputes.

1940
The Germans lose 75 aircraft in the largest air action of the Battle of Britain, during World War II.

1974
President Nixon releases tape transcripts revealing that he had impeded the Watergate investigation.

President Nixon with the Watergate transcripts

August

1777
Colonial soldiers are ambushed by Mohawk Indians and the British, during the Revolutionary War.

1827
The United States and England sign a treaty extending joint occupation of the Oregon Territory.

1862
The Confederate ram, *Arkansas*, is blown up by the Union ironclad, *Essex*, on the Mississippi River, during the Civil War.

1863
The Confederate raider, *Alabama*, captures the Union bark, *Sea Bride*, off the Cape of Good Hope, South Africa, during the Civil War.

1890
Convicted murderer, William Kemmler, becomes the first man to be executed in the electric chair, at Auburn Prison in New York.

1926
Gertrude Ederle of New York becomes the first woman to swim the English Channel.

1945
The United States bomber, *Enola Gay*, drops the first atomic bomb, on Hiroshima, Japan, killing over 80,000 people, during World War II.

1958
Glenn Davis sets a world record of 49.2 seconds for the 400 meter hurdles at a track meet, in Budapest, Hungary.

1973
Vice President Spiro Agnew announces that he is under a Justice Department investigation for receiving kickbacks while serving as Governor of Maryland.

Hiroshima after the atomic bomb

August

1760
After a bitter siege, Fort Loudoun in Tennessee surrenders to Indians, during the French and Indian War.

1782
General George Washington establishes the Purple Heart as a badge of military merit.

1789
The War and Navy Department is created by act of Congress.

1936
The United States proclaims its neutraity in the Spanish Civil War.

1942
United States Marines land on Guadalcanal in the Solomon Islands, the first American amphibious operation during World War II.

1943
Three Japanese destroyers are sunk by an American destroyer group in the Solomon Islands, during World War II.

1953
President Eisenhower signs the Refugee Relief Act of 1953, admitting 214,000 additional refugees.

1959
United States satellite, *Explorer VI*, sends back the first photograph of Earth taken from space.

1978
President Carter declares the Love Canal area near Niagara Falls, New York, a disaster area, due to toxic waste.

1988
The Food and Drug Administration approves the first hair growth drug for general use.

The Earth seen from space

August

1876
Thomas Alva Edison is awarded a patent for the first mimeograph machine.

1883
Chester A. Arthur becomes the first president to officially visit an Indian tribe, meeting with Shoshoni Indian Chief Washaki, at the Wind River Reservation in Wyoming.

1923
A gasoline price war erupts in South Dakota, a result of new oil discoveries in the United States, eventually driving the price of a gallon of gasoline down to 6¢.

1925
Forty thousand white-robed Klu Klux Klansmen march down Pennsylvania Avenue in Washington, D.C., the largest Klan rally in the United States.

1944
Brittany falls to the Allies as the United States First Army begins a drive toward Paris, during World War II.

1945
The United States becomes the first country to sign the UN Charter.

1960
Itsy Bitsy Teeny Weenie Yellow Polka Dot Bikini by Brian Hyland becomes the number one record in the United States.

1966
A team led by Doctor Michael DeBakey, installs the first successful artificial heart pump in a patient at Methodist Hospital, in Houston, Texas.

1988
The first night baseball game at Wrigley field in Chicago is played, and called after four innings because of rain.

Edison's mimeograph machine

1757
French General, Joseph de Montcalm, takes Fort William Henry on Lake George, during the French and Indian War.

1758
Edge Pillock in Burlington County, New Jersey, becomes the first Indian reservation in America.

1841
The steamboat, *Erie*, catches fire on Lake Erie, killing 175 people.

1842
The United States and England sign the Webster-Ashburton Treaty, settling several border matters in eastern Canada.

1862
Two brigades of Union forces are defeated by the Confederates commanded by General Stonewall Jackson at the Battle of Cedar Mountain, Virginia, during the Civil War.

1935
President Roosevelt signs the Motor Carrier Act, giving the Interstate Commerce Commission jurisdiction over interstate bus and truck traffic.

1944
United States forces take Guam after 20 days of fighting, killing 17,000 Japanese soldiers, during World War II.

1945
Forty thousand people are killed as the United States drops a second atomic bomb, on Nagasaki, Japan, during World War II.

1969
Actress Sharon Tate and four others are killed at her Los Angeles home by members of Charles Manson's cult.

1974
Richard M. Nixon becomes the only man to resign from the presidency.

Union troops preparing to attack

August

1622
The province of Maine is established by John Mason and Ferdinando Gorges.

1821
Missouri joins the Union as the twenty-fourth state.

1825
The Osage Indians cede their land in Kansas to the United States.

1856
Four hundred people are killed when a hurricane strikes Last Island, Louisiana.

1861
Union General Nathaniel Lyon is killed at the Battle of Wilson's Creek, Missouri, during the Civil War.

1874
Herbert Hoover, thirty-first President of the United States, is born in West Branch, Iowa.

1921
The *California* is commissioned, becoming the first battleship built on the Pacific Coast.

1927
President Coolidge dedicates Mount Rushmore in South Dakota, as artist, Gutzon Borglum, begins carving the likenesses of Presidents Washington, Jefferson, Lincoln, and Theodore Roosevelt out of the side of the mountain.

1960
The United States signs a treaty designating Antarctica as a peaceful scientific preserve.

1977
David Berkowitz, the "Son of Sam" serial murderer, is arrested in Yonkers, New York.

The Mount Rushmore monument

August

1807
Robert Fulton's steamboat, *Clermont*, makes its first run, on the Hudson River from New York to Albany.

1862
Confederate guerrillas capture Independence, Missouri, during the Civil War.

1902
Oliver Wendell Holmes is appointed to the Supreme Court

1930
The American Lutheran Church is established in Toledo, Ohio.

1940
The Italians attack the main British positions at Tug Argan in East Africa, during World War II.

1942
The British carrier, HMS *Eagle*, is sunk by a German U-boat in the Mediterranean Sea, during World War II.

1965
Thirty-five people are killed in racial riots in the Watts section of Los Angeles.

1970
The Reverend Daniel J. Berrigan, wanted for burning draft records as a protest against the Vietnam War, is captured by the FBI.

1974
Lee Trevino defeats Jack Nicklaus by one stroke to win the PGA golf tournament.

1984
The United States National Team sets a world outdoor record of 37.83 for the 4x100 meter relay.

Robert Fulton's *Clermont*

1658
The first police force in America is formed, in New Amsterdam.

1676
Wampanoag Indian leader, King Philip, is shot, ending King Philip's War.

1852
Isaac Merrit Singer is awarded a patent for his continuous stitching sewing machine.

1896
Gold is discovered in the Klondike area of northwestern Canada, sparking the second gold rush.

1902
The International Harvester Company is established in New Jersey.

1921
Congress passes the Packers and Stockyards Act, outlawing monopolistic practices in the sale of livestock and poultry.

1941
President Roosevelt and British Prime Minister Winston Churchill form the Atlantic Charter, defining each country's war aims, during World War II.

1955
President Eisenhower signs a bill increasing the minimum wage to $1.00 an hour, effective March 1, 1956.

1960
NASA launches *Echo I*, the first telecommunications satellite.

1970
President Nixon signs the Postal Reorganization Act, making the United States Postal Service an independent agency.

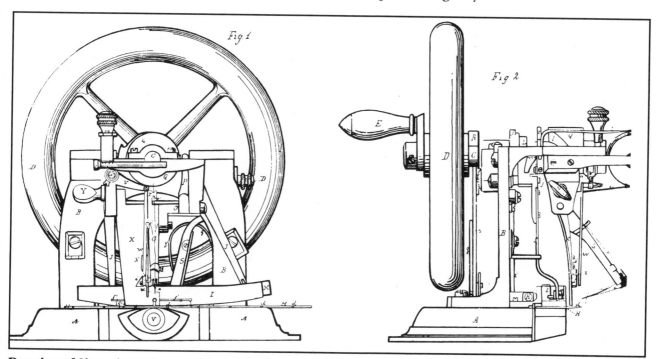

Drawing of Singer's sewing machine

August

1682
The first Welsh settlement in America is established, near Philadelphia.

1846
Commodore David Stockton, along with John Fremont, takes Los Angeles, California.

1856
Free State militia seize the town of Franklin, a pro-slavery strong-hold in the Kansas Territory.

1898
The Philippines surrender to Admiral George Dewey ending hostilities, during the Spanish-American War.

1931
The United States Customs Bureau closes the United States-Mexican border in order to prevent Americans from gambling in Mexico.

1940
The Germans lose 45 aircraft as the Royal Air Force flies more than 700 sorties over the English Channel, during World War II.

1942
General Montgomery assumes command of the British Eighth Army in North Africa, during World War II.

1964
The Columbia Broadcasting System purchases the New York Yankees.

1981
Mary Meagher sets a world record of 2:05.96 for the 200 meter butterfly stroke.

United States Marines landing in Manila

1768
The Cherokee Indians sign the Treaty of Hard Labor, moving the South Carolina frontier further west.

1813
The British brig, *Pelican*, captures the American sloop, *Argus*, in a naval battle off the coast of England, during the War of 1812.

1846
The *California* becomes the first newspaper in California.

1900
Troops from the United States, England, Russia, Germany, and Japan reach Peking, China, and put down the Boxer Rebellion, started by a nationalistic group intent on ridding China of all foreigners.

1908
Governor Charles S. Deneen is forced to declare martial law after race riots break out in Springfield, Illinois.

1928
The Front Page by Ben Hecht opens at the Times Square Theater in New York.

1935
President Roosevelt signs the Social Security Act, establishing a system of old-age benefits.

1962
Thieves take a record $1,551,000 from a mail truck in Plymouth, Massachusetts.

1965
I Got You Babe by Sonny and Cher becomes the number one record in the United States.

United States Marines in Peking

August

1805
The Lewis and Clark Expedition crosses the Continental Divide.

1812
The garrison at Fort Dearborn, led by General Hull, surrenders to the British and is massacred, during the War of 1812.

1918
The Sinking of the Lusitania becomes the first full-length feature cartoon, taking 22 months to produce.

1926
Former Mexican Secretary of War, Enriques Estrada, is arrested along the United States-Mexican border while preparing a revolution in Baja, California.

1935
Humorist and political satirist Will Rogers is killed in a plane crash off Point Barrow, Alaska.

1939
Indian troops arrive at Suez in Egypt to reinforce British forces.

1943
American forces along with three battleships land on Kiska in the Aleutian Islands, during World War II.

1944
The United States Seventh Army invades southern France, during World War II.

1962
The national debt exceeds $300 billion for the first time.

1969
The Woodstock Music and Art Fair opens, near Bethel, New York.

The Woodstock Music Festival

August

1619

The first slaves arrive in Virginia, aboard a Dutch ship.

1777

Two hundred British soldiers are killed at the Battle of Bennington, Vermont, during the Revolutionary War.

1780

The British, under General Cornwallis, defeat the Americans, under General Horatio Gates, at the Battle of Camden, South Carolina, during the Revolutionary War.

1812

Detroit surrenders to the British commanded by General Isaac Brock, during the War of 1812.

1858

President Buchanan sends the first cable message across the Atlantic, to Queen Victoria of England.

1920

Cleveland Indians shortstop Ray Chapman becomes the only baseball player killed in a game, after being hit in the head by a pitch thrown by Carl Mays of the New York Yankees.

1936

The Olympic Games end in Berlin, Germany, with American track star Jesse Owens winning four gold medals.

1981

Mary Meagher sets a world record of 57.93 for the 100 meter butterfly stroke.

1987

Twenty thousand fans make a pilgrimage to Memphis, Tennessee, to mark the tenth anniversary of the death of Elvis Presley.

The Battle of Bennington

August

1788
Judge John Cleeves founds Losantiville, near present-day Cincinnati.

1846
Commodore Stockton declares that the United States has annexed California.

1940
An Italian submarine sinks the Greek cruiser, *Helle*, prompting the Greek armed forces to mobilize, during World War II.

1943
United States forces, commanded by General George S. Patton, enter Messina, Sicily, taking over 100,000 Italian prisoners, during World War II.

1969
Three hundred people are killed and 70,000 left homeless when Hurricane Camille strikes Mississippi, Louisiana, and Alabama.

1978
Max Anderson, Ben Abruzzo, and Larry Newman complete the first successful trans-atlantic balloon crossing, landing in Paris.

1981
Dr. Philip Bjork of the South Dakota School of Mines and Technology discovers the skeleton of a Tyrannosaurus Rex some 65 million years old in Haystack Butte, South Dakota.

1985
The United States National Team sets a world record of 7.13.1 for the 4x100 meter relay in swimming.

1988
Butch Reynolds sets a world outdoor record of 43.39 for the 400 meter run.

Max Anderson (standing) being honored after his flight

August

1587

Virginia Dare is the first English child born in North America, at Roanoke Island, in present-day North Carolina.

1780

American forces are defeated by the British led by Colonel Banastre Tarleton at Fishing Creek, South Carolina, opening the way for a British invasion of North Carolina, during the Revolutionary War.

1862

Chief Little Crow leads a Sioux uprising in Minnesota.

1864

Union troops occupy over a mile of the Weldon Railroad south of Petersburg, Virginia, cutting off the Confederate supply line, during the Civil War.

1873

A team headed by John Lucas becomes the first to scale Mount Whitney, the second highest peak in the United States.

1894

Congress establishes the Bureau of Immigration.

1894

Congress passes the Carey Desert Act authorizing the Federal Government to give each state up to 1 million acres of public land for irrigation.

1942

Japanese reinforcements land in Taivu on Guadalcanal, during World War II.

1985

The United States National Team sets a world record of 3:38.28 for the 4x100 meter medley relay in swimming.

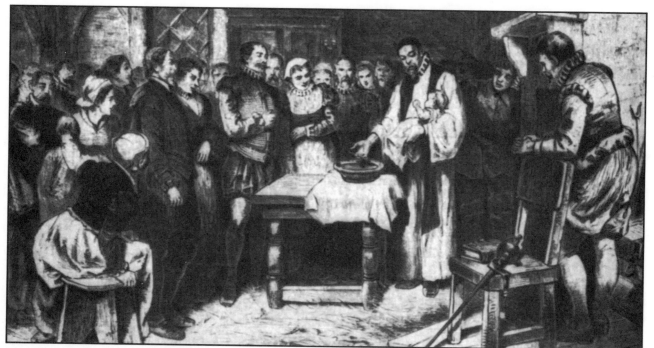

Virginia Dare being baptized

August

1812
The British ship, *Guerriere*, is defeated by the United States frigate, *Old Ironsides*, off the coast of Nova Scotia, during the War of 1812.

1856
Gail Borden is awarded a patent for his process for making evaporated milk.

1914
On Trial by Elmer Rice opens in New York, becoming the first play to use the flashback as a dramatic device.

1915
The English liner, *Arabic*, is sunk by a German submarine near Liverpool, with 2 Americans among those killed.

1929
Amos 'n' Andy debuts on radio station NBC.

1942
Canadian and British troops conduct a disastrous raid on Dieppe in Western Europe, losing over 3600 men and over 60 tanks and landing craft, during World War II.

1981
After being fired on by two Libyan jets, United States Navy fighters shoot them down off the coast of Libya.

1981
Renaldo Nehemiah sets a world outdoor record of 12.93 for the 110 meter hurdles.

1982
Congress authorizes a tax increase of $93.8 billion.

The sinking of the *Arabic*

August

1794

General Anthony Wayne defeats the Indians at the Battle of Fallen Timbers, in the Northwest Territory.

1833

Benjamin Harrison, twenty-third President of the United States, is born in North Bend, Ohio.

1844

President Tyler withdraws from the presidential race to become the first chief executive not to run for a second term.

1847

American forces commanded by General Winfield Scott defeat the Mexicans at Churubusco, Mexico, during the Mexican War.

1866

The first National Labor Congress meets in Baltimore.

1920

Station 8MK in Detroit broadcasts the first radio news bulletins in the United States.

1957

A balloon ascent record of 101,486 feet is set by Major David G. Simons of the USAF.

1982

Eight hundred United States Marines land in Beirut, Lebanon, as part of a multinational force overseeing the withdrawal of PLO fighters.

1987

Patrick Henry Sherrill shoots and kills 14 former co-workers and kills himself in Edmond, Oklahoma, one of the worst mass murders in the United States.

American artillery during the Mexican War

1831
Nat Turner, a slave in Virginia, kills his master and leads a slave insurrection.

1858
The first in a series of debates between Abraham Lincoln and Senator Stephen A. Douglas of Illinois brings Lincoln into the national spotlight.

1863
A force of Confederate raiders commanded by William Quantrill attack Lawrence, Kansas, killing 150 civilians, during the Civil War.

1878
The American Bar Association is formed in Saratoga, New York.

1888
William S. Burroughs of St. Louis is awarded a patent for the adding machine.

1944
Delegates from the United States, Great Britain, China, and the Soviet Union attend the Dumbarton Oaks Conference in Washington, D.C., laying the groundwork for the establishment of the United Nations.

1959
Hawaii joins the Union as the fiftieth state.

1972
Copernicus, an astronomical observatory designed to study the nature of the universe, is launched.

1985
Mary Decker-Slaney sets a world outdoor record of 4:16.71 for the mile.

The Lincoln-Douglas debates

August

1851

The yacht, *America*, defeats 14 British ships to win the first America's Cup.

1861

Confederates seize the Union vessels *W.B. Terry* and *Samuel Orr* in Paducah, Kentucky, during the Civil War.

1864

Union troops occupy over a mile of the Weldon Railroad south of Petersburg, Virginia, cutting off the Confederate supply line, during the Civil War.

1911

President Taft vetoes statehood for Arizona because its constitution permits the recall of judges.

1928

Station WGY in Schenectady, New York, becomes the first television station to broadcast a news event.

1942

Brazil declares war on Italy and Germany, during World War II.

1962

Two United States nuclear submarines make the first rendezvous beneath the North Pole.

1964

Where Did Our Love Go by the Supremes becomes the number one record in the United States.

1974

A joint United States-Soviet Union expedition on Anongula Island, off the coast of Alaska, discovers 9000-year-old artifacts.

1989

Texas Rangers pitcher Nolan Ryan gets his record 5000th strikeout.

The first America's Cup yacht race

1784
East Tennessee declares itself an independent state, named Franklin, in honor of Benjamin Franklin.

1818
The *Walk-in-the-Water* sails from Buffalo, New York, becoming the first steamboat to offer service on the Great Lakes.

1843
Mexico warns the United States that any attempt to annex Texas will be an act of war.

1859
O. Tuft installs the first passenger elevator in a hotel, The Fifth Avenue Hotel, in New York.

1864
After bombardment by Union land batteries, Fort Morgan becomes the last Confederate stronghold at the entrance to Mobile Bay to surrender, during the Civil War.

1912
Alaska becomes an organized United States Territory.

1927
Nicola Sacco and Bartolomeo Vanzetti are executed for a 1920 murder, with many people believing they were framed because of their radical political beliefs.

1939
Germany and Russia sign a non-aggression pact, freeing Hitler to concentrate on Western Europe.

1971
The United States, England, France, and the Soviet Union sign the first Berlin Accord, pledging unhindered passage between West Berlin and West Germany through East German territory.

The capture of the *Tennessee* in Mobile Bay

1814

The British commanded by General Robert Ross rout an American force at the Battle of Bladensburg, near Washington, D.C., during the War of 1812.

1814

The British capture Washington, D.C., setting fire to several buildings, including the Capitol and the White House, during the War of 1812.

1857

The New York branch of the Ohio Life Insurance and Trust Company fails, beginning a national financial panic.

1858

Camp Floyd is established in the Utah Territory to support United States troops sent to keep peace.

1881

The United States establishes a scientific observation post in northern Greenland.

1893

One thousand people are killed as a cyclone strikes Savannah, Georgia, and Charleston, South Carolina.

1912

Congress authorizes the establishment of the parcel post system.

1912

Congress passes the Panama Canal Act, authorizing rebates to American ships.

1929

Bill Tilden wins his seventh United States Lawn Tennis Association singles championship.

1954

President Eisenhower signs the Communist Control Act, stripping the Communist Party of privileges and immunities.

1956

An Army H-21 helicopter makes the first transcontinental flight by a helicopter, flying from San Diego, California, to Washington, D.C.

1963

John Pennel becomes the first person to pole vault 17 feet, with a vault of 17′ ¾ ″, at a track meet in Miami.

1989

Cincinnati Reds manager Pete Rose is suspended from baseball for life, for alleged gambling activities.

The burning of Washington, D.C.

1829

Mexico refuses an offer from President Jackson for the purchase of Texas.

1916

Congress establishes the National Park Service.

1944

Paris is liberated by the Allies, as the German commander General Dietrich von Choltitz surrenders to the French, during World War II.

1950

President Truman orders the railroads seized by the Army, to prevent a strike.

1958

The first law granting pensions to presidents becomes effective.

1967

American Nazi Party leader, George Lincoln Rockwell, is shot and killed by a former aide in Arlington, Virginia.

1980

42nd Street opens at the Winter Garden Theatre in New York a few hours after the director, Gower Champion, dies.

1985

New York Mets pitcher Dwight Gooden becomes the youngest pitcher, at 20 years, 9 months, to win 20 games in the Major Leagues.

1987

The Dow Jones Industrial average reaches an all time high of 2722.42.

The Allies liberating Paris

August

1861
King Kamehameha IV proclaims the Hawaiian Islands' neutrality in the Civil War.

1862
Confederate cavalry commanded by General Fitzhugh Lee enters Manassas Junction, Virginia, beginning the second Battle of Bull Run, during the Civil War.

1891
The first successful attempt at rainmaking in the United States brings a shower to Midland, Texas.

1913
The Koekuk Dam, across the Mississippi River, opens becoming the largest hydroelectric dam in the United States.

1920
The Nineteenth Amendment is enacted, giving women the right to vote.

1932
The Controller of the Currency orders a moratorium on the foreclosure of first mortgages during the Depression.

1935
President Roosevelt signs the Public Utilities Act, requiring public utilities to register with the Security and Exchange Commission.

1935
Congress grants Indian tribes the right of judicial review in cases of treaty violations.

1941
The British take the Abadan area in Iran as the Soviets enter Tabriz, during World War II.

The second Battle of Bull Run

1665
The Bare and Ye Cubb is presented in Acomac, Virginia, becoming the first play to be performed in America.

1774
The Transylvania Company is formed to allow for land speculation in Kentucky.

1776
American General John Sullivan is taken prisoner during the Battle of Long Island, during the Revolutionary War.

1782
The last skirmish of the Revolutionary War takes place, near the Combahee River in South Carolina.

1832
Sauk Chief, Black Hawk, surrenders, ending the Black Hawk War.

1859
Edwin L. Drake strikes oil near Titusville, Pennsylvania, the first oil well in the United States.

1861
A Union expeditionary force lands at Cape Hatteras, North Carolina, giving the Federals an important strategic point to block Confederate shipping, during the Civil War.

1889
The Eastman Dry Plate Company of Rochester, New York, manufactures the first celluloid roll film.

1894
Congress passes the Wilson-Gorman Tariff Act, providing for the first graduated income tax.

1908
Lyndon B. Johnson, thirty-sixth President of the United States, is born in Stonewall, Texas.

The Battle of Long Island

August

1833
England abolishes slavery.

1857
Fort Abercrombie is established in North Dakota to protect settlers from the Sioux Indians.

1861
The Confederates surrender Fort Hatteras, North Carolina, after bombardment by Union naval vessels, during the Civil War.

1867
The Midway Islands in the Pacific Ocean are annexed by the United States.

1867
Midway Island in the Pacific Ocean becomes the first United States Territory outside the North American continent.

1895
The first film to use actors, *The Execution of Mary Queen of Scots*, is shot in West Orange, New Jersey.

1922
The Walker Cup becomes the first American international golf match.

1922
Station WEAF in New York broadcasts the first radio commercial in the United States.

1963
Two hundred thousand people take part in a Freedom March on Washington, D.C., where the Reverend Martin Luther King, Jr. delivers his "I have a dream..." speech.

1978
Donald Vesco sets a motorcycle speed record of 318 mph at the Bonneville Salt Flats in Utah.

Dr. Martin Luther King, Jr. speaking in Washington, D.C.

1779

American forces defeat the Indians and Loyalists led by Chief Joseph Brant at Newtown, during the Revolutionary War.

1864

Former Commander-in-Chief of the Union Army, George B. McClellan, is nominated for President at the Democratic National Convention in Chicago.

1893

Whitcomb L. Judson is awarded a patent for a shoe clasp lock, the forerunner of the zipper.

1941

Fighting ends in Iran, with the British and the Soviet Union occupying key areas, during World War II.

1957

President Eisenhower signs the Civil Rights Act of 1957, providing penalties for violations of voting rights of citizens.

1966

The Beatles give their last public performance in the United States, at Candlestick Park in San Francisco.

1968

Hubert Humphrey is nominated for President at the Democratic National Convention in Chicago as hundreds of anti-war protesters are beaten by police outside the convention center.

1985

Don Baylor of the New York Yankees is hit by a pitch for a record 190th time.

American forces in action against the Indians

August

1645
The New England Confederation signs a peace treaty with the Narragansett Indians.

1778
American forces withdraw from Rhode Island, during the Revolutionary War.

1781
The French fleet commanded by Admiral de Grasse arrives off the coast of Yorktown, Virginia, during the Revolutionary War.

1784
The American ship, *Empress of China*, commanded by Captain John Greene, arrives at the Chinese port of Canton.

1856
Guerrilla warfare rages through the Kansas Territory as the militia attack Osawatomie, Kansas, in the continuing dispute over the status of slavery in the territory.

1861
Union General John C. Fremont declares martial law in Missouri and frees the slaves, against instructions from President Lincoln.

1862
Union troops, commanded by General John Pope, are routed at the Second Battle of Bull Run by Confederate forces, commanded by Generals Robert E. Lee and Stonewall Jackson, during the Civil War.

1926
The first Hambletonian Stakes is run in Syracuse, New York.

1935
Congress passes the Revenue Act, increasing taxes on inheritances and gifts.

1945
General Douglas MacArthur lands in Japan to begin the American occupation, after World War II.

1954
President Eisenhower signs the Atomic Energy Bill, allowing private ownership of atomic reactors to produce electrical power.

1963
The hot line between Washington, D.C. and Moscow in the Soviet Union goes into operation.

1983
Lt. Colonel Guion S. Bluford becomes the first Black astronaut in space, aboard the space shuttle, *Challenger*.

The Battle of Rhode Island

1756
British General Webb gives up the Mohawk Valley in New York to the French, during the French and Indian War.

1895
Latrobe plays Jeanette in the first professional football game, in Latrobe, Pennsylvania.

1910
Theodore Roosevelt delivers his New Nationalism speech stating his Square Deal policy, which supports a graduated income tax, labor protection, and an adequate standing army and navy.

1919
The American Communist Party is formed in Chicago.

1935
President Roosevelt signs the Neutrality Act, forbidding the shipment of arms and munitions to belligerants.

1942
The German advance reaches within 16 miles of Stalingrad in the Soviet Union, during World War II.

1943
United States aircraft carriers attack Marcus Island in the Central Pacific, during World War II.

1949
The Grand Army of the Republic holds its last Civil War veteran's encampment, in Indianapolis, Indiana.

1963
My Boyfriend's Back by the Angels becomes the number one record in the United States.

1983
Edwin Moses sets a world outdoor record of 47.02 for the 400 meter hurdles.

Communist marchers in New York

Edwin Moses winning the 400 meter hurdles

September

1814
A British expeditionary force lands at the mouth of the Castine River in Maine, during the War of 1812.

1821
The Sante Fe Trail opens, with Americans pushing further southwest into regions settled by Spain.

1836
The first American settlement in the Oregon Territory is established, near present day Walla Walla, Washington.

1859
The first sleeping car, built by George Pullman, makes its first run.

1863
Union forces commanded by James G. Blunt capture Fort Smith in western Arkansas, ending hostilities in that region, during the Civil War.

1864
Confederate forces commanded by General John Bell Hood evacuate Atlanta, during the Civil War.

1869
The Prohibition Party is formed during the National Prohibition Convention in Chicago.

1894
Five hundred people are killed as a hurricane strikes Hinckley, Minnesota.

1916
Congress passes the Keating-Owen Act, making interstate transport of items made by child labor, illegal.

1931
The first anthropology laboratory in the United States opens in Santa Fe, New Mexico.

1939
Germany invades Poland, precipitating World War II.

1944
Canadian forces liberate Dieppe in the Western Front, during World War II.

1946
Patty Berg wins the first United States Women's Open golf championship.

1969
The Libyan Arab Republic is proclaimed as Captain Muammar el-Qaddafi leads a military coup against King Idris.

1972
Bobby Fischer defeats Boris Spassky of the Soviet Union to become the first American to win the world chess championship.

1976
Representative Wayne Hays of Ohio resigns from the House of Representatives after the discovery of his affair with former employee Elizabeth Ray.

1979
Pioneer 2 flies past Saturn, discovering two new rings and an eleventh moon.

1983
Soviet jets shoot down a Korean Airlines 747, killing all 269 passengers and crew.

1984
What's Love Got to Do With It by Tina Turner becomes the number one record in the United States.

September

1862
President Lincoln appoints General George B. McClellan to command the Union Army of the Potomac, during the Civil War.

1864
The Union Army commanded by General William T. Sherman occupies Atlanta, during the Civil War.

1901
Emphasizing the need for a strong foreign policy, President Roosevelt says, "Speak softly and carry a big stick."

1914
The Treasury Department establishes the Bureau of War Risk Insurance to provide coverage for merchant shipping.

1937
President Roosevelt signs the National Housing Act, creating the United States Housing Authority.

1945
The Japanese formally surrender aboard the USS *Missouri* in Tokyo Bay, ending World War II.

1947
Delegates from the United States and 18 Western-Hemisphere nations sign the Treaty of Rio, the first regional defense alliance under the United Nations Charter.

1970
Twenty-seven-year-old John Simpson, Jr. becomes the youngest person to win the Hambletonian Stakes trotting classic, driving trotter Timothy T.

1974
President Ford signs the Employee Retirement Income Security Act, bringing private pensions under Federal regulation.

The Japanese surrender aboard the USS *Missouri*

September

1697
The Treaty of Ryswick formally ends King William's War.

1709
The Carolina colony grants 13,500 acres to two new groups of immigrants from Germany and Switzerland.

1783
The Treaty of Paris is signed, officially ending the Revolutionary War.

1813
The term "Uncle Sam" is used for the first time in the Troy *Post* in Troy, New York.

1925
Fourteen people are killed when the United States Army dirigible, *Shenandoah*, is destroyed in a storm near Ava, Ohio.

1930
The first electric passenger train in the United States, developed by Thomas A. Edison, runs between Hoboken and Montclair, New Jersey.

1939
England and France declare war on Germany after its invasion of Poland.

1943
Allied forces cross the Strait of Messina and invade Italy, during World War II.

1954
President Eisenhower signs the Espionage and Sabotage Act of 1954, establishing the death penalty for peacetime sabotage.

1964
President Johnson signs a bill establishing a permanent wilderness system in the United States.

Cartoon depicting the peace proclamation

September

1821
Czar Alexander I of Russia issues an imperial order extending Russia's claims along the Pacific Coast to the 51st parallel.

1862
The Confederate Army of Northern Virginia commanded by General Robert E. Lee crosses into Maryland in an invasion of the North, during the Civil War.

1864
Union forces commanded by General A.C. Gillem shoot and kill Confederate raider John Hunt Morgan in Greeneville, Tennessee, during the Civil War.

1886
Apache Indian Chief Geronimo surrenders to General Nelson A. Miles in the Arizona Territory.

1894
Protesting sweatshop conditions, 12,000 tailors go on strike in New York.

1951
President Truman's speech before the Japanese Peace Treaty Conference becomes the first transcontinental television broadcast.

1961
President Kennedy signs the Foreign Assistance Act of 1961, authorizing over $4 billion for military and economic programs.

1971
One hundred eleven people are killed when an Alaska Airlines jet crashes into a mountain near Juneau, Alaska.

1974
The United States establishes diplomatic relations with East Germany.

Apache Indian Chief Geronimo

September

September

5

1774
The first Continental Congress meets in Carpenters' Hall in Philadelphia.

1781
A French naval fleet, under Admiral de Grasse, drives the British fleet, under Admiral Thomas Graves, back from Chesapeake Bay, during the Revolutionary War.

1855
The fraudulently elected pro-slavery Kansas Territorial Legislature is repudiated at a convention in Big Springs, Kansas.

1877
Sioux Indian Chief Crazy Horse is killed by a soldier at Fort Robinson, Nebraska.

1882
The first Labor Day parade is conducted at Union Square in New York.

1905
Japan and Russia sign the Treaty of Portsmouth, arranged by President Roosevelt, ending hostilities between the two countries.

1914
The German offensive is stopped by the French Army at the Battle of the Marne, during World War I.

1944
The Soviet Union declares war on Bulgaria, during World War II.

1961
President Kennedy signs a bill making air piracy punishable by death.

1972
Arab terrorists kill two Israeli coaches and nine athletes during the Olympics in Munich, Germany.

Bus carrying Israeli hostages to the airport

September

1861

A Union force commanded by General Ulysses S. Grant occupies Paducah, Kentucky, during the Civil War.

1862

Confederates commanded by Stonewall Jackson occupy Frederick, Maryland, north of the Potomac River, during the Civil War.

1869

One hundred eight miners are killed in a coal mine disaster in Avondale, Pennsylvania.

1901

President William McKinley is shot by anarchist Leon Czolgosz at the Pan-American Exposition, in Buffalo, New York.

1939

South Africa declares war on Germany, during World War II.

1941

The head of the German security police, Reinhard Heydrich, orders all Jews in German-occupied lands to wear a Star of David for identification, during World War II.

1942

German Army Group A captures Novorossiysk in the Soviet Union, during World War II.

1961

The Senate approves the creation of the National Wilderness Preservation System, setting aside over 9 million acres of forest as public land.

1975

Rhinestone Cowboy by Glen Campbell becomes the number one record in the United States.

Leon Czolgosz shooting President McKinley

September

1664
Dutch power in America ends when New York Governor, Peter Stuyvesant, surrenders to an English naval force.

1776
The *American Turtle* becomes the first submarine to be used in warfare, attacking the British ship HMS *Eagle* in New York harbor, during the Revolutionary War.

1778
Shawnee Indians attack a settlement at Boonesboro, Kentucky.

1860
The steamship, *Lady Elgin*, collides with the schooner, *Augusta*, on Lake Michigan, killing 400 people.

1876
Jesse and Frank James stage an unsuccessful bank robbery in Northfield, Minnesota, escaping after their gang members are killed.

1881
Jesse James stages his last robbery, in Blue Cut, Missouri.

1896
A. H. Whiting wins the first automobile track race held in the United States at a track in Cranston, Rhode Island.

1916
Congress passes the Workmen's Compensation Act.

1920
The first coast-to-coast airmail delivery service is established.

1921
Fifteen-year-old Margaret Gorman, from Washington, becomes the first and youngest winner of the Miss America beauty pageant in Atlantic City.

Peter Stuyvesant surrendering to the British

September

1565

St. Augustine, founded by Spanish naval officer, Pedro Menendez de Aviles, becomes the first permanent white colony in America.

1598

The parish of St. Augustine, Florida, becomes the first Catholic parish in North America.

1760

A British force led by General Jeffrey Amherst forces the French to surrender at Montreal, during the French and Indian War.

1781

New London, Connecticut, is burned by the British, during the Revolutionary War.

1847

American forces commanded by General Winfield Scott defeat the Mexicans at the Battle of Molino del Rey, Mexico, during the Mexican War.

1900

Six thousand people are killed as a hurricane strikes Galveston, Texas.

1934

One hundred thirty people are killed in a fire aboard the ship, *Morro Castle*, near Asbury Park, New Jersey.

1943

Italy surrenders to Allied forces, during World War II.

1951

Forty-nine nations sign the Japanese Peace Treaty, recognizing Japan's full sovereignty, with the United States retaining the right to maintain military forces there.

1954

The United States and seven other countries sign a treaty establishing the Southeast Asian Treaty Organization.

1971

The Kennedy Center opens in Washington, D.C., with a performance of Leonard Bernstein's *Mass*.

1974

President Ford pardons former President Richard M. Nixon unconditionally, for any unlawful acts he may have committed while in office.

1974

Daredevil Evel Knievel jumps the Snake River Canyon in Twin Falls, Idaho, in a rocket motorcycle.

Laying out St. Augustine, Florida

September

1675
The New England Confederation declares war on the Wampanoag Indians led by King Philip.

1763
George Washington's Mississippi Company receives a grant of 2.5 million acres of land between the Ohio and Wisconsin Rivers.

1776
The Continental Congress passes a resolution replacing "United Colonies" with "United States."

1781
The British, under Colonel Alexander Stewart, defeat the Americans, led by General Nathaniel Greene, at Eutaw Springs, South Carolina, during the Revolutionary War.

The Battle of Eutaw Springs

1850
California joins the Union as the thirty-first state.

1859
Congress establishes the boundaries of Utah.

1895
The American Bowling Congress is established in New York.

1904
Mounted police are used for the first time in New York.

1933
As Thousands Cheer, by Irving Berlin and Moss Hart, opens at the Forrest Theatre in Philadelphia.

1956
Elvis Presley makes his first appearance on the Ed Sullivan Show, singing *Hound Dog* and *Don't Be Cruel*.

1957
Diana by Paul Anka becomes the number one record in the United States.

1960
Thirty people are killed as Hurricane Donna ravages the Eastern Seaboard from Florida to New England.

1965
The Department of Housing and Urban Development is created by act of Congress.

1968
Arthur Ashe wins the men's singles title at the first United States Open tennis championship.

September

1623
The first cargo from the Plymouth Colony is shipped to England.

1753
The Delaware and Iroquois Indians revoke the Treaty of Logstown, which supported French claims to the Ohio Territory.

1813
The American fleet commanded by Oliver Hazard Perry defeats the British at the Battle of Lake Erie, during the War of 1812.

1846
Elias Howe is awarded a patent for his eye-pointed needle sewing machine.

1861
General Albert Sidney Johnston is appointed commander of all Confederate forces in the West, during the Civil War.

1863
Union forces occupy Little Rock, Arkansas, during the Civil War.

1875
The American Forestry Association is formed in Chicago.

1910
Get-Rich-Quick Wallingford by George M. Cohan opens in New York.

1939
Canada declares war on Germany, during World War II.

The Battle of Lake Erie

September

1777
A British force, under General Howe, defeats the Continental Army, led by General George Washington, at the Battle of Brandywine, Pennsylvania, during the Revolutionary War.

1811
The *New Orleans* sets sail down the Ohio River, becoming the first inland steamboat in the United States.

1814
The United States fleet commanded by Thomas Macdonough defeats the British at the Battle of Lake Champlain, New York, during the War of 1812.

1842
Mexican soldiers capture San Antonio, Texas, pushing the Republic of Texas closer to annexation by the United States.

The Bay Area Rapid Transit's inaugural run

1857
One hundred twenty immigrants are killed by Indians at the Mountain Meadows Massacre, in Utah.

1861
Union troops, commanded by General John Reynolds, repulse an attack by the Confederates, commanded by General Robert E. Lee, at Cheat Mountain in western Virginia, during the Civil War.

1912
Philadelphia Athletics second baseman Eddie Collins steals a record six bases in one game. (He repeats this feat on September 22).

1918
The Boston Red Sox defeat the Chicago Cubs in six games, to win the World Series.

1928
The Yelloway Bus Line inaugurates the first transcontinental bus service in the United States, from New York to Los Angeles, California.

1928
The Queen's Messenger, broadcast by station WGY in Schenectady, New York, becomes the first play to be televised in the United States.

1959
Congress passes a bill authorizing the distribution of food stamps to impoverished Americans.

1966
The longest newspaper strike in a major city, beginning on April 24, ends, in New York.

1972
The Bay Area Rapid Transit opens in San Francisco, becoming the first new rapid-transit system in the United States in 50 years.

September

1836

Narcissa Whitman and Eliza Spaulding arrive in Vancouver, Canada, becoming the first white women to cross the North American continent.

1861

A Confederate force commanded by General Sterling Price begins a siege of Lexington, Missouri, during the Civil War.

1866

The Black Crook opens at Niblo's Garden in New York, becoming the first long-running musical on Broadway.

1907

The largest steamship in the world, the *Lusitania*, arrives in New York harbor on its maiden voyage.

1910

Alice Stebbins Wells of Los Angeles becomes the first policewoman in the United States.

1922

The United States Protestant Episcopal Church votes to delete the world "obey" from the marriage service.

1944

The United States First Army pushes five miles into Germany, during World War II.

1959

The *Luna II* becomes the first spacecraft to make a hard landing on the Moon.

1964

The New Hampshire Sweepstakes in Rockingham becomes the first legal sweepstakes in the United States.

1970

Palestinian terrorists blow up a TWA jet in Jordan, after hijacking it and releasing the passengers and crew.

Palestinian terrorists with captured TWA jet.

September

1609

Dutch explorer, Henry Hudson, sails up the Hudson River as far north as Albany, New York.

1759

French General, Joseph de Montcalm, and British General, James Wolfe, are killed on the Plains of Abraham at Quebec, during the French and Indian War.

1788

Congress establishes procedures for the choosing of presidential electors.

1847

American forces commanded by General Winfield Scott take the fortified hill of Chapultepec, Mexico, during the Mexican War.

1861

The Union frigate, *Colorado*, commanded by Lieutenant John H. Russell, attacks the Confederate navy yard in Pensacola, Florida, in the first naval action of the Civil War.

1862

A Union soldier discovers Confederate General Robert E. Lee's plan of the invasion of Maryland, during the Civil War.

1918

United States forces cut off the Germans, taking over 15,000 prisoners in St. Mihiel, France, during World War I.

1940

Italian forces enter Egypt, during World War II.

1970

Gary Muhrcke wins the first New York City Marathon in 2 hours, 31 minutes, and 38.2 seconds.

1977

Oldsmobile introduces the first American-made, diesel-fueled automobiles.

The Battle of the Plains of Abraham

September

1777

A British force under General Burgoyne encamps at Saratoga, New York, after crossing the Hudson River, during the Revolutionary War.

1813

The British ship, *Boxer,* is defeated by the American ship, *Enterprise,* commanded by Captain William Burrows, off the coast of Maine, during the War of 1812.

1814

Fort McHenry in Baltimore withstands a severe bombardment from the British fleet, inspiring Frances Scott Key to write the "Star Spangled Banner," during the War of 1812.

1846

General Santa Anna becomes commander in chief of the Mexican Army.

1847

The American Army commanded by General Winfield Scott enters Mexico City, during the Mexican War.

1862

Confederate forces pull back from Harpers Ferry, Virginia, after Union troops commanded by General William Franklin attack, at the Battle of Crampton's Gap, during the Civil War.

1901

William McKinley, twenty-fifth President of the United States, dies of wounds inflicted by anarchist Leon Czolgosz.

1959

President Eisenhower signs a bill lifting FCC equal time requirements for radio and television news broadcasts.

The bombardment of Fort McHenry

September

1776
The British under General Howe occupy New York after the Continental Army evacuates the city.

1782
Congress adopts the Great Seal of the United States.

1853
Antoinette Brown of South Butler, New York, becomes the first woman minister in the United States.

1853
The first national librarians convention is held in New York.

1857
Brigham Young forbids United States armed forces to enter the Utah Territory, which is under martial law.

1857
William H. Taft, twenty-seventh President of the United States, is born in Cincinnati, Ohio.

1862
Confederate troops commanded by General Stonewall Jackson capture the Federal arsenal at Harpers Ferry, Virginia, during the Civil War.

1923
Governor John C. Walton places Oklahoma under martial law as a result of terrorist activities by the Klu Klux Klan.

1928
Congress establishes Bryce Canyon National Park in Utah.

1930
The United States beats England in the first International Bridge Match.

1942
The Japanese sink the United States aircraft carrier, *Wasp*, off the coast of Guadalcanal, during World War II.

1950
To relieve South Korean forces at Pusan, United States forces land at Inchon, during the Korean War.

1968
Sonny Jurgenson of the Washington Redskins completes an NFL record 99-yard touchdown pass in a game against the Chicago Bears.

General ''Stonewall'' Jackson at Harpers Ferry

September

1766
General George Washington repulses the British at the Battle of Harlem Heights, New York, during the Revolutionary War.

1853
Henry E. Steinway sells his first American-made piano.

1861
Ship Island, Mississippi, is evacuated by the Confederates, becoming an important base for future Union operations along the Gulf Coast, during the Civil War.

1908
General Motors Corporation is formed in New Jersey.

1915
Haiti becomes a United States protectorate.

1924
St. Louis Cardinals Jim Bottomly gets a record 12 RBI's in one game.

1925
No, No, Nanette opens at the Globe Theater in New York.

1953
The Robe is released, becoming the first movie in CinemaScope, an enhanced film process.

1974
Mary Louise Smith becomes the first woman to head the Republican National Committee.

The Battle of Harlem Heights

September

1862
In the bloodiest single day of combat during the Civil War, the Confederate army, commanded by General Robert E. Lee, is forced to retreat in the face of a superior Union force, commanded by General George B. McClellan, at the Battle of Antietam, Maryland.

1902
The United States formally protests to the Romanian Government about its persecution of Jews.

1923
Over a thousand homes are destroyed in a fire near Berkeley, California, killing over 25 people.

1930
Construction is begun on the Hoover Dam near Las Vegas, Nevada.

1931
Long Playing records are demonstrated for the first time by RCA at the Savoy Plaza Hotel in New York.

1944
The Allies begin Operation Market Garden, to seize bridges in Holland, during World War II.

1947
James V. Forrestal becomes the first Secretary of Defense.

1978
President Anwar el-Sadat of Egypt and Prime Minister Menachem Begin of Israel sign a peace treaty at the White House, in Washington, D.C.

1983
Vanessa Williams of New York becomes the first Black to win the Miss America title.

The Battle of Antietam

September

1759
The French surrender Quebec to the British during the French and Indian War.

1850
Congress passes the Fugitive Slave Bill, requiring the return of runaway slaves to their owners.

1851
The New York *Daily Times*, the forerunner of the New York *Times*, begins publication.

1873
The failure of the brokerage firm Jay Cooke & Company triggers the financial panic of 1873.

1900
Minnesota holds the first direct primary election in the United States.

1926
When a hurricane strikes Florida and the Gulf coast, destroying 5,000 homes, 372 people are killed.

1931
The Japanese invade Manchuria, China, in direct violation of the Kellogg-Briand Pact of 1928, signed by 16 nations.

1947
The Department of Defense is created by Congress.

1959
Soviet Premier Khrushchev addresses the United Nations in New York, calling for total nuclear disarmament.

1975
Police capture fugitive, Patricia Hearst, after a 19-month search during which she allegedly joined her Symbionese Liberation Army kidnappers.

Recovering a runaway slave

September

19

1777
British forces threaten Philadelphia, forcing the Continental Congress to leave.

1862
Union forces, commanded by General William S. Rosecrans, defeat the Confederates, commanded by General Sterling Price, in Iuka, Mississippi, during the Civil War.

1864
A Union force, commanded by General Philip Sheridan, defeats the Confederates, commanded by General Jubal A. Early, in Winchester, Virginia, during the Civil War.

1876
Melville R. Bissell of Grand Rapids, Michigan, is awarded a patent for the first carpet sweeper.

1881
James A. Garfield, twentieth President of the United States, dies of wounds suffered after being shot by assassin Charles J. Guiteau, in July.

1928
Steamboat Willie, the first talking cartoon picture, is released by Walt Disney at the Colony Theater, in New York.

1941
The Soviet city of Kiev falls to the German Army, during World War II.

1955
Chicago Cubs shortstop Ernie Banks hits his record fifth grand slam home run in one season.

1957
The first underground nuclear explosion is set off at a test near Las Vegas, Nevada.

1960
The Twist by Chubby Checker becomes the number one record in the United States.

Chubby Checker

September

1850
The District of Columbia abolishes slave trade.

1858
Camp Walbach is established east of the Cheyenne Pass in Wyoming to protect emigrants traveling through the territory.

1861
Union troops, commanded by Colonel Mulligan, surrender to the Confederates, commanded by General Sterling Price, in Lexington, Missouri, during the Civil War.

1863
Union forces, commanded by General William S. Rosecrans, are defeated by the Confederates, commanded by General Braxton Bragg, at the Battle of Chickamauga, Tennessee, during the Civil War.

1944
The United States 82nd Airborne Division takes Nijmegan in the Western Front, during World War II.

1962
Governor Ross R. Barnett denies the application of Black student, James H. Meridith, to the University of Mississippi.

1973
Billie Jean King defeats Bobby Riggs in straight sets in a nationally televised tennis match in the Houston Astrodome.

1984
The United States embassy in Beirut, Lebanon, is bombed by a terrorist, killing two Americans.

1988
Lauro F. Cavazos is named Secretary of Education, becoming the first hispanic member of President Reagan's cabinet.

Bobby Riggs returning a Billy Jean King forehand

1812
Czar Alexander I of Russia offers to mediate in the war between the United States and England.

1833
The United States signs a commercial treaty with the Sultan of Muscat.

1856
The Illinois Central Railroad opens between Chicago and Cairo, Illinois.

1921
Secretary of Commerce, Herbert Hoover, opens a national conference on unemployment, proposing price cuts and public works projects.

1938
A hurricane that strikes the New England states kills 460 people.

1969
Steve O'Neal of the New York Jets kicks an NFL record 98-yard punt in a game against the Denver Broncos.

1977
The American Musical Theater Center is established at Duke University, in North Carolina.

1980
Richard Todd of the New York Jets completes an NFL record 42 passes in a game against the San Francisco 49'ers.

1982
The first professional football players strike begins.

1983
La Cage aux Folles, a musical by Stephen Sondheim and Jerry Herman, opens at the Palace Theatre in New York.

Cartoon depicting Russian mediation of the war

1656

The first women jurors serve in a trial at the General Provisional Court in Patuxent, Maryland.

1711

The Tuscarora Indian War begins in North Carolina, caused by the encroaching of white settlers on Indian land.

1776

Captain Nathan Hale of Connecticut is executed by the British for spying, declaring, "I only regret that I have but one life to lose for my country."

1784

The Russians found their first permanent settlement in Alaska, at Kodiak Island.

1862

President Lincoln issues a preliminary Emancipation Proclamation, calling for all slaves within areas under rebellion to be free on January 1, 1863.

1906

Twenty-one people are killed in Atlanta, Georgia, in one of the worst race riots in the United States.

1950

Dr. Ralph J. Bunche wins the Nobel Peace Prize for his work as a United Nations mediator in the Israeli-Arab conflict.

1964

Fiddler on the Roof opens at the Imperial Theatre in New York.

1975

Sara Jane Moore, an FBI informer, shoots at President Ford in San Francisco, California.

1985

The United States, Japan, France, England, and West Germany agree to take steps to lower the value of the dollar.

Nathan Hale's execution

September

1779
During a naval engagement, John Paul Jones, commanding the *Bonhomme Richard*, says, "I have not yet begun to fight."

1862
Confederate forces commanded by Colonel Henry H. Sibley defeat the Sioux Indians at Wood Lake, Minnesota.

1926
Gene Tunney outpoints Jack Dempsey, to win the heavyweight boxing championship.

1952
Vice presidential candidate, Richard M. Nixon, makes a televised appearance to answer charges of financial impropriety, saying he will never give back his dog Checkers, a campaign gift.

1952
Rocky Marciano knocks out Jersey Joe Walcott in the 13th round, to win the heavyweight boxing championship.

1957
That'll Be the Day by Buddy Holly and the Crickets becomes the number one record in the United States.

1962
Philharmonic Hall opens in New York, becoming the first building to be completed at Lincoln Center for the Performing Arts.

1966
The United States begins aerial defoliation south of the demilitarized zone, to deprive the North Vietnamese of cover, during the Vietnam War.

1972
President Ferdinand Marcos of the Philippines proclaims martial law following a Communist insurgency.

1986
Congress votes to make the rose the official flower of the United States.

Rocky Marciano knocking out Jersey Joe Walcott

September

1789

Congress passes the Federal Judiciary Act, establishing a six-man Supreme Court.

1789

The office of Attorney General is created by act of Congress.

1794

President Washington orders the militia to put down the Whisky Rebellion, caused by Pennsylvania farmers' opposition to an excise tax on liquor.

1821

Czar Alexander I of Russia claims all of the Pacific coast north of the 51st parallel, bisecting land claimed by both the United States and England.

1869

Speculators Jim Fisk and Jay Gould cause a financial panic on Wall Street in an attempt to corner the gold market.

1929

Lieutenant James H. Doolittle makes the first flight using only the instrument panel for guidance at Mitchell Field in New York.

1950

Jim Hardy of the Chicago Cardinals has an NFL record 8 passes intercepted in a game against the Philadelphia Eagles.

1956

The first transatlantic telephone cable system begins operating, between Clarenville, Newfoundland, and Oban, Scotland.

1960

The USS *Enterprise* is launched to become the first nuclear-powered aircraft carrier in the world.

1967

Jim Bakken of the St. Louis Cardinals kicks an NFL record seven field goals in a game against the Pittsburgh Steelers.

Rebels attacking a federal tax collector

1513
Spanish explorer, Vasco Nunez de Balboa, discovers the Pacific Ocean.

1690
Publick Occurrences, printed in Boston, becomes the first newspaper in the Colonies.

1775
Colonel Ethan Allen is captured by the British and sent to England for the duration of the Revolutionary War.

1839
France becomes the first European nation to recognize the Republic of Texas.

1846
United States forces commanded by General Zachary Taylor capture Monterrey, Mexico, during the Mexican War.

1890
Congress establishes Yosemite Park in California.

1919
President Wilson suffers a stroke in Colorado and is unable to perform the duties of President for several weeks.

1957
President Eisenhower orders United States Army troops to Little Rock, Arkansas, to escort nine Black students to public school.

1962
Sonny Liston knocks out Floyd Patterson in the first round, to win the heavyweight boxing championship.

1981
Sandra Day O'Connor becomes the first woman Supreme Court Justice.

Balboa at the Pacific Ocean

1777
The British occupy Philadelphia, during the Revolutionary War.

1789
John Jay becomes the first Chief Justice of the Supreme Court.

1789
Samuel Osgood becomes the first Postmaster General of the United States.

1887
Emile Berliner of Washington, D.C., is awarded a patent for the first disc record player.

1914
Congress establishes the Federal Trade Commission.

1918
At the Battle of Meuse-Argonne, France, during World War I, 1.2 million American troops launch an attach to cut off the German supply line.

1950
United States troops recapture Seoul, during the Korean War.

1957
West Side Story by Leonard Bernstein opens at the Winter Garden Theatre in New York.

1971
Emperor Hirohito meets President Nixon in Anchorage, Alaska, becoming the first meeting between a Japanese emperor and an American president.

1984
The United States yacht, *Liberty*, loses the America's Cup for the first time, to the Australian yacht, *Australia II*.

Chief Justice John Jay

1779
The Continental Congress appoints John Adams to negotiate peace with England, during the Revolutionary War.

1854
Over 150 passengers are killed when the *Arctic* sinks after being hit by a French steamship off the coast of Newfoundland, Canada.

1864
Confederate General Sterling Price leads an unsuccessful attack against a Union force commanded by General Thomas Ewing, Jr., in Pilot Knob, Missouri, during the Civil War.

1909
President Taft sets aside three million acres of oil-rich land for conservation purposes, including Teapot Dome, in Wyoming.

1912
W.C. Handy's "Memphis Blues" becomes the first blues song to be published in the United States.

1939
The Germans take over 150,000 prisoners as Warsaw surrenders, during World War II.

1940
Germany, Italy, and Japan sign the Tripartite Pact, promising to declare war on any third party joining the war against the others.

1944
Operation Market Garden, an Allied invasion of Holland, ends in failure, during World War II.

1963
Gangster Joseph M. Valachi identifies the chiefs of organized crime families during televised testimony before a Senate subcommittee.

Joseph Valachi testifying on Capitol Hill

September

1787
Congress votes to submit the proposed Constitution to the states for ratification.

1850
Brigham Young is named governor of the Utah Territory by President Fillmore.

1863
Union Generals McDowell, McCook, and Crittenden are relieved of their commands and ordered to Indianapolis for a court of inquiry into the Battle of Chickamuga.

1920
Eight players on the Chicago White Sox baseball team are indicted on charges of throwing the 1919 World Series.

1937
President Roosevelt dedicates the Bonneville Dam on the Columbia River in Oregon.

1939
Germany and Russia sign a secret treaty dividing up Poland between them.

1966
The Whitney Museum of American Art opens at its new location in New York.

1968
The Atlanta Chiefs defeat the San Diego Toros 3-0 in the first North American Soccer League championship.

1987
The National Museum of African Art opens as part of the Smithsonian Institution in Washington, D.C.

Banned White Sox player ''Shoeless'' Joe Jackson

September

1789
Congress authorizes the establishment of a 1000-man standing army.

1850
The United States Navy and Merchant Marine bans flogging.

1864
Union forces, commanded by General Ulysses S. Grant, capture Fort Harrison, Virginia, preventing Confederate forces under General Jubal Early from being reinforced, during the Civil War.

1906
The United States assumes military control of Cuba under the Platt Amendment after election disputes cause a revolt.

1938
Announcing he had secured "peace in our time," English Prime Minister Neville Chamberlain signs the Munich Pact, surrendering the Sudetenland to Germany.

1943
Italian Field Marshall Badoglio signs an armistice agreement aboard the HMS *Nelson*, during World War II.

1982
Cyanide put in Tylenol capsules kills several people in Chicago, prompting a nationwide alert and recall of 264,000 bottles.

1983
A Chorus Line has its 3389th performance, becoming the longest-running Broadway show.

1988
The shuttle *Discovery* lifts off, becoming the first United States manned spaceflight in over 3 years.

The launching of the *Discovery*

1800

The Convention of 1800 restores normal diplomatic relations between France and the United States.

1911

Lt. H. H. Arnold becomes the first stuntman in *The Military Air Scout*, a film being shot in New York.

1916

The New York Giants record 26-game winning streak ends, with an 8-3 loss to the Boston Braves.

1939

A Polish government is formed in Paris after the fall of Warsaw to the German Army, during World War II.

1941

German Panzer groups attack and break the Soviet lines east of the Dnieper River in the Soviet Union, during World War II.

1958

Arkansas Governor, Orval Faubus, closes four high schools in Little Rock in defiance of a Supreme Court ruling on segregation.

1962

James H. Meredith becomes the first Black to enroll at the University of Mississippi, after being escorted onto campus by United States marshals.

1965

The National Foundation on the Arts and the Humanities is established.

1970

The *New American Bible* is published in its entirety for the first time.

James Meredith at the University of Mississippi

1768
British troops land in Boston.

1785
The first city directory is published in Philadelphia by John Macpherson.

1800
France and Spain sign the secret Treaty of San Ildefonso, in which Spain returns the Louisiana Territory to France.

1810
The Berkshire Cattle Show in Pittsfield, Massachusetts, becomes the first state fair in the United States.

1880
John Philip Sousa becomes the United States Marine Corps Band's conductor.

1880
The Edison Lamp Works in Menlo Park, New Jersey, begins production of the first light bulbs.

1890
Congress passes the McKinley Tariff Act, establishing tariffs at the highest level ever in the United States.

1891
The University of Chicago is established.

1896
The United States Post Office establishes rural free delivery.

1909
The Model T Ford is introduced, costing $850.

1921
Ten people are wounded when a gunfight erupts at a Klu Klux Klan parade in Lorena, Texas.

1924
James Earl Carter, thirty-eighth President of the United States, is born in Plains, Georgia.

1942
The XP-59 is tested at Muroc Army Base in California, becoming the United States' first jet airplane.

1961
Roger Maris of the New York Yankees hits his 61st home run to surpass Babe Ruth's single season record.

1987
Eight people are killed when an earthquake registering 6.1 on the Richter scale strikes Los Angeles, California.

Roger Maris hitting his 61st home run

October

1780
British Major General John Andre is hanged as a spy after a secret meeting with American General Benedict Arnold, during the Revolutionary War.

1871
The Federal Government arrests Mormon leader Brigham Young for practicing polygamy.

1893
Two thousand people are killed when a cyclone strikes the Gulf Coast of Louisiana.

1932
The New York Yankees defeat the Chicago Cubs in four games, to win the World Series.

1933
Ah, Wilderness! by Eugene O'Neil opens at the Guild Theatre in New York.

1933
The American Federation of Labor sanctions the five-day work week.

1954
The New York Giants defeat the Cleveland Indians in four games, to win the World Series.

1967
Thurgood Marshall becomes the first Black Supreme Court Justice.

1975
The Peachtree Plaza building opens in Atlanta, Georgia, becoming the tallest building in the South.

1980
Michael Joseph Myers of Pennsylvania, becomes the first member of the House of Representatives to be expelled since 1861, after being convicted of bribery in the Abscam investigation.

Justice Thurgood Marshall

October

3

1862
Union forces are driven back by the Confederates commanded by Generals Earl Van Dorn and Sterling Price at the Battle of Corinth, Mississippi, during the Civil War.

1898
Cyrano de Bergerac by Edmond Rostand opens at the Garden Theater in New York.

1910
The Wow-Wows, a vaudeville show starring Charlie Chaplin, opens at the Colonial Theater in New York.

1938
Abe Lincoln in Illinois by Robert E. Sherwood opens in Washington, D.C.

1943
German forces land on Cos in the Aegean taking over 4500 British and Italian prisoners, during World War II.

1951
New York Giants outfielder Bobby Thomson hits a home run in the bottom of the ninth inning to win the pennant against the Brooklyn Dodgers.

1962
Stop the World I Want to Get Off, by Leslie Bricusse and Anthony Newly, opens at the Shubert Theater in New York.

1968
The Great White Hope by Howard Sackler opens at the Alvin Theatre in New York

1974
Frank Robinson signs with the Cleveland Indians, becoming the first Black manager in the Major Leagues.

1984
Richard W. Miller becomes the first FBI agent to be charged with espionage.

Bobby Thomson after his pennant-winning home run

October

4

1812
American forces defeat the British at Ogdensburg, New York, during the War of 1812.

1822
Rutherford B. Hayes, nineteenth President of the United States, is born in Delaware.

1859
The Kansas Territory ratifies an antislavery constitution.

1861
The Confederates sign treaties with the Cherokee, Shawnee, and Seneca Indians, during the Civil War.

1862
The Confederates, commanded by General Earl Van Dorn, are forced to retreat after the Union Army, commanded by General William S. Rosecrans, repels their attack in Corinth, Mississippi, during the Civil War.

1870
Benjamin H. Bristow becomes the first Solicitor General of the United States.

1881
The University of Southern California is founded in Los Angeles.

1895
Horace Rawlins wins the first United States Open golf tournament, at the Newport Golf Club in Newport, Rhode Island.

1955
The Brooklyn Dodgers defeat the New York Yankees in seven games, to win the World Series.

1965
Pope Paul VI addresses the General Assembly of the United Nations in New York.

The United States Open golf tournament

October

1777
The Continental Army under General George Washington loses over 700 men at the Battle of Germantown, Pennsylvania, during the Revolutionary War.

1813
Shawnee Indian Chief Tecumseh, allied with the British, is killed at the Battle of the Thames, in Ontario, Canada, during the War of 1812.

1829
Chester A. Arthur, twenty-first President of the United States, is born in Fairfield, Vermont.

1857
Kansas elects a Legislature banning slavery in the territory.

1864
Confederate troops commanded by General Samuel G. French attack Union positions at Allatoona, Georgia, where they are unsuccessful at an attempt to destroy the railroad bridge there, during the Civil War.

1877
Nez Perces Indian Chief Joseph surrenders to the United States Army in the Bear Paw Mountains in Northern Montana.

1892
The Dalton Gang is broken up when Emmett Dalton is killed during a failed bank robbery attempt in Coffeyville, Kansas.

1921
The World Series is covered on the radio for the first time by station WJZ in Newark, New Jersey.

1930
The Columbia Broadcasting System begins live Sunday radio broadcasts of the New York Philharmonic conducted by Arturo Toscanini.

1931
Hugh Herndon and Clyde Pangborn complete the first nonstop flight across the Pacific Ocean, from Japan to Wenatchee, Washington.

1942
The St. Louis Cardinals defeat the New York Yankees in seven games, to win the World Series.

1944
Bloomer Girl, by Harold Arlen and E.Y. Harburg, opens at the Shubert Theatre in New York.

1953
Earl Warren becomes Chief Justice of the Supreme Court.

Nez Perces Chief Joseph

October

1683
The first German settlers arrive in America, in Philadelphia.

1843
Dr. William T.G. Morton demonstrates the effects of ether at a hospital in Boston.

1884
The United States Naval War College is established in Newport, Rhode Island.

1890
The Mormon Church discontinues the practice of polygamy.

1923
Lieutenant Al Williams sets an air speed record of 243.7 miles per hour in a Curtis racer, in St. Louis, Missouri.

1927
The Jazz Singer, the first successful talking feature film, opens in New York.

1936
The New York Yankees defeat the New York Giants in six games, to win the World Series.

1958
The United States atomic submarine, *Seawolf*, sets an underwater endurance record of 60 days.

1963
The Los Angeles Dodgers defeat the New York Yankees in four games, to win the World Series.

1978
Hannah H. Gray of the University of Chicago becomes the first woman to serve as President of a major university.

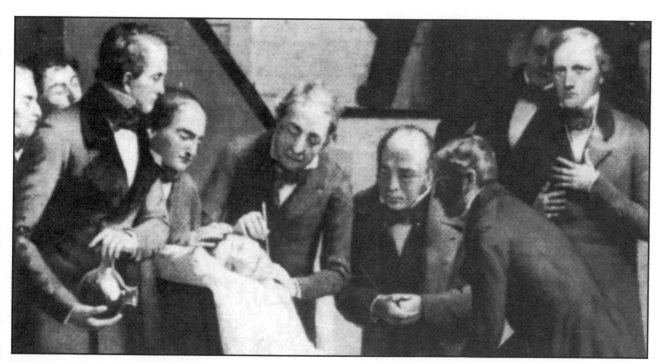

Using anesthesia during an operation

October

1690
English forces attack Quebec, Canada, in the first major military operation of King William's War.

1763
King George III of England signs the Proclamation of 1763, disallowing English settlement west of the Appalachian Mountains.

1777
The Americans rout a British force at the second Battle of Bemis Heights near Saratoga, New York, during the Revolutionary War.

1780
The Americans defeat the British at Kings Mountain, South Carolina, killing their commander, Major Patrick Ferguson, during the Revolutionary War.

1826
A three-mile stretch of track between Quincy, Massachusetts, and the Neponset River becomes the first railroad to be completed in the United States.

1839
Alexander Wolcott takes the first studio photographic portrait in New York.

1856
Cyrus Chambers of Pennsylvania is awarded a patent for the first practical folding machine, used for books and newspapers.

1864
The Union ship, U.S.S. *Wachusett*, captures the Confederate raider, *Florida*, off the coast of Brazil, during the Civil War.

1901
American playwright Booth Tarkington's first play, *Monsieur Beaucaire*, opens in Philadelphia.

1916
Georgia Tech scores a record 222 points in a football game against Cumberland University.

1929
J. Ramsay MacDonald becomes the first British Prime Minister to address the United States Congress.

1933
The New York Giants defeat the Washington Senators in five games, to win the World Series.

1942
The United States and England announce that a United Nations Commission will be established to prosecute Axis war crimes, during World War II.

1950
United States forces invade North Korea, during the Korean War.

1950
The New York Yankees defeat the Philadelphia Phillies in four games, to win the World Series.

1955
The U.S.S. aircraft carrier, *Saratoga*, is launched at the Brooklyn Navy Yard, becoming the most powerful warship in the world.

1976
The Cooper-Hewitt Museum of Design opens in New York.

1982
Cats, a musical by Andrew Lloyd Webber, opens at the Winter Garden Theatre in New York.

1985
American tourist, Leon Klinghoffer, is killed by Palestinian terrorists aboard the cruise ship, *Archille Lauro*, hijacked on the Mediterranean Sea.

October

1633
Dorchester, in the Massachusetts Bay Colony, organizes the first town government in the Colonies.

1862
The Confederates, commanded by General Braxton Bragg, are forced to retreat after an attack by Union forces, commanded by General Don Carlos Buell, in the Battle of Perryville, Kentucky, during the Civil War.

1869
Franklin Pierce, fourteenth President of the United States, dies in Concord, New Hampshire.

1871
Mrs. O'Leary's cow kicks over a lantern, beginning a fire that destroys over 17,500 buildings and leaves 98,500 people homeless in Chicago.

1904
The Vanderbilt Cup race, on Long Island, New York, becomes the first organized automobile race in the United States.

1922
The New York Giants defeat the New York Yankees in four games, to win the World Series.

1927
The New York Yankees defeat the Pittsburgh Pirates in four games, to win the World Series.

1956
New York Yankees pitcher Don Larson becomes the only man to pitch a perfect game in the World Series.

1959
The Los Angeles Dodgers defeat the Chicago White Sox in six games, to win the World Series.

1972
Sargent Shriver becomes Democratic presidential nominee George McGovern's choice for vice president after Thomas Eagleton resigns, following reports that he has undergone psychiatric therapy.

1974
The Franklin National Bank fails, the largest bank failure in the United States.

1988
Columbia defeats Princeton in football, to end its record 44-game losing streak.

1988
Los Angeles Dodgers pitcher Orel Hershiser's record 67 scoreless innings streak ends.

The Chicago Fire

1765
Colonists adopt the Declaration of Rights and Grievances in response to the Stamp Act.

1776
Franciscan missionary Juan Batista de Anza founds the mission of San Francisco de Asis, at present-day San Francisco.

1781
American and French forces begin shelling the surrounded British forces under General Cornwallis at Yorktown, Virginia, during the Revolutionary War.

1812
The British ships, *Detroit* and *Caledonia*, are captured by American forces on Lake Erie, during the War of 1812.

1855
Joshua C. Stoddard of Worcester, Massachusetts, is awarded a patent for his steam calliope.

1862
Confederate cavalry commander J.E.B. Stuart begins a raid in which his force makes a complete circle around the Union Army of the Potomac, during the Civil War.

1865
The first underground oil pipeline in the United States is completed, between Oil Creek and Pithole, Pennsylvania.

1904
The American Tobacco Company is established.

1917
Clarence Saunders of Memphis, Tennessee, is awarded a patent for a self-service method of operating a food store, the first supermarket.

1919
The Cincinnati Reds defeat the Chicago White Sox in eight games, to win the World Series.

1928
New York Yankees outfielder Babe Ruth hits a record three home runs in a World Series game.

1934
The St. Louis Cardinals defeat the Detroit Tigers in seven games, to win the World Series.

1936
Electric power generated by Boulder Dam and drinking water drawn from Lake Meade, created by the dam's construction, reaches Los Angeles.

1946
The Iceman Cometh by Eugene O'Neill opens at the Martin Beck Theatre in New York.

1949
The New York Yankees defeat the Brooklyn Dodgers in five games, to win the World Series.

1960
The United States and Canada sign the Columbia River pact for the joint development of hydro-electric power in the Northwest.

1965
Yesterday by the Beatles becomes the number one record in the United States.

1983
Secretary of the Interior, James Watt, resigns after his remarks describing a commission as "a black, a woman, two jews, and a cripple."

October

10

1774
Lord Dunmore defeats the Shawnee Indians at Point Pleasant on the Ohio River, ending the Shawnee War.

1780
Congress passes a resolution calling for the states to cede their western territories for the creation of new states.

1845
The United States Naval Academy at Fort Severn, Annapolis, Maryland, opens.

1914
President Woodrow Wilson sets off an explosion that completes the waterway across Panama.

1920
Cleveland Indians infielder Bill Wambsganss becomes the only man to make an unassisted triple play in a World Series game.

1924
The Washington Senators defeat the New York Giants in seven games, to win the World Series.

1926
A naval ammunition depot at Lake Denmark, New Jersey, explodes after being hit by lightning, killing 31 people.

1927
The Supreme Court rules that the lease on the Teapot Dome Oil Reserve in Wyoming is invalid, because of the fraudulent negotiations conducted by former Interior Secretary, Albert B. Fall.

1933
The Treaty of Non-Aggression and Conciliation is signed by nations of the Western Hemisphere in Rio de Janiero, Argentina.

1935
Porgy and Bess, an opera by George Gershwin, opens at the Alvin Theatre in New York.

1937
The New York Yankees defeat the New York Giants in five games, to win the World Series.

1944
American carrier force TF 38 destroys many Japanese aircraft on the Ryukyu Islands in the Pacific, during World War II.

1951
President Truman signs the Mutual Security Act of 1951, establishing a Mutual Security Agency.

1956
The New York Yankees defeat the Brooklyn Dodgers in seven games, to win the World Series.

1959
Pan American Airways announces the first global airline service.

1963
Dr. Linus C. Paulding wins the Nobel Peace Prize for his efforts to secure a ban on nuclear testing.

1973
Vice President Spiro Agnew resigns and pleads no contest to income tax evasion charges.

1980
The U.S. National Science Foundation VLA opens in San Augustin, New Mexico, becoming the world's largest radio telescope.

October

1862
The Confederate Congress passes a law making anyone owning more than 20 slaves exempt from military service, during the Civil War.

1906
The San Francisco Board of Education orders the segregation of Oriental schoolchildren.

1913
The Philadelphia Athletics defeat the New York Giants in five games, to win the World Series.

1943
The New York Yankees defeat the St. Louis Cardinals in five games, to win the World Series.

1950
The Federal Communications Commission issues a license to the Columbia Broadcasting System to begin television broadcasts in color.

1968
Apollo 7, with astronauts Walter M. Schirra, Jr., Donn F. Eisele, and Walter Cunningham aboard, becomes the first manned Apollo mission.

1977
John Van Vleck and Philip W. Anderson win the Nobel Prize in Physics for their work in solid state electronics.

1981
LeRoy Irwin of the Los Angeles Rams runs back an NFL record two punts for touchdowns in a game against the Cleveland Browns.

1984
Dr. Kathryn D. Sullivan becomes the first United States woman astronaut to walk in space, during the sixth flight of the space shuttle, *Challenger.*

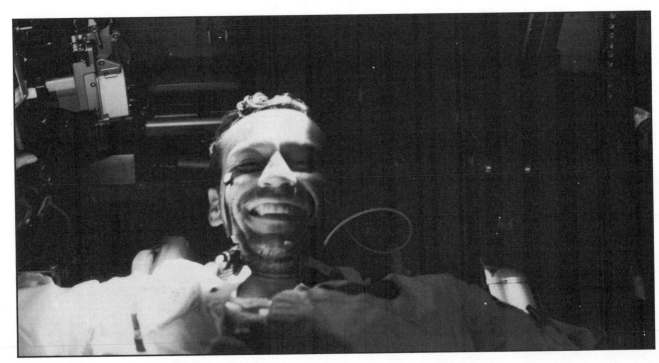

Donn F. Eisele aboard Apollo 7

1492
Christopher Columbus sights land near the Bahamas, going ashore and claiming the territory for the King of Spain.

1641
Samuel Winslow of Massachusetts is awarded the first patent in the Colonies, for his process of manufacturing salt.

1792
The first celebration of Columbus Day is held in New York, on the 300th anniversary of Columbus' discovery.

1837
The Republic of Texas withdraws its request to be annexed by the United States.

1907
The Chicago Cubs defeat the Detroit Tigers in four games, to win the World Series.

1920
The Cleveland Indians defeat the Brooklyn Dodgers in seven games, to win the World Series.

1928
The Iron Lung, designed to treat respiratory failure, is used for the first time at Boston Children's Hospital.

1960
Soviet Premier Nikita Krushchev takes off his shoe and pounds it on the podium during a speech before the United Nations General Assembly in New York.

1967
The St. Louis Cardinals defeat the Boston Red Sox in seven games, to win the World Series.

1971
Jesus Christ Superstar, by Tim Rice and Andrew Lloyd Webber, opens at the Mark Hellinger Theatre in New York.

The landing of Christopher Columbus

October

1775
The Continental Congress authorizes the construction of two warships.

1812
One thousand United States troops are killed or wounded at the Battle of Queenstown Heights, Canada, during the War of 1812.

1864
Maryland adopts a new state constitution banning slavery, during the Civil War.

1903
The Boston Red Sox defeat the Pittsburgh Pirates to win the first World Series.

1914
The Boston Braves defeat the Philadelphia Athletics in four games, to win the World Series.

1921
The New York Giants defeat the New York Yankees in eight games, to win the World Series.

1942
The German Fourth Panzer Army reaches the Volga River in the Soviet Union, during World War II.

1944
The British 46th Division takes Carpineta in Italy, during World War II.

1960
The Pittsburgh Pirates defeat the New Yankees in seven games, to win the World Series.

1974
Dennis Morgan of the Dallas Cowboys returns a punt 98 yards, an NFL record, in a game against the St. Louis Cardinals.

The Battle of Queenstown Heights

October

1641
French explorer, Samuel de Champlain, founds Montreal.

1890
Dwight D. Eisenhower, thirty-fourth President of the United States is born in Denison, Texas.

1899
William McKinley becomes the first President to ride in an automobile.

1905
The New York Giants defeat the Philadelphia Athletics in five games, to win the World Series.

1912
Presidential candidate Theodore Roosevelt is shot and wounded at a political rally in Milwaukee, Wisconsin.

1922
The first mechanical telephone switchboard in the United States is installed in New York.

1929
The Philadelphia Athletics defeat the Chicago Cubs in five games, to win the World Series.

1933
Germany withdraws from the Disarmament Conference and announces its resignation from the League of Nations.

1947
The Bell X-1 becomes the first aircraft to break the sound barrier, reaching a speed of 714.5 mph.

1961
How to Succeed in Business Without Really Trying, by Abe Burrows and Frank Loesser, opens at the Forty-Sixth Street Theatre in New York.

1964
The Reverend Martin Luther King, Jr. wins the Nobel Peace Prize for his work in the Civil Rights Movement.

1965
The Los Angeles Dodgers defeat the Minnesota Twins in seven games, to win the World Series.

1984
The Detroit Tigers defeat the San Diego Padres in five games, to win the World Series.

President McKinley riding in an automobile

October

15

1863
Union troops enter Canton, Mississippi, during the Civil War.

1864
Confederate President Jefferson Davis puts General Braxton Bragg in command of forces in Wilmington, Delaware, during the Civil War.

1881
American Angler, edited by William C. Harris, becomes the first fishing journal published in the United States.

1900
Symphony Hall opens in Boston with a performance of Beethoven's *Solemn Mass in D.*

1914
Congress passes the Clayton Anti-trust Act, providing organized labor with bargaining power in negotiations with management.

1915
American bankers, led by J.P. Morgan, agree to loan a record $500 million to the English and French Governments.

1917
The Chicago White Sox defeat the New York Giants in six games, to win the World Series.

1941
The Soviet army evacuates Odessa after holding out for several weeks behind lines, during World War II.

1943
Canadian troops from the Eighth Army take Vinchiaturo in Italy, during World War II.

1946
The St. Louis Cardinals defeat the Boston Red Sox in seven games, to win the World Series.

1946
Former German Field Marshal, Hermann Goering, commits suicide before his scheduled execution in Nuremberg, Germany.

1964
Aleksei Kosygin becomes Premier of the Soviet Union, after Nikita Krushchev is ousted.

1966
The Department of Transportation is created by act of Congress.

1970
The Baltimore Orioles defeat the Cincinnati Reds in five games, to win the World Series.

1970
President Nixon signs the Organized Crime Control Act, authorizing Federal funds to combat organized crime.

1972
The Water Pollution Control Act is passed by Congress, over President Nixon's Veto.

1974
Paul J. Flory of Stanford University wins the Nobel Prize in Chemistry for his work in developing new synthetic materials.

1977
You Light Up My Life by Debbie Boone becomes the number one record in the United States.

1978
Congress passes the National Energy Act of 1978, regulating natural gas prices and setting fuel efficiency standards.

October

1689
Count Frontenac returns to Canada from France with a plan to conquer New England, setting the stage for King William's War.

1701
Yale University is founded as Collegiate School, in Killingworth, Connecticut.

1710
The British capture Port Royal, Nova Scotia, during the second French and Indian War.

1829
The Tremont House in Boston becomes the first hotel equipped with private bathrooms.

1839
Joseph Saxton takes the earliest known surviving photograph in the United States with his home-made camera.

1859
A group led by abolitionist John Brown seizes the Federal arsenal at Harpers Ferry, Virginia.

1863
President Lincoln appoints General Ulysses S. Grant commander of the newly created Military Division of the Mississippi, during the Civil War.

1891
American sailors on leave from the U.S.S. *Baltimore* are attacked by a mob in Chile, threatening a war between the two countries.

1891
The first correspondence school in the United States opens in Scranton, Pennsylvania.

1900
England and Germany sign the Anglo-German Treaty, agreeing to support the "open door" policy of the United States.

1900
The Automobile Club of America is formed.

1901
President Roosevelt alienates the South when he invites Black leader, Booker T. Washington, to the White House.

1909
The Pittsburgh Pirates defeat the Detroit Tigers in seven games, to win the World Series.

1916
Margaret Sanger opens the first birth control clinic in Brooklyn, New York.

1925
Texas bans the teaching of evolutionary theory in its public schools.

1957
Two aluminum pellets sent aloft by the United States Air Force become the first American objects in space.

1962
The New York Yankees defeat the San Francisco Giants in seven games, to win the World Series.

1969
The New York Mets defeat the Baltimore Orioles in five games, to win the World Series.

1973
Maynard Jackson of Atlanta, Georgia, becomes the first Black mayor of a major Southern city.

October

1777
The British General Burgoyne surrenders over 5600 troops to General Horatio Gates at Saratoga, New York, during the Revolutionary War.

1855
The first conference of rabbis in the United States meets in Cleveland, Ohio.

1863
President Lincoln calls for an additional 300,000 volunteers for Union armies, during the Civil War.

1931
Chicago gangster Al Capone is convicted of tax evasion and sentenced to 11 years in prison.

1933
Scientist Albert Einstein arrives in the United States seeking refuge from the anti-semitism of Hitler's Germany.

1960
Quiz show contestant, Charles Van Doren, is arrested on charges of perjury after he stated to a grand jury that he did not receive answers beforehand to questions on *21*, the popular quiz show.

1971
The Pittsburgh Pirates defeat the Baltimore Orioles in seven games, to win the World Series.

1978
Arno A. Penzias and Robert W. Wilson win the Nobel Price in Physics for their discovery of weak electromagnetic radiation.

1988
Gertrude B. Elion and George H. Hitchings win a share of the Nobel Prize in Medicine for their discoveries of principles for drug treatment.

British General Burgoyne's surrender

October

1648
The "Shoomakers of Boston" become the first labor organization in America.

1685
French settlers begin arriving in South Carolina after King Louis XIV revokes the Edict of Nantes, which guaranteed religious freedom to Protestants.

1770
The Cherokee Indians sign the Treaty of Lochobar, moving the Virginia boundary line further west.

1790
The Ohio Indians attack an expedition of Americans near Fort Wayne, Indiana, beginning hostilities in the Northwest Territories.

1862
Confederate cavalryman John Hunt Morgan routs Union cavalry forces and occupies Lexington, Kentucky, during the Civil War.

1939
President Roosevelt orders all United States ports closed to submarines of belligerent nations.

1951
Dr. Max Theiler of the Rockefeller Institute wins the Nobel Prize in Medicine for his development of a yellow fever vaccine.

1955
Scientists at the University of California discover a new atomic subparticle, the antiproton.

1962
Dr. James Watson of Harvard University wins a share of the Nobel Prize in Medicine for his discovery of the molecular structure of DNA.

1968
Bob Beamon sets a world outdoor record of 29' 2½ " in the long jump.

1969
The Department of Health, Education and Welfare announces a ban on the use of cyclomates.

1976
William N. Lipscomb, Jr. of Harvard University wins the Nobel Prize in Chemistry for his studies on the structure of boranes.

1977
New York Yankees outfielder Reggie Jackson hits a record three home runs in a World Series game, tying Babe Ruth's record.

Bob Beamon long jumping at the Olympics

October

1781
The British under General Cornwallis surrender their 8000 man army at Yorktown, Virginia, ending major hostilities, during the Revolutionary War.

1863
Union cavalry, commanded by General Judson Kilpatrick, are defeated by Confederate cavalry, under General Jeb Stuart, at Buckland Mills, Virginia, during the Civil War.

1864
In the northernmost action of the Civil War, Lieutenant General Bennet Young leads a Confederate force on a raid into St. Albans, Vermont.

1939
Germany incorporates western Poland into the Reich and establishes the first Jewish ghetto in Lublin, during World War II.

1941
Joseph Stalin announces that he is remaining in Moscow to defend the city from German attacks, during World War II.

1959
The Miracle Worker by William Gibson opens at the Playhouse in New York.

1987
The New York Stock Exchange Dow Jones Industrial average falls a record 508 points in the worst stock market crash in history.

1988
Leon M. Lederman, Melvin Schwartz, and Jack Steinberger win the Nobel Prize in Physics for their work with laboratory made neutrino beams.

Traders watching the Dow Jones Industrials

October

1864
President Lincoln issues a proclamation making the last Thursday in November a day of Thanksgiving.

1928
The Republican Party coins the phrase, "a chicken in every pot..."

1933
Thomas Hunt Morgan wins the Nobel Prize in Medicine for his discovery of the chromosome link in heredity.

1942
Congress passes a tax bill designed to raise a record $6.8 billion, during World War II.

1944
General Douglas MacArthur returns to the Philippines, as United States forces land at Leyte, during World War II.

1947
The House Un-American Activities Committee begins its investigation into Communist infiltration of the entertainment industry.

1964
Herbert Hoover, thirty-first President of the United States, dies in New York.

1968
The United States Olympic Team sets a world outdoor record of 2:56.16 for the 4x400 meter relay.

1972
John Bardeen, Leon N. Cooper, and John R. Schrieffer win the Nobel Prize in Physics for their development of the theory of super-conductivity.

1982
The St. Louis Cardinals defeat the Milwaukee Brewers in seven games, to win the World Series.

General MacArthur returning to the Philippines

October

1519
Portuguese explorer Ferdinand Magellan enters the strait named after him, while searching for a route to the West Indies.

1769
A group of Spanish explorers discover San Francisco Bay.

1861
Nineteen hundred Union soldiers are killed at Balls Bluff in Leesburg, Virginia, after being ambushed by the Confederates, during the Civil War.

1867
Leaders of the Southern Plains tribes sign a peace treaty with a congressional commission at Medicine Lodge Creek in southwestern Kansas, ending the First Sioux War.

Magellan crossing the Strait

1907
A run on the Knickerbocker Trust Company in New York causes a national financial panic.

1915
The American Telephone & Telegraph Company makes the first transatlantic transmission of speech, from Arlington, Virginia, to Paris.

1917
The first American troops arrive at the front lines at Sommervillier, France, during World War I.

1918
Margaret B. Owne sets a speed typing record of 170 words per minute in New York.

1944
The Allies take Aachen, Germany, after 7 days of house-to-house fighting, during World War II.

1959
The Solomon R. Guggenheim Museum, designed by Frank Lloyd Wright, opens in New York.

1970
Dr. Norman E. Borlaug wins the Nobel Peace Prize for his work in helping Third World nations boost food production.

1972
My Ding-a-Ling becomes Chuck Berry's only number one record in the United States.

1973
The Oakland Athletics defeat the New York Mets in seven games, to win the World Series.

1979
Roy Green of the St. Louis Cardinals runs back a kickoff 106 yards, an NFL record, in a game against the Dallas Cowboys.

October

1746
Princeton University is founded as the College of New Jersey.

1784
All territory west of the Niagara River is ceded to the United States by the Six Iroquois Nations, in the Treaty of Fort Stanwix.

1836
Sam Houston becomes the first President of the Republic of Texas.

1861
The Confederacy establishes the Department of Virginia with General Joseph E. Johnston in command, during the Civil War.

1864
Confederate forces commanded by General Sterling Price attack Union positions near Independence, Missouri, during the Civil War.

1883
The Metropolitan Opera House opens in New York with a performance of Gounod's *Faust*.

1883
The first New York Horse Show opens at Gilmore's Gardens in New York.

1903
In a bitter labor dispute, the Amalgamated Copper Company of Montana shuts down, putting more than half of the wage earners in Montana out of work.

1962
President Kennedy reveals the existence of missile sites in Cuba in a national television address.

1972
The Oakland Athletics defeat the Cincinnati Reds in seven games, to win the World Series.

The first New York Horse Show

October

1850
The first national women's rights convention is held, in Worcester, Massachusetts.

1855
The Kansas Free State sets up the Topeka Constitution outlawing slavery in the territory and giving Kansas two governments.

1864
Confederate forces, commanded by General Sterling Price, are forced to retreat after an attack by Union troops, commanded by General Samuel Curtis, at the Battle of Westport, Missouri, during the Civil War.

1910
The Philadelphia Athletics defeat the Chicago Cubs in five games, to win the World Series.

1924
President Coolidge delivers a speech in the first national radio network broadcast in the United States.

1952
Dr. Selman A. Waksman of Rutgers University wins the Nobel Prize in Medicine for his discovery of streptomycin.

1961
Runaround Sue by Dion and the Belmonts becomes the number one record in the United States.

1970
Gary Gabelich sets a new land speed record of 622.4 mph at the Bonneville Salt Flats in Utah.

1973
Ivar Giaver of the General Electric Company wins a share of the Nobel Prize in Physics for his work in microelectronics.

1983
When a truck loaded with explosives blows up outside a building at their headquarters in Beirut, Lebanon, 241 United States Marines are killed.

Women's rights convention

October

1861
The first transcontinental telegraph message is sent from San Francisco to Washington, D.C.

1862
Major General William S. Rosecrans replaces General Don Carlos Buell as commander of Union forces in Kentucky, during the Civil War.

1864
General William T. Sherman assumes command of the Union Army of the Tennessee, during the Civil War.

1910
Naughty Marietta by Victor Herbert opens in Syracuse, New York.

1931
The George Washington Bridge opens, linking New York and New Jersey.

1940
The Fair Labor Standards Act goes into effect, establishing the 40-hour work week.

1941
The German Army takes Kharkov in the Soviet Union, during World War II.

1949
The permanent headquarters of the United Nations opens, in New York.

1962
President Kennedy authorizes a naval blockade of Cuba to halt Soviet military shipments.

1974
Equus by Peter Shaffer opens at the Plymouth Theatre in New York.

Opening ceremonies at the George Washington Bridge

October

1812

The United States frigate, *United States*, commanded by Captain Stephen Decatur, captures the British frigate, *Macedonian*, off the Madeira Islands, during the War of 1812.

1813

An American force commanded by General Wade Hampton defeats a British force at the Battle of Chateugay, near Montreal, during the War of 1812.

1850

The Southern Rights Association is established, with its goal the end of slavery.

1867

Maimonides College in Philadelphia becomes the first rabbinical school in the United States.

1926

The Supreme Court rules that the President has the authority to remove executive officers.

1939

Albert Brandt of Lockport, New York, scores a record 886 for three games in the ABC league bowling tournament.

1957

Gangster Albert Anastasia is shot and killed by two gunmen at a barber shop in New York.

1962

John Steinbeck wins the Nobel Prize for Literature for his entire body of works.

1983

United States forces invade Grenada after a bloody coup by pro-Cuban Marxists threatens American students on the island.

1987

The Minnesota Twins defeat the St. Louis Cardinals in seven games, to win the World Series.

Hand-to-hand combat during the War of 1812

October

1825

The Erie Canal, connecting Lake Erie with the Hudson River, officially opens.

1861

Union troops commanded by General Kelley take Romney in western Virginia, during the Civil War.

1881

Marshal Virgil Earp, along with his brother Wyatt and "Doc" Holliday, attack and kill three men at the OK Corral in Tombstone, Arizona Territory.

1911

The Philadelphia Athletics defeat the New York Giants in six games, to win the World Series.

1931

Mourning Becomes Electra by Eugene O'Neil opens at the Guild Theatre in New York.

1944

The Battle of Leyte Gulf ends with the defeat of the Japanese, the largest naval battle of World War II.

1959

Emilio Segre and Owen Chamberlain of the University of California win the Nobel Prize in Physics for their discovery of the antiproton.

1971

Bobby Fischer becomes the first American to qualify for the world chess championship.

1975

President Anwar el-Sadat becomes the first Egyptian president to visit the United States.

1982

President Reagan announces a record $110 billion budget deficit for the fiscal year 1982.

The gunfight at the OK Corral

1492
Christopher Columbus discovers Cuba.

1787
The Federalist, a series of essays on political theory, written by Thomas Jefferson, Alexander Hamilton, James Madison, and others, begins publication.

1795
Spain agrees to relinquish two forts on the Mississippi River and open it up to navigation, in the Treaty of San Lorenz.

1810
President Madison annexes West Florida.

1858
Theodore Roosevelt, twenty-sixth President of the United States, is born in New York.

1869
Two hundred people are killed in a fire aboard the steamboat, *Stonewall*, on the Ohio River.

1873
General E.R.S. Canby is killed by Modoc Indians, led by Captain Jack, after the failure of their negotiations regarding Indian settlements.

1904
The first section of the New York City subway system opens.

1917
Violinist Jascha Heifetz makes his American debut at Carnegie Hall in New York.

1985
The Kansas City Royals defeat the St. Louis Cardinals in seven games, to win the World Series.

Thomas Jefferson

October

1636
Harvard College is founded by the General Court of Massachusetts.

1776
The Continental Army led by General George Washington suffers heavy losses at the Battle of White Plains, New York, during the Revolutionary War.

1790
England and Spain negotiate the Nootka Sound Convention, reinforcing disputed British claims to territory in the Oregon region.

1863
Union cavalry occupy Arkadelphia near Little Rock, Arkansas, during the Civil War.

1954
Ernest Hemingway wins the Nobel Prize for Literature.

1962
Soviet Premier Khrushchev agrees to withdraw all missile bases from Cuba.

1962
Y.A. Tittle of the New York Giants throws an NFL record seven touchdown passes in a game against the Washington Redskins.

1965
The Gateway to the West monument is completed in St. Louis, at 630 feet, the world's tallest.

1972
President Nixon signs a bill establishing the Consumer Product Safety Commission.

1982
The Los Angeles Dodgers defeat the New York Yankees in six games, to win the World Series.

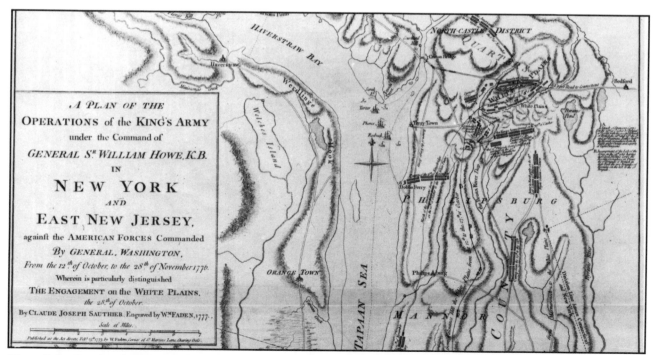

Map of the Battle of White Plains

October

1652

The Massachusetts Bay Colony declares itself an independent commonwealth.

1796

Captain Ebenezer Dorr becomes the first American to explore the California coast, aboard the *Otter.*

1923

Runnin' Wild opens on Broadway, introducing the Charleston.

1929

The New York Stock Market crashes, with a record of more than 16 million shares traded, on "Black Tuesday."

1945

The first ball-point pen in the United States goes on sale at Gimbel's department store in New York, selling for $12.50.

1950

Wally Triplett of the Detroit Lions gets an NFL record 294 yards in kickoff returns in a game against the Los Angeles Rams.

1956

Opera star Maria Callas makes her American debut in *Norma* at the Metropolitan Opera in New York.

1964

The 565 carat "Star of India" sapphire is stolen from the Museum of Natural History in New York.

1978

James Schelich becomes the first person to win a payoff from a slot machine, in Las Vegas, Nevada.

The Massachusetts Bay Colony

1735

John Adams, second President of the United States, is born in Braintree, Massachusetts.

1768

The Wesley Chapel in New York becomes the first Methodist Church in America.

1888

Paddy Duffy defeats Joey Giambra, to win the first welterweight boxing championship.

1930

Dr. Karl Landsteiner of the Rockefeller Institute wins the Nobel Prize in Medicine for his discovery of human blood groups.

1938

Orson Welles' radio performance of H.G. Wells' *War of the Worlds* causes panic when listeners believe there is an invasion from Mars.

1958

Joshua Lederberg and George W. Beadle win the Nobel Prize in Medicine for their studies of the genetic organization of bacteria.

1968

Lars Onsager of Yale University wins the Nobel Prize in Chemistry for his work in thermodynamics.

1969

Dr. Murray Gell-Mann of the California Institute of Technology wins the Nobel Prize in Physics for his work in elementary particles.

1974

Muhammad Ali knocks out George Foreman in the 8th round, to win the heavyweight boxing championship.

Orson Welles broadcasting *War of the Worlds*

1753
Governor Robert Dinwiddie, of Virginia, sends a force led by George Washington to demand French withdrawal from the Ohio Territory.

1861
Union General Winfield Scott, hero of the War of 1812 and the Mexican War, retires as commander in chief of the United States Army.

1864
Nevada joins the Union as the thirty-sixth state.

1873
The United States steamer, *Virginius*, is captured by a Spanish gunboat because it is carrying supplies to Cuban revolutionaries.

1932
The Governor of Nevada orders a 12-day banking holiday in an effort to save the State's banks.

1952
The United States detonates the first experimental H-bomb, on the Pacific atoll of Eniwetok.

1956
Auntie Mame by Jerome Lawrence opens at the Broadhurst Theatre in New York.

1957
Dr. Tsung Dao Lee of Columbia University wins the Nobel Prize in Physics for his study of subatomic particles.

1961
Robert Fitzgerald wins the first Bollingen Prize for translation, for Homer's *Odyssey*.

Washington's mission to the French

The explosion of an H-bomb

November

1743
French explorer Pierre de la Verendrye reaches the Rocky Mountains.

1784
Georgia moves its boundaries west in a treaty with the Creek Indians.

1788
The Congress under the Articles of Confederation adjourns, leaving the United States temporarily without a central Government.

1861
President Lincoln names General George B. McClellan commander in chief of the United States Army, during the Civil War.

1879
Thomas Alva Edison of Menlo Park, New Jersey, is awarded a patent for the first electric lamp.

1890
Mississippi becomes the first state to put restrictions on Black suffrage.

1895
The American Motor League becomes the first motoring association in the United States.

1913
The first Army-Notre Dame football game is won by Notre Dame, 35-10.

1918
One hundred people are killed in a subway derailment on the Brighton Beach line in Brooklyn, New York.

1944
Harvey by Mary Coyle Chase opens at the Forty-Eighth Street Theatre in New York.

1950
President Truman is unhurt when two Puerto Rican nationalists kill a White House guard in an unsuccessful assassination attempt.

1956
William Shockley, Walter Brattain, and John Bardeen of Bell Telephone Laboratories win the Nobel Prize in Physics for their discovery of the transistor effect.

1957
The Mackinac Straits Bridge opens, connecting Michigan's upper and lower peninsulas and becoming the longest suspension bridge in the world.

Edison's electric generator

November

1783
George Washington issues his "Farewell Address to the Army," in Rocky Hill, New Jersey.

1795
James Polk, eleventh President of the United States, is born in North Carolina.

1865
Warren G. Harding, twenty-ninth President of the United States, is born in Corsica, Ohio.

1889
North and South Dakota join the Union as the thirty-ninth and fortieth states.

1903
The United States Navy prevents Columbia from landing troops in Panama.

1904
Evangeline Booth is made commander of the Salvation Army of the United States.

1914
England declares the entire North Sea a military area, subjecting neutral shipping to seizures, during World War I.

1921
The American Birth Control League is formed by Margaret Sanger and Mary Ward Dennett.

1929
The Embassy in New York becomes the first theater to show newsreels in the United States.

1950
The Columbia Broadcasting System begins the first color television broadcasts in the United States.

1983
Congress designates the third Monday in January as a Federal holiday, honoring Dr. Martin Luther King, Jr.

Washington's Farewell Address

1762

King Louis XV of France gives Spain all French territory west of the Mississippi in the secret Treaty of Fountainebleau.

1900

The first automobile show in the United States opens, at Madison Square Garden, New York.

1917

German forces attack American troops near the Rhine-Marne Canal in France, the first engagement of World War I for American forces.

1927

A Connecticut Yankee, by Richard Rodgers and Lorenz Hart, opens at the Vanderbilt Theatre in New York.

1930

All Quiet on the Western Front wins the Academy Award for Best Picture of 1929-1930.

1941

Joseph Grew, the United States Ambassador to Japan, cables Washington, D.C. that the Japanese may be planning a surprise attack on the United States.

1960

Willard F. Libby of the University of California wins the Nobel Prize in Physics for his discovery of a method of radioactive carbon dating.

1966

President Johnson signs the Clean Waters Restoration Act.

1973

Mariner 10 becomes the first United States probe of the planet Mercury.

1986

A Lebanese magazine reveals that the United States has been secretly selling arms to Iran, beginning the Iran-Contra affair.

The first New York Automobile Show

November

4

1862
Richard J. Gatling is awarded a patent for the Gatling Gun, a rapid fire cannon.

1864
Confederate forces commanded by General Nathan Bedford Forrest attack Union supply transports at Johnsonville, Tennessee, during the Civil War.

1879
James J. Ritty of Dayton, Ohio, is awarded a patent for the first cash register.

1937
Golden Boy by Clifford Odets opens at the Belasco Theatre in New York.

1939
President Roosevelt signs the Neutrality Act of 1939, designed to allow the United States to aid its European allies, England and France, during World War II.

1942
The German 90th Light Division retreats after attacks by the British X Corps at El Alamein in North Africa, during World War II.

1954
Fanny by Joshua Logan opens at the Majestic Theatre in New York.

1967
American forces break a North Vietnamese assault at Loc Ninh, near the Cambodian border, during the Vietnam War.

1976
Reggie Jackson signs with the New York Yankees in baseball's first free-agent draft.

1979
The American Embassy in Teheran, Iran, is seized by militants, who take 65 American hostages.

Iranian students outside the United States Embassy

November

1653
The Iroquois Indians sign a peace treaty with the French, ending the Iroquois War in the Northwest Territories.

1768
Southwestern New York, western Pennsylvania, and parts of West Virginia, Tennessee, and Kentucky are sold by the Leàgue of Iroquois.

1862
President Lincoln names General Ambrose Burnside to replace General George B. McClellan as commander of the Army of the Potomac, during the Civil War.

1911
Calbraith P. Rodgers lands in Pasadena, California, completing the first cross-country flight.

1927
Walter Hagen wins his record fourth straight PGA golf tournament.

1930
Sinclair Lewis becomes the first American to win the Nobel Prize for Literature, for his novel, *Babbitt*.

1956
The United States arranges a ceasefire in the Sinai Peninsula to stop fighting by England, France, and Israel against Egypt.

1966
The Fantasticks becomes the longest running musical in New York.

1966
Last Train to Clarksville by the Monkees becomes the number one record in the United States.

Iroquois Indians attacking a village

1793

The British violate United States neutrality by ordering that any ship carrying French goods can be impounded.

1860

Abraham Lincoln is elected President of the United States.

1861

Jefferson Davis is elected President of the "permanent" Government of the Confederacy, running unopposed, during the Civil War.

1869

Rutgers beats Princeton 6-4 in the first intercollegiate football game in the United States.

1882

Famed English actress, Lillie Langtry, makes her American debut in Shakespeare's *As You Like It* at the Fifth Avenue Theatre in New York.

1903

The United States recognizes the independence of Panama.

1923

Colonel Jacob Schick is awarded a patent for the electric shaver.

1928

The first animated electric sign in the United States is installed on top of the Times Building in New York's Times Square.

1941

President Roosevelt announces that the United States will lend the Soviet Union $1 billion to finance the acquisition of military supplies, during World War II.

Princeton's football team in action

1811

A force of American soldiers commanded by William Henry Harrison defeats the Indians at the Tippecanoe River, in Indiana.

1836

California declares independence from Mexico.

1861

Union forces commanded by Lieutenant Thomas W. Sherman capture Port Royal Island along the South Carolina coast, during the Civil War.

1874

Harper's Weekly publishes the first political cartoon depicting an elephant to symbolize the Republican Party.

1915

Twenty-seven Americans are among the dead when an Austrian submarine sinks the Italian liner, *Ancona*.

1933

Ending 16 years of Tammany Hall control over local politics, Fiorello LaGuardia is elected mayor of New York City.

1940

A suspension bridge over Puget Sound in Washington collapses due to wind vibration.

1942

United States forces commanded by General Dwight D. Eisenhower land in North Africa, during World War II.

1944

President Roosevelt is reelected for an unprecedented fourth term.

1959

The 116-day steel strike ends, becoming the longest strike in the United States.

The Battle of Tippecanoe

November

1805
The Lewis and Clark expedition reaches the Pacific Ocean.

1861
Confederate Commissioners James Mason and John Slidell, aboard the British ship, *Trent*, are seized by the USS *San Jacinto*, commanded by Captain Charles Wilkes, in the Bahamas, during the Civil War.

1880
Noted French actress Sarah Bernhardt makes her American debut at Booth's Theatre in New York.

1884
The first newspaper syndicate is formed by Sidney McClure.

1889
Montana joins the Union as the forty-first state.

1905
The Chicago and Northwestern Railroad's *Overland Limited* becomes the first train to have electric lamps.

1910
Victor L. Berger of Dutchess County, in New York, becomes the first Socialist elected to Congress.

1929
The Museum of Modern Art opens in New York.

1933
The Civil Works Administration is established, with $400 million set aside to provide employment for 4 million people.

1939
Life With Father, by Howard Lindsay and Russel Crouse, opens at the Empire Theatre in New York.

Sarah Bernhardt

November

1861
The Confederate raider, *Nashville*, captures and burns the Union clipper ship, *Harvey Birch*, in the Atlantic Ocean, during the Civil War.

1862
Major General Ambrose Burnside assumes command of the Army of the Potomac, during the Civil War.

1906
Theodore Roosevelt becomes the first President to visit a foreign country, sailing on the battleship, U.S.S. *Louisiana*, to Panama.

1918
Kaiser Wilhelm II of Germany abdicates his throne.

1935
John L. Lewis establishes the Committee for Industrial Organization after breaking away from the American Federation of Labor.

1938
Jewish homes and businesses are attacked by Nazi thugs in Germany on the *Kristallnacht*.

1939
Ernest Orlando of the University of California wins the Nobel Prize in Physics for his development of the cyclotron.

1941
The German army takes Tikhvin in the Soviet Union, cutting the rail route into the city, during World War II.

1942
The Australian 25th Brigade takes Gorari in New Guinea, cutting off Japanese forces, during World War II.

1965
New York, Pennsylvania, and parts of New England and New Jersey are without power for over 13 hours after the failure of a generating plant near Niagara Falls, New York.

General Ambrose E. Burnside

November

1766
Rutgers University is established in New Brunswick, New Jersey.

1775
The Continental Congress organizes two battalions of marines, during the Revolutionary War.

1799
Napoleon Bonaparte becomes First Consul of France.

1808
The Osage Indians sign the Osage Treaty with the United States, ceding all of their land in present-day Missouri and Arkansas.

1845
Representative John Slidell of Louisiana is sent to Mexico to attempt to restore diplomatic relations.

1865
Confederate Captain Henry Wirz, commandant of the Andersonville prisoner of war camp, is executed for mistreatment of Union soldiers, during the Civil War.

1911
The Carnegie Foundation is established by Andrew Carnegie, becoming the first major charitable foundation in the United States.

1927
Arthur H. Compton of the University of Chicago is awarded a share of the Nobel Prize in Physics for his discovery of the Compton effect, which occurs when gamma rays collide with x-rays.

1931
Cimarron wins the Academy Award for Best Picture of 1931.

1938
The Good Earth by Pearl S. Buck wins the Nobel Prize for Literature.

1950
William Faulkner wins the Nobel Prize in Literature.

1951
The New Jersey Bell System inaugurates the first transcontinental direct-dial telephone service.

1975
The parents of comatose Karen Anne Quinlan lose a bid in New Jersey Supreme Court to have their daughter's respirator turned off.

The first United States Marines

November

11

1831
Virginia slave, Nat Turner, is hanged for killing his master and leading a slave uprising.

1865
Mary E. Walker, the first woman surgeon in the United States Army, becomes the first woman to be awarded the Medal of Honor.

1868
The New York Athletic Club holds the first indoor track meet in the United States, at the Empire Skating Rink in New York.

1885
Stanford University is founded in Palo Alto, California.

1889
Washington joins the Union as the forty-second state.

1918
The German Government signs an armistice treaty in a railroad car in the forest of Compiegne, France, ending World War I.

1918
Private Harry Gunther of Baltimore becomes the last American killed during World War I.

1921
After lying in state at the Capitol, the unknown soldier of World War I is buried at Arlington National Cemetery in Virginia.

1924
Desire Under the Elms by Eugene O'Neill opens at the Greenwich Village Theatre in New York.

1925
Physicist Robert A. Millikan of the California Institute of Technology announces the isolation of cosmic rays.

The Germans surrendering in France

November

1896
The Amateur Hockey League becomes the first ice hockey league in the United States.

1921
In an attempt to reduce armaments, the major naval powers begin the Conference for Limitation of Armaments, in Washington, D.C.

1936
The San Francisco-Oakland Bridge opens, becoming the longest bridge in the United States.

1936
Eugene O'Neil wins the Nobel Prize for Literature.

1942
President Roosevelt lowers the draft age to 18, during World War II.

1945
Former Secretary of State Cordell Hull wins the Nobel Peace Prize for his work in establishing the United Nations.

1946
The first drive-in bank in the United States is opened by the Exchange National Bank of Chicago.

1970
Sleuth by Anthony Shaffer opens at the Music Box Theatre in New York.

1980
Voyager I flies within 77,000 miles of the planet Saturn, discovering many more rings than previously known.

1983
The Cabbage Patch doll is created in Haywood, California.

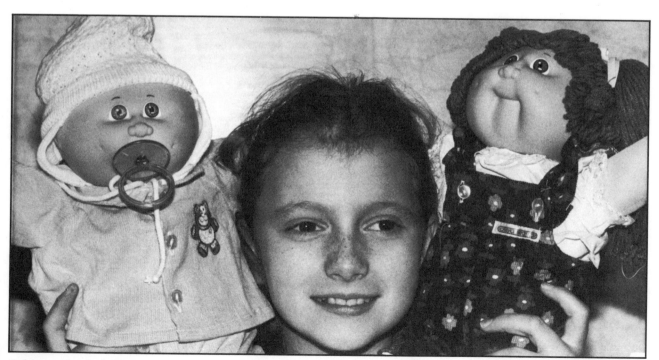

Cabbage Patch dolls

1749
The University of Pennsylvania is established in Philadelphia.

1775
American Brigadier General Richard Montgomery occupies Montreal, during the Revolutionary War.

1840
The Republic of Texas and England sign a commercial treaty.

1909
President Taft's Secretary of the Interior, Richard A. Ballinger, is forced to resign, after charges of favoritism in granting claims to Alaskan coal lands.

1909
In an explosion at the St. Paul mine in Cherry, Illinois, 259 miners are killed.

1927
The Holland Tunnel, connecting New York and New Jersey, opens, becoming the first underwater automobile tunnel in the United States.

1946
The first successful artificial seeding of clouds to produce rain takes place over Mount Graylock, Massachusetts.

1956
The Supreme Court rules that segregation on interstate buses is unconstitutional.

1967
Hair, by James Rado, Gerome Ragni, and Galt MacDermot, opens at the Public Theater in New York.

1977
The last installment of the comic strip *L'il Abner* appears.

The first car through the Holland Tunnel

November

1910
Pilot Eugene Ely becomes the first man to take off in an airplane from the deck of a ship, the United States light cruiser, *Birmingham*.

1940
Factories and many historic buildings are destroyed as the German Air Force attacks Coventry, England, during World War II.

1943
Sid Luckman of the Chicago Bears throws an NFL record seven touchdown passes in a game against the New York Giants.

1946
John Raleigh Mott and Emily Greene Balch win the Nobel Peace Prize, he for his work with the YMCA relief programs for prisoners of war, and she for her work with the Women's International League for Peace and Freedom.

1946
Percy Williams Bridgeman of Harvard University wins the Nobel Prize in Physics for his work in high-pressure physics.

1961
President Kennedy increases the number of United States advisors in South Vietnam from 1000 to 16,000.

1967
Congress passes the Air Quality Act, providing over $428 million to fight air pollution.

1972
The Dow Jones Index closes above 1000 for the first time.

1987
Investor Ivan F. Boesky agrees to pay the Government $100 million as a penalty for illegal insider trading activities.

Sid Luckman (left) in action

November

1777
The Continental Congress adopts the Articles of Confederation.

1796
France announces the suspension of diplomatic relations with the United States.

1806
The *Literary Cabinet*, published at Yale University, becomes the first college magazine.

1806
American explorer Zebulon Pike discovers Pike's Peak, in present-day Colorado.

1827
The Creek Indians cede their remaining land in the Southeast to the United States.

The American Navy in action against the Japanese

1900
The Carnegie Institute of Technology is established in Pittsburgh, Pennsylvania.

1901
Miller Reese Hutchinson of New York is awarded a patent for the first electric hearing aid.

1907
The comic strip *Mutt and Jeff* is published in the *San Francisco Chronicle*.

1922
Dr. Alexis Carrel announces his discovery of white corpuscles, the agents that help prevent the spread of infections.

1934
Harold Clayton Urey wins the Nobel Prize in Chemistry for his discovery of deuterium, an isotope of hydrogen.

1942
The United States fleet defeats the Japanese task force off the coast of Guadalcanal, during World War II.

1961
The Metropolitan Museum of Art in New York purchases Rembrandt's *Aristotle Contemplating the Bust of Homer* for a record $2.3 million.

1964
Len Dawson of the Kansas City Chiefs fumbles an AFL record seven times in a game against the San Diego Chargers.

1969
Two hundred fifty thousand people take part in an antiwar rally in Washington, D.C., to protest United States involvement in the Vietnam War.

1776
The flag of the United States is saluted for the first time at St. Eustatius, Dutch West Indies.

1776
The British take over 2000 prisoners after capturing Fort Washington on Manhattan Island, during the Revolutionary War.

1813
The British extend their naval blockade of the Atlantic coast to Long Island, during the War of 1812.

1864
The Union Army, commanded by General William T. Sherman, begins a march to the sea from Atlanta in order to cut the Confederacy in two, during the Civil War.

1887
Jack McAuliff defeats Jem Carney, to win the first lightweight boxing championship.

1907
Oklahoma joins the Union as the forty-sixth state.

1933
The United States announces the resumption of diplomatic relations with Russia.

1952
The United States Atomic Energy Commission announces the completion of hydrogen bomb testing in the Marshall Islands.

1973
President Nixon signs the Alaska Pipeline Act, authorizing the construction of the Alaska Pipeline from the North Slope to Valdez.

General Sherman's troops on the march

1734
John Peter Zenger, editor of the *New York Weekly Journal*, is imprisoned for articles critical of New York Governor, William Cosby.

1744
The Philadelphia Troop of Light Horse becomes the first military group in the colonies.

1764
Chief Pontiac's forces surrender at the Muskingham River in the Ohio Territory, during the French and Indian War.

1800
The first Congress to sit in Washington convenes.

1856
Fort Buchanan is established as the first military post, on land acquired by the United States in the Gadsden Purchase.

1880
The United States and China sign the Chinese Exclusion Treaty, giving the United States the right to regulate the immigration of Chinese nationals.

1889
The Union Pacific Railroad inaugurates service between Chicago; Portland, Oregon; and San Francisco.

1962
Big Girls Don't Cry by The Four Seasons becomes the number one record in the United States.

1969
The United States and the Soviet Union open the first round of the Strategic Arms Limitation Talks in Helsinki, Finland.

The Capitol of the United States

November

1820
American sailor Nathaniel B. Palmer, Captain of the sloop, *Hero*, discovers Antarctica.

1883
Congress divides the United States into standard time zones.

1886
Chester A. Arthur, twenty-first President of the United States, dies in New York.

1901
The United States and England sign the Hay-Pauncefote Treaty, giving the United States control of the canal linking the Atlantic and Pacific Oceans.

1903
The United States signs the Hay-Bunau-Varilla Treaty, giving the United States complete control over the Panama Canal Zone.

1909
United States warships are sent to Nicaragua after two Americans, along with hundreds of Nicaraguan revolutionaries, are killed by dictator Jose Santos Zelaya.

1932
Grand Hotel wins the Academy Award for Best Picture of 1931.

1933
Roberta by Jerome Kern opens at the New Amsterdam Theatre in New York.

1966
The United States Roman Catholic Church announces it will no longer require abstinence from eating meat on Fridays, except during Lent.

1977
The first National Women's Conference in Houston, Texas, draws 1442 delegates, calling for the passage of an Equal Rights Amendment.

Nat Palmer in Antarctica

1831
James A. Garfield, twentieth President of the United States, is born in Ohio.

1863
President Lincoln delivers his Gettysburg Address at the military cemetery on the Gettysburg battlefield.

1893
The first color newspaper supplement is published in the *New York World*.

1919
The United States Senate refuses to ratify the treaty of Versailles disagreements with its allies.

1941
The British 7th Armoured Division suffers heavy casualties during an attack by the German 21st Panzer Brigade in North Africa, during World War II.

1958
Tom Dooley by the Kingston Trio becomes the number one record in the United States.

1961
New York Governor Nelson Rockefeller's son Michael disappears off the coast of New Guinea.

1966
Michigan State and Notre Dame, both undefeated, play a 10-10 tie in a football game, in East Lansing, Michigan.

1969
Astronauts Charles Conrad, Jr. and Alan L. Bean become the third and fourth men to walk on the Moon during the Apollo 12 mission.

Lincoln at Gettysburg

November

1789
New Jersey becomes the first state to ratify the Bill of Rights.

1798
The American schooner, *Retaliation*, is seized by the French off the coast of Guadaloupe.

1811
Construction of the Cumberland Road, to connect Cumberland, Maryland, with Wheeling, West Virginia, begins.

1817
Florida Indians are attacked by settlers retaliating for Indian raids, beginning the First Seminole War.

1919
The first municipal airport in the United States opens in Tucson, Arizona.

1920
President Woodrow Wilson wins the Nobel Peace Prize for his efforts in promoting the League of Nations.

1941
The British 4th Armoured Brigade is attacked by the German 15th Panzer Brigade in North Africa, suffering heavy casualties, during World War II.

1943
United States forces land on Tarawa in the Gilbert Islands, during World War II.

1945
The trial of 21 German war criminals begins in Nuremberg, Germany.

1948
The United States Army Signal Corps sets a balloon altitude record of 140,000 feet.

1962
President Kennedy lifts the naval blockade of Cuba, after being assured by Soviet Premier Khrushchev that all missiles will be removed within 30 days.

1965
Two hundred forty American troops are killed in battles in the Iadrang Valley of South Vietnam, during the Vietnam War.

1966
Cabaret, by John Kander and Fred Ebb, opens at the Broadhurst Theatre in New York.

1968
Seventy-eight miners are killed in a coal mine explosion in Farmington, West Virginia.

1969
The Department of Agriculture bans the use of DDT in residential areas.

1969
A group of Indians representing more than 20 tribes seize Alcatraz Island in San Francisco Bay, calling for the establishment of an educational center there.

1977
Walter Payton of the Chicago Bears rushes for an NFL record 275 yards in a game against the Minnesota Vikings.

1985
President Reagan and Soviet General Secretary Gorbachev conduct their first summit meeting in Geneva, Switzerland.

1620
Pilgrims sign the Mayflower Compact, the first social contract for a New England colony.

1789
North Carolina becomes the twelfth state to ratify the Constitution.

1862
James A. Seddon is appointed Confederate Secretary of War by President Jefferson Davis, during the Civil War.

1934
Anything Goes, featuring music by Cole Porter, opens at the Alvin Theatre in New York.

1940
Greek forces enter Koritza, capturing over 2,000 Italians, during World War II.

1964
The Verrazano-Narrows Bridge connecting Staten Island with Brooklyn opens, becoming the longest suspension bridge in the world.

1974
Congress passes the Freedom of Information Act, expanding public access to Government files.

1979
One United States marine is killed as the American Embassy in Islamabad, Pakistan, is besieged.

1980
Eighty-four people are killed in a fire at the MGM Grand Hotel in Las Vegas, Nevada.

1981
Physical by Olivia Newton-John becomes the number one record in the United States.

Signing the Mayflower Compact

November

1704

The first Delaware assembly convenes in New Castle.

1924

The University of California plays Stanford University in the first football game watched by over 100,000 people.

1935

Pan American Airways inaugurates service from San Francisco to Manila in the Philippines.

1950

The Fort Wayne Pistons beat the Minneapolis Lakers by a score of 19-18, the lowest scoring game in NBA history.

1961

A Man for All Seasons by Robert Bolt opens at the ANTA Theatre in New York.

1963

John F. Kennedy, twenty-fifth President of the United States, dies after being shot by Lee Harvey Oswald while driving in a motorcade in Dallas, Texas.

1967

United States forces take Hill 875 near Dak To after a bloody 19-day assault, during the Vietnam War.

1969

Scientists at Harvard University announce the isolation of a single gene, the basic unit of heredity.

1981

Kellen Winslow of the San Diego Chargers catches an NFL record five touchdown passes in a game against the Oakland Raiders.

Still from a recording of the Kennedy assassination

November

1804
Franklin Pierce, fourteenth President of the United States, is born in Hillsboro, New Hampshire.

1863
The Confederate siege of Chattanooga, Tennessee, is broken by Union forces commanded by General Ulysses S. Grant, forcing the Confederates to evacuate the state, at the Battle of Chattanooga, during the Civil War.

1889
The first juke box is installed at the Palais Royal Saloon in San Francisco.

1903
Enrico Caruso makes his American debut at the Metropolitan Opera House in New York.

1914
United States forces are withdrawn from Mexico.

1936
The first practical application of fluorescent lighting is made at a dinner celebrating the United States Patent Office's centennial.

1941
The town of Klin in the Soviet Union is captured by German Panzer divisions, during World War II.

1970
The United States and Mexico sign a treaty settling long-standing border disputes.

1985
American scholar, Gary Taylor, discovers a previously unknown poem by William Shakespeare in the library at Oxford University, Oxford, England.

Union artillery at the Battle of Chattanooga

1784
Zachary Taylor, twelfth President of the United States, is born in Virginia County, New York.

1832
South Carolina declares the United States tariff null and void in a test of states' rights against the Federal Government.

1835
The Texas Provincial Government forms the Texas Rangers, a mounted police force.

1862
Confederate President Jefferson Davis appoints General Joseph E. Johnston commander of the Army of the West, during the Civil War.

1865
Mississippi establishes the Black Codes, a series of discriminatory measures against the newly freed Blacks.

1904
The first gallery to exhibit photographs is opened by Alfred Stieglitz and Edward Steichen in New York.

1953
Senator Joseph McCarthy accuses the former Truman Administration of "crawling" with Communists in a radio and television broadcast.

1960
Wilt Chamberlain of the Philadelphia Warriors gets an NBA record 55 rebounds in a game against the Boston Celtics.

1963
Jack Ruby shoots and kills President Kennedy's assassin, Lee Harvey Oswald, as he is being escorted by Dallas police, while millions watch on television.

The Texas Rangers

November

1758

The French blow up Fort Duquesne to prevent it from falling into the hands of the English, during the French and Indian War.

1783

The last British troops leave New York.

1863

The Union Army commanded by General Ulysses S. Grant storms Missionary Ridge in Tennessee, routing the Confederates under General Braxton Bragg, during the Civil War.

1864

Confederate raiders unsuccessfully attempt to burn New York, during the Civil War.

1876

An Army detachment commanded by Colonel Ranald Mackenzie attacks the Cheyenne village of Dull Knife in the Montana Territory, discovering numerous items belonging to General George Custer's massacred Seventh Cavalry.

1876

The Greenback Party is formed in Indianapolis with a platform that features the inflation of United States currency.

1941

The German Army captures Istra, northwest of Moscow, during World War II.

1942

The Greek resistance, led by British agents, blows up the viaduct along the Athens-Salonika railroad used by German General Rommel's troops, during World War II.

1943

Three Japanese ships are sunk off Cape St. George, New Britain, by an American destroyer force, during World War II.

1952

George Meany becomes the President of the American Federation of Labor.

The Battle of Missionary Ridge

1791
President Washington conducts the first Cabinet meeting.

1832
The New York & Harlem Railroad begins operating the first streetcar in the United States.

1855
Fifteen hundred pro-slavery Border Ruffians threaten Lawrence, Kansas, in the Wakarusa War.

1861
A convention in Wheeling in western Virginia votes to secede from Virginia and create a new state called West Virginia.

1863
The Union Army of the Potomac crosses the Rapidan River in Virginia, in an attempt to turn the right flank of the Confederate Army of Northern Virginia, commanded by General Robert E. Lee, during the Civil War.

1940
The Germans begin construction of a Jewish ghetto in Warsaw, Poland, during World War II.

1941
The United States demands that Japan withdraw from China and recognize the Chinese Nationalist Government.

1942
The British 78th Division drives the Germans out of Medjez el Bab in Tunisia, during World War II.

1955
Sixteen Tons by Tennessee Ernie Ford becomes the number one record in the United States.

1969
President Nixon signs a bill establishing a lottery for Selective Service draftees.

The first streetcar

November

1755
Joseph Salvador establishes the first Jewish settlement in America, in South Carolina.

1826
American explorer Jedediah Smith arrives in San Diego to become the first man to cross the Mohave Desert enroute to California.

1863
Confederate raider John Hunt Morgan escapes from the Ohio State Penitentiary, during the Civil War.

1868
The Seventh Cavalry, commanded by Lieutenant Colonel George Custer, attacks a Cheyenne Indian village on the Upper Washita River, killing Chief Black Kettle.

1873
The Hoosac Tunnel in western Massachusetts is completed, becoming the longest railroad tunnel in the United States.

1930
Former Secretary of State, Frank B. Kellogg, wins the Nobel Peace Prize for his role in negotiating the Kellogg-Briand Peace Pact of 1928.

1939
Key Largo by Maxwell Anderson opens at the Ethel Barrymore Theatre in New York.

1966
Charlie Gogolak of the Washington Redskins kicks an NFL record nine points after touchdowns in a game against the New York Giants.

1974
Louis B. Russel, Jr., dies in Richmond, Virginia, after surviving a record six years with a heart transplant.

1977
The Concorde SST makes its first landing in the United States at John F. Kennedy International Airport in New York.

The Concord landing at JFK International Airport

November

1519

Portuguese explorer Ferdinand Magellan reaches the Pacific Ocean, while searching for a route to the West Indies.

1775

The Continental Navy is established, during the Revolutionary War.

1785

The United States denies legitimacy to the state of Franklin and returns the territory to the Cherokee Indians.

1895

Charles and Frank Duryea win the first automobile race in the United States, from Chicago to Evanston, Illinois.

1925

The Grand Ole Opry opens in Nashville, Tennessee.

1928

An expedition led by Richard Byrd reaches the South Pole.

1929

Ernie Nevers of the Chicago Cardinals scores an NFL record 40 points in a game against the Chicago Bears.

1942

Four hundred eighty-seven people are killed in a fire at the Coconut Grove nightclub in Boston, one of the worst fires in the United States.

1957

Look Homeward Angel by Ketti Frings opens at the Ethel Barrymore Theatre in New York.

1964

Leader of the Pack by the Shangri-Las becomes the number one record in the United States.

Uniforms of the Continental Navy

1745
The French burn an English settlement at Saratoga, New York, during King George's War.

1760
Detroit falls to the English, during the French and Indian War.

1775
The British ship, *Nancy*, carrying guns and ammunition, is captured by the American cruiser, *Lee*, during the Revolutionary War.

1863
Confederate forces, commanded by General James Longstreet, are forced to withdraw after an unsuccessful assault on Union positions in Fort Sanders, Tennessee, during the Civil War.

1864
Union troops commanded by Colonel Chivington massacre a party of Cheyenne Indians in Sand Creek, Colorado.

1890
Navy beats Army 24-0 in their first annual football game.

1929
Lt. Commander Richard E. Byrd makes the first successful flight over the South Pole.

1941
Coffee rationing begins in the United States, during World War II.

1941
German tank forces commanded by General Reinhardt reach the Moscow-Volga Canal, during World War II.

1987
Venice Glen of the San Diego Chargers returns a pass interception an NFL record 103 yards in a game against the Denver Broncos.

Symbols of the Army and Navy football teams

1861
The British Government communicates its displeasure at the seizure of Confederate commissioners James Mason and John Slidell aboard the British ship, *Trent*.

1864
The Confederate Army of Tennessee commanded by General John Bell Hood launches a disastrous assault against Union positions, sustaining over 6200 casualties at the Battle of Franklin, Tennessee, during the Civil War.

1915
Sabotage is suspected in an explosion at the DuPont munitions plant in Wilmington, Delaware.

1917
The United States "Rainbow" Division arrives in France, with soldiers from every state in the Union.

1924
The Radio Corporation of America demonstrates the first wireless transmission of photographs, from London to New York.

1926
The Desert Song, an operetta by Oscar Hammerstein and Frank Mandel, opens at the Casino Theatre in New York.

1939
Russian forces invade Finland, beginning the Russo-Finnish War.

1956
Floyd Patterson knocks out Archie Moore in the 5th round, to win the heavyweight boxing championship.

1979
Sugar Ray Leonard stops Wilfredo Benitez in the 15th round, to win the welterweight boxing championship.

Union cavalry at the Battle of Franklin

1660
The English Parliament passes the first Navigation Act, designed to govern colonial trade.

1861
The United States gunboat *Penguin* captures the Confederate blockade runner *Albion* near Charleston, South Carolina, during the Civil War.

1903
The Great Train Robbery becomes the first western film.

1915
The United States requests that Germany remove its military attaches from its Embassy in Washington, D.C.

1918
American and British troops cross into Germany on their way to occupying Coblenz, during World War I.

1942
Nationwide gasoline rationing goes into effect, during World War II.

1943
The Teheran Conference in Iran ends, with President Roosevelt, British Prime Minister Churchill, and Soviet Premier Stalin setting a strategy for the invasion of Europe.

1955
Rosa Parks, a Black woman from Montgomery, Alabama, is arrested after refusing to give up her seat on a city bus, testing the city's racial segregation laws.

1958
Flower Drum Song, by Richard Rodgers and Oscar Hammerstein II, opens at the St. James Theatre in New York.

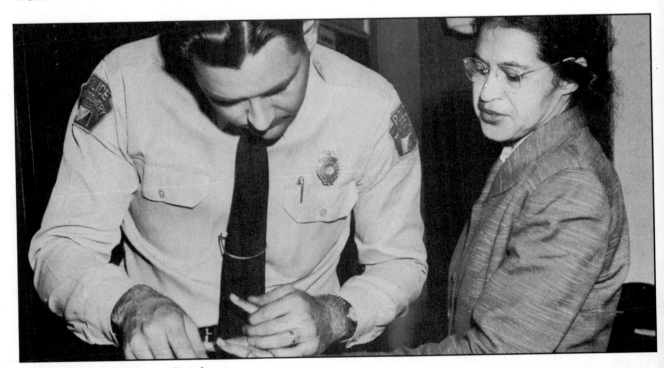

Rosa Parks being fingerprinted

1761

English Secretary of State, Lord Egremont, issues a proclamation requiring royal approval of all land grants in Indian territory.

1823

President Monroe presents his Monroe Doctrine to Congress, proclaiming that the Americas are no longer open to European colonization and interference.

1859

Abolitionist John Brown is hanged for murder, conspiracy, and treason, becoming a martyr in the Northern states.

1901

King Camp Gillette of Boston is awarded a patent for the first safety razor.

1908

The Federal Council of the Churches of Christ in America is established, in Philadelphia.

1924

The Student Prince, an operetta by Sigmund Romberg, opens at the Fifty-Ninth Street Theatre in New York.

1942

The first self-generated chain reaction of a uranium-graphite atomic pile takes place in a squash court at the University of Chicago.

1954

Senator Joseph McCarthy is condemned by a special session of the Senate for his conduct in Senate committees.

1961

Fidel Castro announces that Cuba will become a Communist nation.

1979

A mob attacks the American Embassy in Tripoli, Libya, damaging two floors.

1980

President Carter signs the Alaska National Interest Lands Conservation Act, preserving 56 million acres.

1982

Barney Clark of Des Moines, Iowa, receives the first artificial heart, at the Utah Medical Center in Salt Lake City.

1987

President Reagan and Prime Minister Brian Mulroney of Canada sign a free trade agreement.

President James Monroe

1775
The first official American flag is raised for the first time, aboard the flagship, *Alfred*.

1818
Illinois joins the Union as the twenty-first state.

1833
Oberlin Collegiate Institute in Oberlin, Ohio, becomes the first women's college in the United States.

1838
Republican Joshua Giddings of Ohio becomes the first abolitionist to enter the House of Representatives.

1863
Confederate forces evacuate Knoxville, leaving all of Tennessee under Union control, during the Civil War.

1868
The treason trial of former Confederate President Jefferson Davis begins in Richmond, Virginia.

1947
A Streetcar Named Desire by Tennessee Williams opens at the Ethel Barrymore Theatre in New York.

1950
Tom Fears of the Los Angeles Rams catches an NFL record 18 passes in a game against the Green Bay Packers.

1984
Seventeen hundred people are killed after an explosion at a Union Carbide chemical plant in Bhopal, India.

Raising the flag aboard the *Alfred*

December

4

1674
Father Marquette establishes a mission near present-day Chicago.

1865
Congress establishes a Joint Committee on Reconstruction with Senator Thaddeus Stevens of Pennsylvania as chairman.

1883
The Sons of the American Revolution is formed in New York.

1902
Gold is discovered on Columbia Mountain in Nevada, leading to the establishment of the Goldfield, Nevada, Mining District.

1918
President Wilson sails for Europe as head of the United States delegation to the Peace Conference.

1933
Tobacco Road by Jack Kirkland opens in New York.

1952
Walter P. Reuther is chosen President of the CIO.

1968
The American Medical Association formulates a new definition of death, to resolve controversies surrounding organ transplants.

1981
President Reagan authorizes the CIA to conduct covert intelligence operations.

Father Marquette with the Indians

December

5

1776
The Phi Beta Kappa fraternity is founded at the College of William and Mary.

1782
Martin Van Buren, eighth President of the United States, is born in Kinderhook, New York.

1792
George Washington is reelected President of the United States.

1865
Sir Henry Bessemer is awarded a patent for a method of converting iron into steel.

1906
Reverend Algernon S. Crapsey, of the St. Andrew's Protestant Episcopal Church in Rochester, New York, is convicted of heresy and expelled from the ministry.

1933
The Twenty-First Amendment is adopted, officially ending prohibition in the United States.

1941
Hitler orders a halt to the German offensive in the Soviet Union because of the growing weakness of the German forces there, during World War II.

1955
The AFL and CIO formally merge, headed by George Meany.

1964
Captain Roger H.C. Donlen becomes the first Vietnam Veteran to win the Congressional Medal of Honor.

Unloading beer in New York City

December

6

1790
Philadelphia becomes the Capital of the United States.

1825
President John Quincy Adams delivers the first annual presidential message to Congress.

1847
Representative Abraham Lincoln of Illinois takes his seat in the House of Representatives.

1864
President Lincoln names former Secretary of the Treasury, Salmon P. Chase, Chief Justice of the Supreme Court.

1869
The Colored National Labor Convention becomes the first national Black labor group in the United States.

1877
Thomas Alva Edison of Menlo Park, New Jersey, makes the first sound recording, a recital of "Mary Had A Little Lamb."

1907
In Monongah, West Virginia, 361 miners are killed in an explosion.

1922
An official Government message is broadcast over the radio for the first time.

1923
President Coolidge makes the first official presidential address to be broadcast over the radio.

1925
The John Simon Guggenheim Foundation is established to promote scholarship and the arts.

1933
A Federal judge lifts the ban on the previously censored *Ulysses* by James Joyce.

1956
Fidel Castro invades Cuba with a force of 82 men in an attempt to remove President Fulgencio Batista from power.

1973
Gerald R. Ford becomes the first vice president to take office under the terms of the Twenty-Fifth Amendment.

1987
John Telchik of the Philadelphia Eagles kicks an NFL record 15 punts in a game against the New York Giants.

Fidel Castro

December

1787
Delaware becomes the first state to ratify the Constitution.

1862
Union forces, commanded by General James Blunt, defeat the Confederates, under General Thomas Hindman, at the Battle of Prairie Grove, Arkansas, during the Civil War.

1874
Seventy Blacks are killed after protesting the ejection of a carpetbag sheriff, in Vicksburg, Mississippi.

1915
President Wilson calls for a standing army of 142,000 men, and a reserve of 400,000.

1917
The United States declares war on Austria-Hungary.

1931
The White House turns away hundreds of marchers with an employment-seeking petition as breadlines begin forming throughout the United States during the Depression.

1941
The United States battleships, *Arizona*, *California*, *Oklahoma*, and *Utah*, are sunk during a surprise attack by Japan on the United States naval base at Pearl Harbor, Hawaii.

1942
The Soviets gain bridgeheads over the River Chir and threaten German air bases in the Soviet Union, during World War II.

1946
In a fire at the Winecoff Hotel in Atlanta, Georgia, 127 people are killed.

The USS *Arizona* at Pearl Harbor

December

1863
President Lincoln issues a proclamation of amnesty and reconstruction, offering to pardon anyone taking part in the rebellion who will take a loyalty oath.

1887
The American Federation of Labor is established, with Samuel Gompers as its first President.

1914
Watch Your Step, Irving Berlin's first musical, opens in New York.

1925
The Coconuts, by George S. Kaufman and Irving Berlin, starring the Marx Brothers, opens at the Lyric Theatre in New York.

1941
The United States declares war on Japan following the Japanese surprise attack on Pearl Harbor on December 7.

1963
Frank Sinatra, Jr., is kidnapped in Lake Tahoe, Nevada, and released three days later after a $240,000 ransom is paid.

1971
The United States gives 40 million acres of land to the Eskimos, Indians, and Aleuts, under the provisions of the Native Lands Claims Act.

1980
Former Beatle, John Lennon, is shot and killed outside his apartment in New York by Mark Chapman.

1987
President Reagan and Soviet Union General Secretary Gorbachev sign the first treaty reducing nuclear arsenals, in Washington, D.C.

Samuel Gompers

1835

The Texas Army commanded by Colonel Benjamin Milan captures San Antonio.

1864

The United States ship, *Otsego*, is sunk by a torpedo on the Roanoke River in Virginia, during the Civil War.

1878

Joseph Pulitzer buys the St. Louis *Dispatch*, his first newspaper.

1940

The British, commanded by General O'Conner, launch an offensive against the Italians in North Africa, during World War II.

1941

The Japanese occupy Bangkok, Thailand, during World War II.

1942

Australian troops storm Japanese positions at Gona in new Guinea, sustaining heavy casualties, during World War II.

1943

The Allies further consolidate their gains around Monte Cassino in Italy after repelling German attacks, during World War II.

1963

Dominique by the Singing Nun becomes the number one record in the United States.

1969

Charles M. Manson is indicted for the murders of actress Sharon Tate and five others by his followers on August 9.

1975

Judge W. Arthur Garrity places South Boston High School under Federal court receivership for failing to comply with a court-ordered busing plan.

Charles Manson being led back to prison

1778

John Jay is appointed President of the Continental Congress.

1817

Mississippi joins the Union as the twentieth state.

1832

President Jackson issues a proclamation to South Carolina, calling its nullification of United States tariff laws an act of rebellion.

1869

Wyoming becomes the first territory or state to grant women's suffrage in the United States.

1898

The United States and Spain sign the Treaty of Paris, formally ending the Spanish-American War.

1904

The Bethlehem Steel Corporation is established in New Jersey.

1910

Giacomo Puccini's opera, *La Fanciulla Del West*, opens at the Metropolitan Opera in New York, becoming the first opera based on an American theme.

1913

Elihu Root is awarded the Nobel Peace Prize for his work with the Carnegie Endowment for International Peace.

1915

The one-millionth Model T Ford rolls off the assembly line at the Ford plant in Detroit, Michigan.

1926

Vice President Charles G. Dawes wins the Nobel Peace Prize for his work on the restructuring of the German war debt.

1941

The Japanese invade Luzon in the Philippines, during World War II.

1943

The first American planes arrive in the Solomon Islands, during World War II.

1974

Representative Wilbur D. Mills of Arkansas resigns his chairmanship of the Ways and Means Committee after being linked with Fanne Fox, a burlesque dancer.

1984

United States astronomers announce the discovery of a planet outside the solar system.

The women's suffrage movement

December

1789
The University of North Carolina is chartered in Chapel Hill.

1816
Indiana joins the Union as the nineteenth state.

1838
The House of Representatives adopts the Atherton Gag, automatically tabling any petition to discuss slavery.

1862
Union troops commanded by General Ambrose Burnside build two pontoon bridges across the Rappahannock River in Virginia and occupy Fredericksburg, during the Civil War.

1882
At the Bijou Theatre in Boston, Gilbert and Sullivan's *Iolanthe* becomes the first show to be performed in a theater lit by incandescent electric lights.

1930
The Bank of the United States closes as a result of the deepening financial crisis in the United States.

1936
King Edward VIII of England abdicates his throne to marry American divorcee, Wallis Simpson.

1937
Italy withdraws from the League of Nations.

1941
Germany and Italy declare war on the United States.

1954
The aircraft carrier, U.S.S. *Forrestal*, is launched in Newport News, Virginia, becoming the largest warship ever built.

The U.S.S. *Forrestal*

December

12

1787
Pennsylvania becomes the second state to ratify the Constitution.

1831
Henry Clay becomes the first candidate to be nominated at a major party convention.

1862
The Union ironclad ship *Cairo* strikes a mine and sinks on the Yazoo River in Mississippi, during the Civil War.

1863
Confederate submarine *H.L. Hunley* sinks in Charleston Harbor killing its inventor, H.L. Hunley, during the Civil War.

1906
Oscar S. Strauss becomes the first Jew to serve in a Cabinet post after being appointed Secretary of Commerce and Labor by President Roosevelt.

1925
The Motel Inn in San Luis Obispo, California, becomes the first motel in the United States.

1927
Oklahoma Governor Henry S. Johnston calls out state troops to prevent legislators from conducting an impeachment hearing against him.

1928
The International Civil Aeronautics Conference opens in Washington, D.C., with 31 countries in attendance.

1937
Two American sailors are killed when the United States gunboat, *Panay*, is sunk by Japanese war planes in Chinese waters.

1957
Major Adrian E. Drew of the USAF sets a jet speed record of 1207.6 mph in an F-101 Voodoo, over the Mojave Desert in California.

Henry Clay

December

1759
Michael Hillegas of Philadelphia opens the first music store in America.

1816
The Provident Institution for Savings in Boston becomes the first savings bank in the United States.

1862
The Union Army commanded by General Ambrose Burnside suffers a costly defeat, sustaining over 12,000 casualties at the Battle of Fredericksburg, Virginia, during the Civil War.

1896
Italo Marcioni of New Jersey is awarded a patent for a mold to produce ice cream cones.

1913
Congress passes the Owen-Glass Act, setting up the Federal Reserve System.

1939
The British submarine, *Salmon*, sinks the German cruiser, *Nurnberg*, in the North Sea, during World War II.

1940
Adolph Hitler issues Directive 20, calling for the invasion of Greece, during World War II.

1941
British forces withdraw from Hong Kong, during World War II.

1942
The British Eighth Army captures Mersa Brega in Libya, forcing German General Rommel to withdraw, during World War II.

1944
The United States heavy cruiser *Nashville* is attacked by Japanese Kamikaze pilots, sustaining many casualties, during World War II.

The Battle of Fredericksburg

December

1774
Major John Sullivan leads a band of militia in the break-in at the arsenal at Fort William and Mary in New Hampshire, the first military action of the Revolutionary War.

1778
The Continental Congress appoints Benjamin Franklin to represent the United States in France.

1782
British forces evacuate Charleston, South Carolina.

1790
Alexander Hamilton presents a plan for a Bank of the United States to Congress.

1799
George Washington, first President of the United States, dies at his home in Mount Vernon, Virginia.

1819
Alabama joins the Union as the twenty-second state.

1861
General H.H. Sibley assumes command of Confederate forces in the New Mexico and Arizona Territories, during the Civil War.

1942
American forces take Buna Village in New Guinea as the Japanese withdraw, during World War II.

1962
Mariner II passes within 21,000 miles of Venus, becoming the United States' first successful interplanetary mission.

1968
I Heard it Through the Grapevine by Marvin Gaye becomes the number one record in the United States.

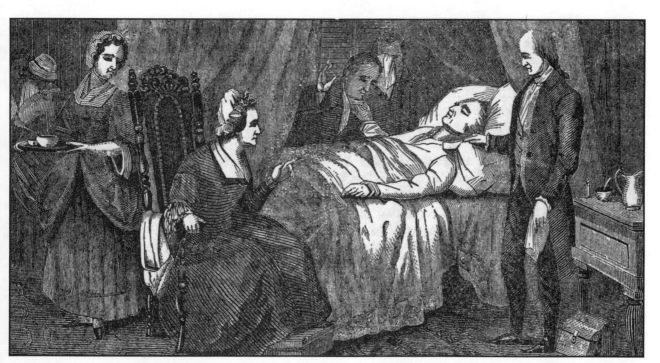

The death of George Washington

1835

President Santa Ana of Mexico issues a constitution for all Mexican territories, including Texas.

1864

Union forces, commanded by General George H. Thomas, defeat the Confederate Army of Tennessee, commanded by General John Bell Hood, at the Battle of Nashville, Tennessee, during the Civil War.

1875

The House of Representatives approves a resolution banning a third term for presidents.

1890

Sioux Indian Chief, Sitting Bull, is killed by United States soldiers near the Grand River in South Dakota.

1944

United States forces land at San Augustin in the Philippines, during World War II.

1965

The Gemini 6 space capsule completes the first successful space rendezvous, coming within six feet of *Gemini 7.*

1967

Forty-six people are killed when the Silver Bridge, between Point Pleasant, West Virginia, and Kanauga, Ohio, collapses during the rush hour.

1970

The United States returns 48,000 acres of land in the Blue Lake area of New Mexico to the Taos Pueblo Indians.

1978

Cleveland, Ohio, becomes the first major American city to default on its loan obligations since the Depression.

The death of Chief Sitting Bull

December

1773

The Boston Tea Party occurs when colonists disguised as Indians dump tea from three British ships into Boston Harbor.

1811

An earthquake strikes in Missouri, changing the course of the Mississippi River and creating Reelfoot Lake in Tennessee.

1864

The Confederates, commanded by General John Bell Hood, are routed by Union forces, commanded by General George Thomas, at the Battle of Nashville, Tennessee, during the Civil War.

1900

The National Civic Federation is established to deal with confrontations between labor and management.

1907

Sixteen battleships, known as the Great White Fleet, steam out of Hampton Roads, Virginia, on a voyage around the world to demonstrate the naval power of the United States.

1930

Golfer Bobby Jones wins the first Amateur Athletic Union James E. Sullivan Memorial Trophy as the outstanding athlete of the year.

1944

The German Army breaks through Allied lines in the Ardennes, in the Battle of the Bulge, during World War II.

1953

United States Air Force Major Chuck Yeager sets an airplane speed record of 1600 mph in a Bell X-1A rocket plane.

The Boston Tea Party

December

1777
General George Washington leads his troops into winter quarters at Valley Forge, Pennsylvania.

1903
Orville Wright makes the first airplane flight, lasting 12 seconds and reaching a height of 12 feet, at Kitty Hawk, North Carolina.

1927
Forty men are killed when the United States submarine, *S-4*, collides with the Coast Guard destroyer, *Paulding*, off the coast of Provincetown, Massachusetts.

1933
The Chicago Bears defeat the New York Giants 23-21 in the first National Football League championship.

1939
The German battleship, *Graf Spee*, is sunk off the coast of Montevideo, Uruguay, during World War II.

1941
Admiral Chester Nimitz becomes commander of the United States Pacific Fleet, during World War II.

1957
The United States launches the first Atlas rocket, produced by General Dynamics.

1969
Singer Tiny Tim marries Victoria Budinger, in a ceremony on Johnny Carson's *The Tonight Show*.

1980
Amadeus opens at the Broadhurst Theatre in New York.

Washington at Valley Forge

December

1787
New Jersey becomes the third state to ratify the Constitution.

1860
The Crittenden Compromise is proposed by Senator John J. Crittenden of Kentucky, in a last ditch effort to keep the Southern States from seceding.

1864
President Lincoln calls for an additional 300,000 troops, during the Civil War.

1869
William F. Semple of Ohio is awarded a patent for chewing gum.

1908
The first Red Cross Christmas Seals are sold, raising $135,000.

1917
Congress passes the Eighteenth Amendment, barring the sale or distribution of alcoholic beverages.

1931
Gangster "Legs" Diamond is shot to death in Albany, New York.

1942
The Allies take Cape Endiadere in New Guinea, with Australian troops leading the way, during World War II.

1961
The Lion Sleeps Tonight by the Tokens becomes the number one record in the United States.

1972
The United States resumes full scale bombing of North Vietnam, after the Paris Peace Talks stall.

The body of "Legs" Diamond leaving Lodging House

1732
Benjamin Franklin's *Poor Richard's Almanac* is published, in Philadelphia.

1766
The English Parliament suspends the New York Legislature for voting against the Quartering Act.

1892
The University of Oklahoma is established in Norman.

1914
Earl Hurd is awarded a patent for the first animating technique.

1941
Adolph Hitler becomes commander in chief of the German Army, during World War II.

1942
Soviet forces take Kontemirovka, prompting German General Manstein to order a withdrawal, during World War II.

1957
The Music Man by Meredith Wilson opens at the Majestic Theater in New York.

1959
Walter Williams, the last living Civil War veteran, dies at 117.

1987
Texaco agrees to pay Pennzoil damages of $3 billion to settle a lawsuit arising from Texaco's merger with the Getty Oil Company.

Benjamin Franklin

December

1860
South Carolina becomes the first state to secede from the Union.

1861
Congress establishes a Joint Committee on the Conduct of the War to oversee President Lincoln, during the Civil War.

1864
Confederate forces commanded by General William Hardee evacuate Savannah, Georgia, during the Civil War.

1951
The U.S. Reactor Testing Station in Idaho becomes the first atomic-powered generator to produce electricity.

1957
Pan American Airways puts the first Boeing 707 jet into service.

1967
United States troop strength reaches a high of over 474,000 men.

1972
The Sunshine Boys by Neil Simon opens at the Broadhurst Theatre in New York.

1984
Bell Laboratories announces the development of a memory chip able to store more than one million bits of electronic data.

1987
Janet Evans sets a world record of 4:04.45 for the 400 meter freestyle.

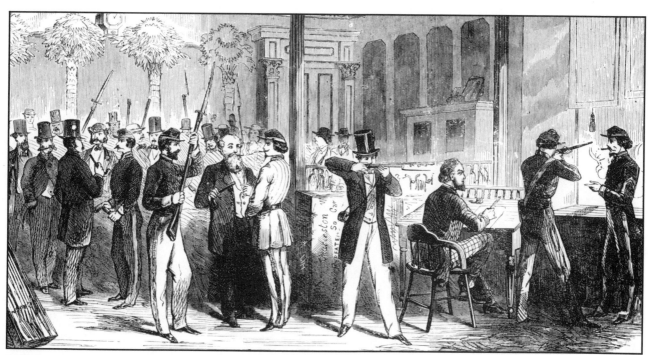

Volunteers in South Carolina after the secession

December

1624
The South Company of Sweden establishes the first Swedish colony in America in present day Delaware.

1790
Samuel Slater begins production in the first American cotton mill, in Pawtucket, Rhode Island.

1864
The Confederates commanded by General William J. Hardee evacuate Savannah, Georgia, during the Civil War.

1866
A party of Sioux, Cheyenne, and Arapaho Indians ambush and kill Captain William Fetterman's army regiment near Fort Phil Kearny, during the First Sioux War.

1913
The first crossword puzzle is published in the *New York World*.

1920
Sally by Jerome Kern opens at the New Amsterdam Theatre in New York.

1936
The first major ski resort in the United States opens in Sun Valley, Idaho.

1937
Snow White and the Seven Dwarfs, Walt Disney's first full-length, animated film, opens in Los Angeles, California.

1942
The Supreme Court rules that Nevada divorces are valid in all states.

1979
Congress passes a bill authorizing a Federal bailout of the ailing Chrysler Corporation, providing $1.5 billion in loan guarantees.

A New England Cotton Mill

December

1775
Esek Hopkins is appointed commander in chief of the Continental Navy.

1789
North Carolina cedes Tennessee to the United States to become a separate state.

1894
The United States Golf Association is formed.

1941
The Japanese take Wake Island after a 15-day stand by United States Marines, during World War II.

1944
American General Anthony McAuliffe replies, "Nuts!" to a German demand to surrender his troops, trapped in the Ardennes at the Battle of the Bulge, during World War II.

1956
The first gorilla born in captivity is born at the Columbus Zoo in Ohio.

1961
Specialist 4 James Davis becomes the first American soldier killed in battle during the Vietnam War.

1964
Twenty-two people are killed as California, Oregon, Idaho, Washington, and Nevada are declared disaster areas after severe flooding.

1984
Like a Virgin by Madonna becomes the number one record in the United States.

1985
Stephone Paige of the Kansas City Chiefs gains an NFL record 309 yards in a game against the San Diego Chargers.

Destroyed German tanks during the Battle of the Bulge

December

23

1775
King George III of England issues a proclamation closing the American Colonies to all trade.

1783
George Washington officially resigns his commission as commander in chief of the Continental Army.

1939
The first Canadian troops arrive in England, during World War II.

1941
Wake Island surrenders to the Japanese, during World War II.

1948
Former Japanese Premier, Hideki Tojo, and six others are hanged in Tokyo, for war crimes.

1962
The Cuban Government releases prisoners captured in the Bay of Pigs invasion in exchange for $50 million in aid.

1970
The World Trade Center in lower Manhattan is topped out, becoming the tallest building in the world.

1978
Bryan Trottier of the New York Islanders scores an NHL record six points in one period in a game against the New York Rangers.

1986
The experimental airplane, *Voyager*, completes the first nonstop around-the-world flight, landing at Edwards Air Force Base in California.

King George III

December

1784
James Madison publishes *Remonstrances Against Religious Assessments*, advocating the separation of church and state.

1784
The Methodist Church is formed in Baltimore.

1814
The United States and England sign the Treaty of Ghent, ending the War of 1812.

1851
Two thirds of the books at the Library of Congress in Washington, D.C., are destroyed in a fire.

1862
Union forces occupy Galveston, Texas, during the Civil War.

1865
The Klu Klux Klan is founded in Pulaski, Tennessee.

1893
Henry Ford completes construction of his first gasoline engine.

1906
The National Electric Signalling Company of Brant Rock, Massachusetts, presents the first radio broadcast in the United States.

1938
The Declaration of Lima is signed by 21 Western Hemisphere nations, reaffirming the principle of mutual consultation.

1943
General Dwight D. Eisenhower is named Supreme Commander of Allied Forces for the invasion of Europe, during World War II.

Three Klansmen after the Civil War

December

1831
Louisiana and Arkansas become the first two states to celebrate Christmas as a legal holiday.

1837
An American force commanded by General Zachary Taylor defeats the Seminole Indians at Okeechobee Swamp, Florida, during the Second Seminole War.

1843
The first matinee is performed, at the Olympic Theater in New York.

1865
The Union Stockyards open in Chicago, making that city the center of transcontinental commerce.

1868
President Johnson grants unqualified amnesty to all those who participated in the "rebellion."

1875
The Chicago Daily News is founded by Melville E. Stone.

1928
In Old Arizona becomes the first western talking film.

1934
Santa Anita opens, becoming the first licensed race track in California.

1940
The British cruiser, *Berwick*, is hit during an attack by the German cruiser, *Admiral Hipper*, in the North Atlantic, during World War II.

1942
British forces in Hong Kong surrender to the Japanese, during World War II.

General Jackson in Florida

December

1620
Pilgrims reach Plymouth, Massachusetts, aboard the *Mayflower.*

1776
General George Washington captures 1000 Hessian troops at the Battle of Trenton, New Jersey, during the Revolutionary War.

1812
The British announce a naval blockade of Chesapeake and Delaware Bays, during the War of 1812.

1861
The United States decides to release Confederate commissioners James Mason and John Slidell, seized aboard a British ship, acknowledging the capture as illegal.

1862
Thirty-eight Santee Sioux Indians are hanged after a six-week rampage in Minnesota that resulted in the deaths of 400 settlers.

1865
James Nason of Franklin, Massachusetts, invents the first percolator for brewing coffee.

1908
Jack Johnson becomes the first Black heavyweight boxing champion, stopping Tommy Burns in 14 rounds.

1917
A proclamation by President Wilson authorizes the Federal Government to take control of the nation's railroads as a war measure.

1931
Of Thee I Sing by George Gershwin opens at the Music Box Theatre in New York.

1972
Harry S. Truman, thirty-third President of the United States, dies in Kansas City, Missouri.

American troops in action in New Jersey

1817
General Andrew Jackson takes command of American troops, during the First Seminole War.

1832
The United States and Russia sign a treaty of commerce, at St. Petersburg.

1927
Show Boat, by Oscar Hammerstein II and Jerome Kern, opens at the Ziegfeld Theater in New York.

1932
Radio City Music Hall opens in New York.

1941
American authorities declare Manila an open city, during World War II.

1944
The British XXX Corps drive the Germans out of Celles on the Western Front, during World War II.

1945
The World Bank is established by 24 countries at a meeting in Washington, D.C.

1947
Eighty people are killed when a record 25.8 inches of snow falls in the Northeast.

1950
The United States and Spain resume diplomatic relations.

1985
Five Americans are killed during a terrorist attack at Rome Airport, Italy.

Radio City Music Hall

1832
St. Louis University becomes the first Catholic university west of the Allegheny Mountains.

1835
Seminole Indians massacre American troops commanded by General Wiley Thompson at Fort King, Florida, during the Second Seminole War.

1846
Iowa joins the Union as the twenty-ninth state.

1856
Woodrow Wilson, twenty-eighth President of the United States, is born in Staunton, Virginia.

1860
President Buchanan refuses to recognize commissioners from South Carolina after the State's secession.

1900
Prohibitionist Carrie Nation breaks into a bar in Wichita, Kansas, destroying furniture and a major oil painting by John Noble.

1930
The State Capitol building in Bismarck, North Dakota, is destroyed in a fire along with most of the state's documents.

1941
The Germans inflict severe losses on the British 22nd Armoured Brigade in North Africa, during World War II.

1942
President Roosevelt confirms his policy of not sharing atomic information with the British.

1942
Arthur Rodzinski becomes the Musical Director and Conductor of the New York Philharmonic Symphony Orchestra.

Wrecked German tank in North Africa

1778
The British under Colonel Archibald Campbell occupy Savannah, Georgia, during the Revolutionary War.

1808
Andrew Johnson, seventeenth President of the United States, is born in Raleigh, North Carolina.

1812
The British frigate, *Java*, is destroyed by the United States frigate, *Constitution*, off the coast of Brazil, during the War of 1812.

1837
Canadian authorities seize the American Ship *Caroline* near Buffalo, for running supplies to Canadian revolutionaries.

1845
Texas joins the Union as the twenty-eighth state.

1846
American forces commanded by General Zachary Taylor occupy Victoria, Mexico, during the Mexican War.

1851
The first Young Men's Christian Association is established, in Boston.

1890
In the last major engagement between Indians and the United States Army, more than 300 Sioux Indians, including Chief Big Foot, are killed at Wounded Knee Creek in South Dakota.

1913
The Adventures of Kathleen opens in Chicago, becoming the first movie serial in the United States.

1972
Life Magazine suspends publication after 36 years.

An early YMCA building

1813
A British force commanded by General Gordon Drummand burns Buffalo, New York, along with the Black Rock Navy Yard, during the War of 1812.

1853
The United States and Mexico sign the Gadsten Purchase, with the United States acquiring almost 30,000 square miles of territory in southern Arizona and New Mexico.

1854
The Pennsylvania Rock Oil Company of New Haven, Connecticut, becomes the first oil company in the United States.

1860
Troops from South Carolina seize the Federal arsenal at Charleston.

1862
The Union ironclad, *Monitor*, sinks in a storm off the coast of North Carolina, during the Civil War.

1903
In Chicago, 588 people are killed in a fire at the Iroquis Theatre.

1948
Kiss Me, Kate by Cole Porter opens at the New Century Theatre in New York.

1959
The U.S.S. *George Washington* is commissioned in Groton, Connecticut, becoming the first nuclear submarine capable of launching missiles.

1969
President Nixon signs a tax reform bill reducing individual annual tax rates by 5%.

The U.S.S. *George Washington*

1781
Congress establishes the Bank of North America, with a capitalization of $400,000.

1862
The Confederates, commanded by General Braxton Bragg, attack Union forces, commanded by General William S. Rosecrans, on the first day of the two-day Battle of Murfreesboro, Tennessee, during the Civil War.

1901
Thomas Estrada Palma becomes Cuba's first President under its new Constitution.

1904
For the first time, crowds gather in New York's Times Square to celebrate the coming of the new year.

1935
Parker Brothers is awarded a patent for its game of Monopoly.

1943
The New York police are called to control crowds at a Frank Sinatra concert at the Paramount Theatre in Brooklyn.

1970
President Nixon signs the National Air Quality Control Act.

1974
The United States lifts a 41-year ban on private ownership of gold.

1984
The United States withdraws from The United Nations Educational, Scientific, and Cultural Organization in a dispute over mismanagement.

1986
Ninety-five people are killed during a hotel fire in Puerto Rico, set by a disgruntled employee.

Times Square on New Year's Eve

The Battle of Murfreesboro